Changing Authoritarian Rule and Public Policy in Argentina, 1930-1970

Changing Authoritarian Rule and Public Policy in Argentina, 1930-1970

Benjamin A. Most

with an introduction by Luigi Manzetti

GSIS Monograph Series
in World Affairs

THE UNIVERSITY OF DENVER

Lynne Rienner Publishers   Boulder & London

Published in the United States of America in 1991 by
Lynne Rienner Publishers, Inc.
1800 30th Street, Boulder, Colorado 80301

and in the United Kingdom by
Lynne Rienner Publishers, Inc.
3 Henrietta Street, Covent Garden, London WC2E 8LU

Library of Congress Cataloging-in-Publication Data
Most, Benjamin A., d. 1986.
  Changing authoritarian rule and public policy in Argentina,
1930-1970 / by Benjamin A. Most ; with an introduction by Luigi
Manzetti   (GSIS monograph series in world affairs)
  Includes bibliographical references and index.
  ISBN 1-55587-246-8 (alk. paper)
  1. Argentina—Politics and government—1910–1943. 2. Argentina—
Politics and government—1943-1955. 3. Argentina—History
—20th century. I. Title.
JL2024.M67 1990
321.9'0982—dc20   90-42342
                                                        CIP

British Cataloguing in Publication Data
A Cataloguing in Publication record for this
book is available from the British Library.

Printed and bound in the United States of America

The paper used in this publication meets the requirements
of the American National Standard for Permanence of
Paper for Printed Library Materials Z39.48-1984.

Contents

List of Tables and Figures   vii

Foreword   *Harvey Starr*   ix

1   Introduction: The Study of Changing Authoritarian
    Political Systems   *Luigi Manzetti*   1

2   Setting the Stage:
    Political Change and Public Policy   19

3   The Theoretical Framework:
    Authoritarianism, Incrementalism, and
    Constraints on Decisionmakers   23

4   Who Governed When in Argentina?
    Coalitions, Presidents,
    Cabinet Officers, and Public Employees   45

5   Policies Toward the State, the Military, and Society   67

6   Industrialization and Foreign Policies   81

7   Labor Policies   111

8   Expenditure and Revenue Policies   135

9   Conclusion   177

References   185
Index   199
About the Book and the Authors   206

Tables and Figures

Tables

7.1   Labor Policies: Impact of the 1952 Transition   115

7.2   Labor Policies: Summary of the 1952 Transition: From Populist Authoritarian Rule to the Era of the Hegemonic Crisis   116

7.3   Labor Policies: Examination of a Possible 1949 Transition   118

7.4   Labor Policies: Impact of the 1943 Transition   120

7.5   Labor Policies: Summary of the 1943 Transition: From Traditional to Populist Authoritarian Rule   122

7.6   Labor Policies: Impact of the 1966 Transition   124

7.7   Labor Policies: Summary of the 1966 Transition: From the Era of the Hegemonic Crisis to Bureaucratic-Authoritarian Rule   125

7.8   Labor Policies: Examination of the 1966 Transition Using 1950 Starting Points   127

7.9   Labor Policies: Overall Summary   130

8.1   Budget Policies: Impact of the 1952 Transition   140

8.2   Budget Policies: Summary of the 1952 Transition: From Populist Authoritarian Rule to the Era of the Hegemonic Crisis   143

8.3   Budget Policies: Examination of Possible Shifts in 1945 and 1948   147

8.4   Budget Policies: Summary of the Possible Shifts in 1945 and 1948   148

8.5   Budget Policies: Impact of the 1943 Transition   151

8.6   Budget Policies: Summary of the 1943 Transition: From Traditional to Populist Authoritarian Rule   153

8.7   Budget Policies: Impact of the 1966 Transition   158

8.8   Budget Policies: Summary of the 1966 Transition: From the Era of the Hegemonic Crisis to Bureaucratic-Authoritarian Rule   159

8.9   Budget Policies: Overall Summary   164

Figures

7.1	Real Income	132
7.2	Gross Domestic Product Share	132
7.3	Labor Strikes	133
7.4	Government Employment Levels	133
8.1	Total Expenditures in 1960 Pesos	167
8.2	Total Expenditures in Current Pesos	168
8.3	Total Revenues in 1960 Pesos	169
8.4	Defense Spending in 1960 Pesos	169
8.5	Defense Expenditures in Current Pesos	170
8.6	Defense Spending–Total Spending Ratio	171
8.7	Cost-of-Living Index	172
8.8	Change in the Cost-of-Living Index	173
8.9	Deficit in 1960 Pesos	173

Foreword

HARVEY STARR

It is not unusual to see a reference to the odyssey a book has taken from its conception and research to its final form. Unfortunately, the journey taken by this book includes tragedy as well. Ben Most was in the process of revising this manuscript, accepted for publication in the Monograph Series in World Affairs, when he died in November 1986.

This book was only one of the projects to which Ben devoted his considerable energy. He was engaged with coauthors in major research projects on the diffusion of international conflict, as well as a study on the logic of inquiry in international relations. Indeed, most political scientists will automatically think of Ben Most as an important student of international politics. Yet his first significant research interest was in Latin American and comparative public policy. His dissertation was on Argentine public policy, codirected by John V. Gillespie and David Collier. He had also conducted fieldwork in Argentina, Bolivia, and Mexico.

One of Ben's earliest publications was "Authoritarianism and the Growth of the State in Latin America," in *Comparative Political Studies*. Later came "Resource Allocation: The Case of Latin America," in *The Politics of Resource Allocation* edited by Groth and Wade. At Brown University, where he taught in 1977–1981 before moving to the University of Iowa, he offered courses such as Latin American Politics, Foreign Policies of the Latin American Nations, Introduction to Comparative Public Policy, and Advanced Topics in Comparative Public Policy. He also produced papers such as "Corporatism, Authoritarianism, and the State in Latin America: An Assessment of Their Impacts on Public Policies" and "Bridging the Islands of Theory: Policy Analysis in the American State, Comparative Foreign and Third World Settings."

The title of this latter paper is instructive, for Ben Most was extraordinarily concerned with bridging subfields and methodological traditions as well as islands of theory. The present book is exemplary of all Ben wished to do with his scholarship. It is a major statement of his convergent interests in public policy, Latin America, the comparative study of political phenomena, and the application of diverse but appropriate methodologies to the investigation of those political phenomena. While it will interest students of Argentina and Latin America, it will also say much to those concerned with political and economic development and with the study of bureaucracies and public institutions, in terms of both theory and case study material. Ben's analysis of the policy process also reflects his important work on the logic of inquiry and research design and indicates how the issues raised later in terms of the study of international relations also apply to the comparative study of public policy.

Transforming an accepted manuscript into a final book is always a considerable task. In this instance it would have been impossible except for the assistance of a number of individuals. At Indiana University, Christi Barbour provided outstanding editorial work, helping to translate the recommendations of the referees and the series editor into the reality of a streamlined manuscript. Kevin Middlebrook read the edited manuscript and provided useful comments, especially regarding the form of an introduction. Peter Snow of the University of Iowa did likewise, recommending Luigi Manzetti to write the introduction. At that time I had decided the manuscript needed an introductory chapter that would place the analysis of Argentina in 1930–1970 within an updated theoretical and political context, juxtaposing Most's earlier conclusions with more recent theoretical work by such scholars as Guillermo O'Donnell and with events in Argentina since 1970. I thus needed someone who knew Argentina and the work on Latin American development. Luigi Manzetti matched my needs perfectly: he received his Ph.D. in political science from the University of Iowa, with a specialty in Latin American politics; he had also been Ben's student. His willingness to take on this project—and his commitment to it—require a special acknowledgment. And as the reader will see from his chapter, Most's work stands up well to the test of time.

Finally, this book would not have become a reality without the support and assistance of Karen A. Feste, editor of the GSIS Monograph Series in World Affairs, and Lynne Rienner of Lynne Rienner Publishers. In addition to all their help, they have both put up with the various delays on my part and maintained a commitment to this project throughout its extended odyssey. I thank you. And Ben thanks you.

Harvey Starr
Columbia, South Carolina

ONE

Introduction: The Study of Changing Authoritarian Political Systems

LUIGI MANZETTI

The relationship between regime type and public policy has long been one of the main concerns of political science. In the Latin American context, the chronic instability of democratic institutions has routinely raised the question of whether authoritarian regimes are more effective than democratic ones in promoting economic development and, recently, stabilization policies.

The series of military coups that swept South America in the mid-1960s and early 1970s brought to power a new breed of military officers especially concerned with issues of economic growth and national security: Brazil in 1964–1985, Argentina in 1966–1973 and 1976–1983, Uruguay in 1973–1985, Chile in 1973–1989, Peru in 1968–1980. The distinctive nature of the military regimes in some of these countries and the policies they promoted raised again the questions: Do military regimes produce policies that are different from those of civilian regimes? Are these policies more effective in accomplishing developmental or stabilization goals? The ability of the Brazilian and Argentine authoritarian regimes to stabilize their economies in the short run in the late 1960s fostered a more benevolent attitude in the United States toward authoritarianism abroad, to the point that the Rockefeller Report on the Western Hemisphere stated in 1969:

> The new military officers are motivated by increasing impatience with corruption, inefficiency, and stagnant political order. . . . They are searching for ways to bring education and better standards of living to their people while avoiding anarchy and violent revolution. In many cases, it will be more useful for the United States to try to work with them in these efforts, rather than to abandon or insult them because we are conditioned by arbitrary stereotypes. (Rockefeller 1969, 17)

Some scholars, too, suggested that the increased professionalism and middle-class backgrounds of the officers' corps, along with their emphasis on economic development, were strong indicators that the military could become an effective modernizing force (Halpern 1962; Pye 1962; Shils 1962). Subsequent analyses of Brazil and Peru (considered by many to be the role models of conservative and reformist military regimes, respectively), found instead that the armed forces acted "above class lines." According to some studies these military regimes' concern with development problems could be explained by their pursuit of corporate self-interests (Stepan 1973; Einaudi and Stepan 1974; Collier 1976).

Other scholars argued that the military was constrained by external forces and unable to implement effective development policies: it was either unprepared to promote economic planning and institution building or it was too closely tied with, or dependent on, powerful interest groups (Lieuwen 1961; Johnson 1962; Needler 1969; Willner 1970; Lissak 1975). A third approach (Huntington 1971) posited that the policies of a military regime depended on the level of social and economic development in a country. In less-developed countries the military would be expected to promote modernization; in more developed ones, where interest groups were more differentiated and influential, the armed forces would play a conservative role. Central to Huntington's analysis was the relationship between political participation and the degree of political institutionalization: when popular participation overwhelmed the capacity of political institutions to satisfy people's demands, military intervention would probably occur. Such intervention would take the form of a moderating force or direct rule by the armed forces.

Huntington's model, however, failed to explain why military intervention differed in length, policies, and style. Nordlinger (1970) found empirical support for Huntington's hypothesis that the military was more likely to promote modernization in the less-developed countries. His results led him to conclude in favor of Huntington's contention; but in general, the economic outcomes of the policies enforced by the military tended to be negative. Later, Jackman (1976) replicated Nordlinger's study using a more sophisticated technique. Jackman contended that Nordlinger's statistical analysis was flawed with methodological problems and that military rule, regardless of geographic area or level of economic development, had no positive effects on social change indicators (energy consumption, health care, mass communication, and school enrollment).

Two further cross-national studies using larger data sets were performed by McKinlay and Cohan (1975, 1976). The first study, comparing civilian and military regimes by changes in exports, food production, military spending and size, primary education, and per capita GNP, found that military regimes performed slightly better in the less-developed countries than did civilian regimes, particularly in primary education. In their second study, McKinlay and Cohan added political indicators to socioeconomic variables and found that military regimes experienced higher levels of political change and lower levels of political activity than did civilian regimes.

Whereas all this literature emphasized the pros and cons of military rule, with the rise of "dependency" scholarship in the late 1960s the importance of the nature of political regimes in explaining public policy began to be questioned. Advocates of dependency theory argued that the constraints imposed by the international economy, the interaction of internal and external elements in dependency relations, the persistence of the underdevelopment status of Third World countries, cultural beliefs, the internal decisionmaking apparatus, and social structures were more important than regime dichotomies in explaining policy in Latin America (Frank 1966, 1967; Cardoso and Faletto 1969; Dos Santos 1970; Jaguaribe et al. 1970; Cockcroft, Frank, and Johnson 1972;).

Others dismissed, on different grounds, the argument that military and civilian regimes pursued distinctive public policies (Nun 1969; Ronfeldt 1974; Schmitter 1975; Ayres 1975). Furthermore, in their influential studies both Anderson (1967) and Schmitter (1971) were unable to draw any clear conclusion about the success of different types of political regimes in promoting development.

Bureaucratic–Authoritarianism and Public Policy

The debate over the relationship between regime type and public policies is central to Guillermo O'Donnell's *Modernization and Bureaucratic-Authoritarianism* (1973). In this work, heavily influenced by the writings of Gershenkron (1952, 1966), Cardoso and Faletto (1969), Apter (1965, 1969, 1971), and Hirschman (1961, 1968), O'Donnell rejected the modernization theorists' (above all Lipset's) contention that increasing modernization led to democracy, arguing that greater levels of literacy, urbanization, social mobility, industrialization, and political participation created the conditions, instead, for a new form of authoritarian regime he labeled *bureaucratic-authoritarianism* (B-A). Interestingly for a political scientist, O'Donnell's model elaborated an economic explanation for what was in the end a true political phenomenon.

Basing his argument on the experiences of Brazil and Argentina, O'Donnell contended that in the aftermath of the Great Depression, populist coalitions came to the foreground of Latin American politics with a distinctive set of policies. Despite the heterogeneous nature of these coalitions, their supporters were united in their opposition to the traditional elites and the foreign interests tied to them. Once in power, the populist governments abandoned the laissez faire economic policies that the elites had enforced until 1930 and instead promoted import substitution industrialization (ISI), which was to be sustained by the expansion of the domestic market and by real increases in the purchasing power of wage and salary earners. According to O'Donnell, the exhaustion of the "easy" phase of the industrialization process brought with it a phase of industrial "deepening," which meant shifting from consumer goods to capital goods production. This, in turn, resulted in political crisis. In fact, the deepening process called for an economic restructuring based on criteria of efficiency and increased productivity, which penalized the members of the middle class and working class who had previously benefited from the populist policies. The refusal of these sectors of the society to renounce their demands in terms of both political power and consumption standards caused polarization in the political arena. This, for O'Donnell, led the "propertied classes" to coalesce with the military, excluding a popular sector increasingly impatient with the "incompetent" policies of the populist administrations and creating a new ruling coalition made up of development-minded officers and bourgeois technocrats devoted to a "technical" and "rational" approach to problem solving (as compared to the "political" style adopted by populist governments) and the goal of economic stability. More broadly, O'Donnell's argument posited that the modernization process in developing countries was associated with socioeconomic crisis. As a crisis arose, a new ruling coalition emerged that would produce distinct public policies as compared to those implemented by the previous ruling coalition.

Despite its widespread appeal, the B–A model was increasingly challenged, perhaps most notably in a collections of articles edited by David Collier (1979). In the Collier volume, Hirschman criticized the B–A model for being overdeterministic in its economic explanation of the political phenomena under study. He suggested that political variables, such as the Cuban revolution, could have been factors encouraging the military's intervention in Argentina and Brazil. From an economic standpoint, Hirschman questioned O'Donnell's assumption that the exhaustion of the "easy" phase of ISI was instrumental in bringing to power the new coalition of military officers and technocrats that was sought in order to implement the structural changes needed to solve the crisis. First, he pointed out that at the time of the coups the economies concerned still showed room for "horizontal" expansion. Second, the collapse of the ISI strategy resulted not so much in its inability to sustain itself but in poor policy implementation by populist regimes. Third (and equally important), Hirschman raised doubts about the necessity to create a B–A regime to carry out austere stabilization policies.

In the same volume, Serra (1979) reexamined the ability of the B–A model to explain the case of Brazil. Looking specifically at the hypotheses derived from the model concerning the exploitation of the working class, the industrial "deepening," and the "economic rationality" pursued by the B–A regime, he found all three "mistaken." Robert Kaufman (1979) concurred with Hirschman and Serra, casting doubts on the hypothesis that the necessity of "deepening" the industrialization process was instrumental in the creation of the B–A regime. However, he seemed to agree with O'Donnell that the political and economic instability created by the populist regimes left few alternatives open and may have been crucial in the creation of the military–technocratic coalition.

In the volume's concluding chapter, Collier added his own criticisms to those articulated in earlier chapters. First, he found no systematic evidence that socioeconomic changes constituted sufficient or necessary conditions for the political transformations posited by O'Donnell's model. Second, he questioned the explanatory power of the "bureaucratic" variable in the model and its causal relationship with the installation of the authoritarian regime. Third, he found that the model was unable to account for the timing between industrial and social changes and the coming to power of the B–A regime. And last, he pointed out that the addition of new variables to explain differing developments in further cases was done without incorporating those variables into the original model.

Other scholars criticized O'Donnell on similar grounds. Merkx and Remmer (1982) questioned the linkage between the degree of repression and prior levels of threat, elite cohesion, economic performance, political alignments, and the deactivation of the popular sector by pointing to the lack of empirical evidence. Like Collier, they criticized the "ideal type" approach used by O'Donnell in constructing his argument. Although useful in identifying basic similarities across countries, such an approach—in their view—led to a confusion of concepts, definitions, and explanatory variables that failed to explain variations among cases or to strengthen the overall theoretical argument.

Although O'Donnell (1978, 1979, 1982) responded to his critics, he did not satisfy their plea for clarification. To the disappointment of many, he claimed that their criticisms failed to disprove his model and declined to refine his argument further. In 1988 O'Donnell returned to these issues in a book focusing specifically on the Argentine experience between 1966 and 1973. In this latest work, political variables (such as the incorporation of the popular sector, the perception of threat, and institutions and public policies that led to the B–A regime) are emphasized over economic determinants and bureaucratic linkage. The emergence of bureaucratic–authoritarianism is ascribed to more specific variables of a less-structural nature. Nonetheless, his renewed emphasis on the importance of the pre-coup crisis, whose elements were peculiar to the Argentine case, added a large degree of individual explanation to the dynamic of the B–A regime and thus weakened the strength of the argument as a generalization.

Regime Type and Economic Stabilization

Was the establishment of an authoritarian regime a precondition for economic stabilization? Did this kind of regime fare better than democratic ones in promoting austerity policies? In the late 1970s, the focus began to shift from policy outputs to policy outcomes and regime performance. From his comparative analysis of Mexico, Argentina, and Brazil, Skidmore (1977) found that only authoritarian regimes were able to carry out stabilization programs successfully. Looking at the same set of countries, Kaufman (1985) came to similar conclusions: the exclusionary policies of the military regimes in Argentina and Brazil were more successful than those of civilian governments, although only in the short term. Cohen (1985), in his comparison of Argentina, Brazil, and Colombia, found that authoritarian regimes showed greater effectiveness in promoting stabilization policies and economic growth. However, his analysis was flawed by statistical and methodological problems that made his conclusions doubtful.

Other studies openly contradicted the linkage between military regimes and stabilization policies. Commenting on the state of research on regime type in Latin America in the 1960s and 1970s, Remmer (1978) came to the conclusion that no strong relationship could be established between particular types of regime and specific sets of public policy outcomes. Remmer instead recommended a focus on policy outputs and specific governmental policies, rather than on system performance. A study by Haggard (1985) looked at thirty stabilization programs carried out with the assistance of the International Monetary Fund (IMF) between 1975 and 1984 in twenty-four developing countries. Haggard rejected the hypothesis that the need for economic stabilization led to "authoritarian or repressive responses" and discounted the argument that authoritarian regimes were more successful in implementing stabilization policies. Rather than focusing on regime type as an explanatory variable, he emphasized factors such as the cohesiveness and ideological orientation of interest groups and elites, their economic power, the administrative constraints on policymakers, and the availability of resources at the disposal of a given government. Similar conclusions had been previously reached by Nelson (1984).

Most recently, Remmer (1986) in her empirical analysis of the IMF programs carried out by nine Latin American countries, showed that authoritarian regimes did not achieve better results than civilian regimes, nor were the policies that they implemented more austere. While downplaying the importance of the regime type as an explanatory variable, Remmer did argue that regime change could make a difference in the implementation of successful policies. The collapse of a given regime could create enough room for bold stabilization policies in contrast to the (perceived or real) political inaction of the previous government.

In an effort to explain and synthetize such different findings, Hughes and Mijeski (1984) contended that depending on the policy area, the nature of the regime could make a difference. Regime type seemed to be a strong explanatory variable in the case of political and civil rights policies, but not in areas such as military and education expenditures.

In their study of public policy of post-1964 Brazil, Hayes (1972, 1975), Ames (1973, 1975), and Ames and Goff (1975) showed that after its inauguration, the military regime behaved very much like its civilian predecessors, increasing expenditures to reward its supporters. In a subsequent cross-national study, Ames found evidence for what he called the "military coup cycle":

> The year in which the coup occurs should be associated with a decline in spending: the first year after the coup should witness a surge; subsequent years should be associated with declines. . . . In certain cases—Panama after 1968, Brazil between 1968 and 1973, Peru from 1968 until 1975, and Argentina between 1969 and 1973—the military expanded the scope of government activities rather sharply.
>
> After early surges in spending, right-wing military regimes face various options. In relatively simple economies, the military is fiscally conservative. In more complex economies (where the government is inevitably a major economic force), the military remains antistatist and conservative as long as the economy performs acceptably. If the economy falters, the military seems willing to replace a failed economic team with one committed to expansionist policies. The only exception is Pinochet's Chile, where neoliberal economists were so well entrenched in policymaking positions that failures led to more rigorous application of the same policies. (Ames 1987, 18)

The bottom line of Ames's argument is that military regimes behaved very much like civilian ones, at least in their first year in office. Subsequently, the degree of orthodoxy of their fiscal and monetary policies increased in relation to the consolidation of their power. What is critical in Ames's empirical findings is that contrary to what O'Donnell and others emphasized, B–A regimes were not characterized by a "distinctive approach to public spending" (Ames 1987, 29).

The Constraint Argument and Public Policy

This literature on regime type and public policy has been plagued by conceptual, causal, operational, and statistical problems.

Conceptualization. Both dependent and independent variables have often been loosely defined. Some have focused on public policy in terms of outputs whereas others have looked at outcomes without clearly specifying what either outputs or outcomes are meant to be. Terms like *modernization, devel-*

opment, and *economic orthodoxy* have often remained vague, thus complicating their operationalization. Furthermore, scholars have continued to look for *always-true* policy patterns that could be ascribed to certain regimes across space and time even though the evidence suggested that the existence of such patterns was slim at best.

Causality. Scholars have often failed to investigate *whether* certain policies were causally related to specific types of regime. They have concentrated on the indicators that were assumed to determine public policy outcomes but ignored *how* they were related to one another specifically and to public policies more generally. Too often, military and civilian regimes were assumed to be synonymous with certain kinds of public policies, without investigating whether such a causal relationship existed to begin with. Moreover, both military and civilian regimes were regarded as unified actors. This discounted a priori the possibility of internal divisions among the regime decisionmakers that could lead to policy outputs or outcomes different from those hypothesized.

Operationalization. A set of gross indicators such as changes in per capita GDP, electricity consumption, military expenditures, public works expenditures, schooling rates, and so on have commonly been used. However, taken alone, such indicators were often misleading, as they did not automatically translate into the policy priorities of a given regime. Moreover, cross-national studies based on such indicators did not control for other intervening endogenous variables (wage and price controls, devaluations, interest rates, strikes, and political repression) and exogenous variables (oil prices, fluctuations in commodity prices, and foreign investments) that could not be captured by budgetary figures alone.

Statistical problems. The availability of data and their reliability have troubled the design of quantitative testing. To complicate things, many studies have been flawed by multicollinearity problems, model misspecification, and autocorrelation.

Within this context, Benjamin Most's work in the following chapters is a significant step forward, addressing some of the shortcomings mentioned above. Most begins by reviewing the two main arguments concerning public policy and regime change in Latin America: *bureaucratic–authoritarianism* and *incrementalism.* According to O'Donnell, changes in public policies should have ensued whenever different coalitions came to power. Following this logic, Argentina should have experienced major policy changes when new coalitions arose in 1943, 1952, and 1966. Incrementalism, on the contrary, contended that the changes in who governed were unimportant and that previous policies were the best predictor of current policy. According to this view, it was the bureaucrats who carried out the policies, rather than the new coalition members, that really mattered.

From a conceptual standpoint, Most's work is remarkable, since it tried to reconcile some of the tenets of these two contending arguments. It aimed at specifying under what conditions new dominant coalitions could have an impact on public policy. Accordingly, his "constraint argument" posited that policies initiated by a ruling coalition would be the result of bargaining and compromise between interests rather than the imposition of a given coalition. Four main factors were expected to constrain the menu of choice of Argentine coalitions over time: (1) limitations on the political elites' ability to press their policy demands, (2) the existence of a crisis of hegemony, (3) the growth of a large public sector, and (4) limitations on the availability of previously uncommitted resources. As a matter of fact, the interrupted time series analysis supported Most's constraint argument. As policy constraints intensified, the capacity of Argentine coalitions to direct or redirect public policy diminished, as predicted. In fact, changes in ruling coalitions in 1943 and 1952 had greater effects on public policy than in 1966, contrary to what we could have expected following O'Donnell's reasoning. Therefore, coalition changes, as time went by, had only marginal effects in the shaping of public policy. Most's synthesis of the B–A and incremental models successfully links the islands of theory by developing a model that holds true only under explicitly prescribed conditions. Furthermore, although the work is devoted to the analysis of the Argentine case, the logic on which it is based can be useful in the examination of other cases as well. Last, by concentrating on the micro level, Most was able to disaggregate the state as an analytical tool. This was a point advocated by Collier (1979) and Merkx and Remmer (1982) in their criticism of O'Donnell but never translated into practice by either O'Donnell or his critics.

In terms of operationalization, Most's model has the advantage of clearly specifying both dependent and independent variables in a fashion suitable for the empirical test. Of course, the aggregate nature of some indicators (real income of salary and wages, government employment, defense expenditures, government revenues, government expenditures, and so on) reflect the same shortcomings of studies reviewed above. However, Most tried to remedy this problem by a qualitative analysis of the events (see Chapters 4 and 5). In addition, dummy variables were included in the analysis to control for endogenous factors. The main shortcoming of the time series analysis rests on the exclusion of exogenous factors that could easily have affected the shaping of domestic policies. Nor does the analysis control for the effects of political repression in carrying out public policies; but this is partly due to the scarcity of such data for the period examined.

As for causality, the relationship between policy indicators and policy outcomes is well examined; and the parameters of evaluation chosen do respond to those specified by O'Donnell. Statistically, Most provided concrete evidence in support of his own argument while casting serious doubts on the validity of O'Donnell's.

Post-1970 Argentina

Juan Carlos Ongania, hand-picked by the military after the removal of President Arturo Illia in 1966, was himself deposed by the commanders in chief of the armed forces in June 1970. A common explanation for Ongania's downfall has been that the riots that started in the city of Cordoba a year before (commonly referred as Cordobazo) convinced the military that Ongania was no longer able to foster economic stabilization policies without paying an unbearable political cost. However, a more plausible explanation is that the military commanders, particularly General Alejandro Lanusse, was increasingly preoccupied with the possibility that Ongania could become another *caudillo* like Franco in Spain. This could mean that the armed forces would become a subordinate player, something that Lanusse, who aspired to become president himself, could not tolerate. In other words, the military used the Cordobazo as an excuse to get rid of a man who had become too independent. When Ongania tried to dismiss Lanusse, he found that he had lost control of the armed forces and had to leave office.[1]

In the aftermath of the coup, the military did not know what to do next. Although the army fostered Lanusse's presidential candidacy, the navy and air force joined forces to block it, since they were afraid that Lanusse would act like Ongania. As a compromise, it was decided to recall a little-known military attaché in Washington, General Roberto Levingston, to occupy the presidency for an unspecified period of time. Levingston, instead of acting as a spokesman of the military, attempted to consolidate his power and to distance himself from the armed forces in order to gain civilian support. This effort prompted the quick reaction of the armed forces' commanders; and after only eight months in power Levingston was deposed and replaced with Lanusse, who now had gained enough support among the armed forces to achieve his presidential ambitions. Contrary to Ongania's commitment to economic stabilization, first Levingston and then Lanusse used redistributive and expansionary economic policies to gain support from interest groups and to pave the way for a return to democracy. Lanusse, aware of the likelihood of a Perónist victory in a free election (the military had vetoed the participation of the Perónists in the electoral process since Perón's demotion in 1955), tried to convince conservative and centrist parties to form an anti-Peronist block. When this attempt failed, Lanusse, facing a mounting economic crisis coupled with increasing urban terrorism, decided to speed up the election process.

Hector Campora, Perón's hand-picked candidate (Perón was still exiled in Madrid), won the presidential elections in early 1973. A few months later, Campora stepped down and called for new elections so that Perón could return to power after eighteen years. In October 1973 Perón won his third term, with his wife, María Estela Martínez de Perón, becoming vice-president. Upon taking power, Perón continued to support the "social pact" previously agreed on by the Campora administration with business and labor organizations. The social pact was a formal agreement supervised by the government devised to promote growth, price stability, and progressive income redistribution. After an across-the-board wage increase, unions pledged to comply with a voluntary wage freeze for two years, while business agreed to refrain from price increases. For a few months the social pact was effective in establishing price stability, but it collapsed soon after Perón's death in July 1974. His wife, who succeeded him, quickly alienated both industrialists and trade unions by erratic and contradictory policy choices. By early 1976 the country was on the verge of stagflation, while leftist and rightist terrorist groups were claiming victims daily.

It was only in March 1976, when it was clear that there was widespread support to end the incompetent and corrupt administration of Ms. Perón, that the military intervened and deposed the president. This time, however, the military did not entrust authority to one man as it had to Ongania. The commanders in chief of the three armies, following the post-1964 Brazilian military regime, decided that the military would rule the country as an institution for an indefinite period of time.

The military junta that took control of the government soon after the coup called for the inauguration of a Process of National Reorganization. Congress was closed, parties and trade unions banned, and all political activities disallowed. The Proceso, as it came to be known in Argentina, set for itself three main goals: (1) the eradication of terrorism, (2) the establishment of price stability and a positive balance of trade, and (3) the redefinition of the institutional framework in order to give the country more stable political and social institutions. Using a type of "state terrorism" that became sadly known for its brutality, the military took charge of the fight against urban guerrillas. The regime appointed José Alfredo Martínez de Hoz, a well-known entrepreneur, to design a strategy to achieve the economic goals. Martínez de Hoz served as economy minister from 1976 to 1981; his predecessors since 1952 had enjoyed, on the average, a tenure of nine months. General Jorge Videla, the army commander, who became the first military president, gave Martínez de Hoz wide powers on economic affairs that made him the most powerful man in Argentina, second only to the president (Pion-Berlin 1985, 1989). The neoconservative approach espoused by Martínez de Hoz proposed

> not only stabilization policies to restore basic macroeconomic equilibrium but a development strategy based on the following: (1) an outward-oriented growth policy; (2) the maximum use of market mechanisms to allocate

resources, rather than administrative controls; and (3) replacement of the state by the private sector as the principal dynamic agent for growth, the state retiring to a subsidiary role. Such a strategy encompassed not only a price-stabilization program but an opening of trade and finances to the outside world as well; at the same time, it aimed to reduce the size and role of government. (Ramos 1986, 44)

Although the policies were conceptually similar in many respects to the neo-conservative approach adopted by the military regimes in Chile and Uruguay since 1973, their application was far less orthodox. After embarking on an austere stabilization plan with the assistance of the IMF in mid-1976, Martínez de Hoz was able to achieve some price stability and positive trade balance by the end of 1977. From 1978 on, the government passed a number of measures aimed at trade and financial liberalization, which, instead of accomplishing economic efficiency and price stability, provoked the economic collapse that shook up the country between 1980 and 1981.

The clear failure of Martínez de Hoz's policies convinced General Roberto Viola, who succeeded Videla as president in 1981, to appoint a new economic team with a different philosophy. Lorenzo Sigaut, Viola's economy minister, tried desperately to remedy a situation that was already compromised. Through massive devaluations, Sigaut successfully restored a positive balance of payments; but he was unable to temper inflationary expectations and capital flight.

In the face of deep economic crisis and increasing political pressure by civilian groups for a quick return to democracy, Viola slowly began a process of political liberalization. However, such an attempt was short-lived; for the hard-line sectors of the military, headed by army commander Leopoldo Galtieri, deposed Viola.

Galtieri, who replaced Viola in the presidency, appointed a new economic team, which began to employ a series of orthodox stabilization policies. Politically, while repressing opposition, Galtieri began to portray himself as a new *caudillo*. His aim was to create a conservative block that under his guidance could defeat the Peronists and the Radicals in an open election to be held at an unspecified date in the future.

Despite the ban imposed on them, political party leaders joined in the Multipartidaria, a multiparty coalition including Radicals, Peronists, Christian Democrats and other minor groups. Labor unions also remained active; in late March 1982 they staged a general strike to protest the government stabilization policies and to ask for a return to democracy. The following April, the Falklands/Malvinas War broke out. Some argued that the rationale behind the invasion was to rally public support behind an increasingly discredited regime (Vacs 1986). Right after the occupation of the islands, a tide of nationalism swept Argentina and Galtieri experienced for a moment a popular support that only Perón had seen before. However, the tragic end of the war and the incompetent manner in which the military commanders conducted the operation put a de facto end to the military regime. Retired general Reynaldo Bignone was appointed as the new ad interim president to guide the transition to civilian rule. At the end of 1983, the military handed power over to a civilian administration. Of the three goals stated by the Proceso, only the eradication of terrorism was achieved by 1978—through brutal repression. According to independent sources about thirty thousand people had disappeared, most presumed dead. By 1983, the country was on the verge of an economic collapse: inflation was running at an increase of 350 percent a year; and the country was not able to service the interest payments on its foreign debt, which had grown from $8,279 million in 1976 to $44,377 million in 1983. The third objective—the creation of new political and social institutions—remained, as it had during the authoritarian period of 1966–1973, a dead letter. The military had proven, once more, that it was ill equipped for the task of institution building. It had based its legitimacy on the argument that it was better suited to assure economic stability, law, and order than civilian politicians. The record, by 1983, clearly proved that this was not the case.

The 1983 elections saw two main contenders: Italo Luder for the Peronist party and Raul Alfonsín for the Radicals. The Peronists, who had never lost a fair election, were shocked when Alfonsín came out as the winner. Alfonsin's victory was credited to his broad appeal not only among the middle sectors (which traditionally made up the bulk of the Radical electoral base) but also among the upper class and some sectors of the working class. Moreover, poor campaign strategies and weak leadership on the part of the Peronist ticket convinced many undecided voters to opt for Alfonsín. During his campaign, Alfonsín promised to (1) prosecute those guilty of human rights violations during the "dirty war," (2) abandon the recessionary policies of the Bignone administration and pursue economic policies aimed at economic growth and income redistribution, and (3) reestablish public confidence in the institutions of the democratic system.

However, on taking office in December 1983, it was clear that the new administration lacked any clear plans to tackle the economic crisis. Initially, a piecemeal and gradualist approach was adopted. Large wage increases were granted to make up for previous losses, and credit was eased to encourage investments; these efforts (predictably) provoked even more inflation and public deficit. As he promised during the presidential campaign, Alfonsín initially took a tough stand on the renegotiation of the foreign debt and interest payments on the debt were suspended at the end of 1983. By December 1984 a further deterioration in the balance of payments, coupled with an inflationary outburst, convinced Alfonsín of the necessity of an agreement with the IMF establishing a strict stabilization plan. However, the implementation of the plan was delayed until there was widespread political consensus for a drastic solution. Alfonsín moved gradually. He first appointed a new economic team in February but waited until June to announce the Austral Plan. By that time, the rate of inflation was increasing at 30 percent a month.

The Austral Plan was an instant success. It combined some features of orthodox monetary and fiscal policy with more unorthodox measures, such as wage and price freezes, compulsory savings, and the creation of a new currency, the austral. Inflation dropped from 30 percent in June to 3 percent in August, and price stability continued through the first half of 1986. It appeared as if Argentina had broken an inflationary cycle that had lasted for three decades. Beginning in March 1986, the administration, under heavy pressure from trade unions and business interests, began to promote economic growth at the expense of price stability. This proved to be a crucial mistake. As soon as price and wage controls were lifted, it became evident that inflation had been suppressed but not eliminated. From the second part of 1987 on, the growth in the rate of inflation returned to monthly double-digit levels, declining only moderately at the end of 1988. In short, political pressure on the administration to reactivate the economy too soon prejudiced the early achievements.

In his effort to initiate military trials, Alfonsín acted firmly at first; but he found it more and more difficult to do so in the face of military opposition, which resulted in three military uprisings between 1987 and 1988. In December 1986 Congress passed the Ley de Punto Final (which set a sixty-day deadline for the filing of criminal charges against military and civilians suspected of having committed crimes) and in June 1987 the Due Obedience Law (acquitting officers who had acted under superiors' orders). In the end, only a few senior officers were convicted. The concessions made by the Radicals to the armed forces in the face of military threats tarnished the image of the administration. In fact, many early supporters of Alfonsín felt as if the president's promise to bring criminals before the law had been betrayed.

Alfonsín tried to convince his fellow citizens that only through tolerance, respect for the rules spelled out in the constitution, and negotiation, could democracy be restored in Argentina. He wanted to portray himself as a president above party lines; but that aim often contrasted with the necessity to foster the interests of the Radical party and its candidates, particularly in the gubernatorial and congressional elections of 1987 and the presidential campaign of 1989.

Recent Scholarship and Findings on Argentina

Most's analysis, unfortunately, spanned only the years 1930 to 1970. An extension of this work to include critical coalition changes in the 1970s and

1980s could add much to the scholarly debate. During this period there were three critical coalition changes: 1973 (the populist administrations of the Peronist period), 1976 (the Proceso), and 1983 (the Radical administration). These were crucial periods in Argentine history, particularly the military regime of 1976–1983, which comes closer to resembling the bureaucratic-authoritarian model than the 1966–1970 Ongania administration and constitutes an even better testing ground for O'Donnell's hypothesis.

Although no quantitative public policy analyses of the kind carried out by Most were performed for the 1970–1988 period, a number of studies exist that are closely related to both O'Donnell's and Most's arguments. Economic and political analyses of the 1973–1976 Peronist administrations show that the policies implemented were not new and did not represent a clear departure from previous policies (Canitrot 1978; De Pablo 1980; Di Tella 1983; Epstein 1987; Wynia 1978, 1986). In fact, under Levingston and Lanusse salary earners and interest groups had been partially compensated for the losses incurred during the Ongania administration (Wynia 1978). Moreover, price and wage freezes and voluntary compliance had been tried by populist and authoritarian governments before. A combination of inadequate resource availability, exogenous factors (the 1973 oil shock crisis), and political constraints severely restricted the environment of choice of the Peronist policymakers. Even the social pact, which officially collapsed with Perón's death in July 1974, ran into serious trouble in March of the same year when salary increases were granted prematurely in order to retain the unions' support. Thereafter, economic policies became less redistributive and resorted to conventional monetary and fiscal means to fight the inflationary spiral.

As for the policies carried out by the military regime under Videla, the evidence is mixed. Studies by Frenkel and O'Donnell (1978), Frenkel and Fanelli (1987), and Schvarzer (1983) have emphasized a strong relationship between neoconservative economic policy and the bureaucratic–authoritarian regime. According to these scholars, the new government designed and carried out a distinct set of economic policies to solve the stalemate that the country had reached by 1976. Other works have seriously questioned such a relationship. Studies on the neoconservative approach to economic stabilization in Argentina by Canitrot (1979, 1981), Heymann (1983), Ramos (1986), Wogart (1983), and Sourrouille (1983), although different in approach and emphasis, found the economic policies of Martínez de Hoz much less orthodox than previously hypothesized. On the presumed coherence of military regime's economic policies, Wogart commented,

> What started out as demand-oriented orthodox price stabilization, benefiting business in general and agriculture in particular at the cost of lower real wages and reduced public outlays, ended up as a supply-widening restructuring program, punishing business (particularly agriculture), selling tradable goods at the benefit of business engaged in non-traded goods—especially in nontradable services. (1983, 470)

Martínez de Hoz's stabilization program in 1976 and 1977 tried to avoid a "shock treatment" (as had resulted under the civilian administrations of President Arturo Frondizi in 1959 and Ongania in 1967). The purchasing power of salary and wage earners declined sharply; but unemployment levels and public investments remained steady, while self-employment increased (Ramos 1986). The inability of the economy minister to "rationalize" the state sector was due to the vetoes imposed by the military, particularly when it came to curtailing expenditures of companies linked to the large, military-controlled industrial sector. Therefore, although parties and labor unions had been muted, this did not mean, as many assumed, that "politics" per se had disappeared. Military managers, representing various vested interests, in part replaced the civilian interests that had thwarted the implementation of economic policies under previous civilian and authoritarian regimes. The reversal of some of Martínez de Hoz's economic policies when Viola succeeded Videla was a clear sign that the military was all but committed to the neoconservative approach. Nor can reversal be ascribed to an attempt to implement a coherent set of economic policies, as O'Donnell would argue.

Again, under Alfonsín no clear policy pattern emerged. Analyses by Heymann (1987), Canavese and Di Tella (1987), and Rodriguez (1987) showed the different paths chosen by the Radical administration as the events unfolded. First, redistributional policies and economic growth were pursued. When such policies became untenable, the government turned to the Austral Plan and austere economic measures. As the economic situation improved, emphasis was placed again on growth at the expense of price stability. After a few months the economic picture deteriorated; and the government went back to enforce a new set of anti-inflationary measures, first in 1987 with the Australito Plan and again in mid-1988 with the Plan Primavera. In short, domestic political and economic problems, along with external constraints such as the debt servicing, placed severe limitations on the Alfonsín administration's capacity to redirect policies in the long run. The Austral Plan was an attempt in this direction but did not last long for the reasons explained.

The record for the 1970–1988 period suggests that the room available to new ruling coalitions for the carrying out of distinctive public policies was small. Incrementalism and policy shifts within the same kind of regime best describe the Argentine situation. The evidence shows that similar factors led to different policy responses by the same political regimes, while different policy processes ended with similar results under different regimes. Most's work, in the pages to come, attempts to make some sense out of this puzzle and constitutes a stride forward both theoretically and methodologically. The conclusions reached by this work can be a useful point of departure for students of public policy in Latin America. Building on the analysis presented in these pages, researchers may find it useful to conceptualize more rigorously how domestic policy constraints limit the environment of choice of policymakers and, in turn, how domestic and external constraints are inter-related to each other. The emphasis, therefore, should be placed on the decisionmaker's perception of the policy options available, the expected utility ensuing from each option, and the decisionmaker's willingness to favor one choice over another (Most and Starr 1984). In this way we could come to an explanation of why similar factors across space and time can result in different policies, while different processes can trigger similar outcomes, regardless of differences in regime type.

Durham, N.C.
December 1988

Notes

1. Interview with Adalbert Krieger Vasena, Buenos Aires, August 1987.

TWO

Setting the Stage: Political Change and Public Policy

Since Guillermo O'Donnell's (1973) work on the linkages between economic crisis, regime type, and public policy, research on Latin America took off in several new and rewarding directions. His study suggested that the nations in that region are not "progressing" toward the development of either pluralist–democratic or totalitarian political institutions and practices. Rather, urbanization, industrialization, and middle-class growth combine with certain socioeconomic crises to produce a dialectical interplay of forces (Collier 1978), which leads the Latin American nations along a "third path"[1]—the development and elaboration of new forms of authoritarian rule.[2]

O'Donnell argued that particular types of economic and social crisis are associated with each phase of modernization. Each phase brings a new dominant coalition to power and produces a different type of authoritarian government. Each government then pursues a distinct set of public policies in its efforts to solve the social, economic, and political problems it confronts. Two linkages are important here: between type of problem (or crisis) and dominant coalition and between type of coalition and particular policies.

The second link, however, implies an orderly image of political change that is not consistent with standard descriptions of the policy process in Latin America. For instance, it has been noted that political elites in the region tend to exaggerate the novelty and innovation of their policies, that wide gaps often develop between policies proclaimed and those actually adopted, that bureaucratic inertia typically thwarts policymakers' efforts to change policies, and that the most general characteristic of policymaking in the region is chronic failure to achieve policy goals.

I shall address the questions raised when these awkward features of the Latin American policy process are juxtaposed with the smooth model of policy change suggested by O'Donnell's research. Is the match between types of economic and social problems, types of authoritarian rule, and public policies really as orderly as has been assumed? Although it may be useful to classify these governments as authoritarian, how successful are they in exercising authority when they attempt to implement public policies? Is policy

19

change more (or less) erratic than the literature on authoritarian politics suggests? Do policies follow a pattern of slow, incremental change marginally influenced by major changes in government, or do policy trends change sharply when one coalition replaces another? Does it really matter which coalition dominates?

I examine these questions from the perspective of two competing arguments. The first, derived primarily from O'Donnell's original treatment of authoritarian rule in Latin America, focuses on who governs. Dominant coalitions determine what policies are made, for whom, and at whose expense. The replacement of one dominant coalition by another should produce fundamental shifts in public policies. The alternative argument, drawn from North American research on public policy, asks, "who cares who governs?" It assumes that the policy preferences, class backgrounds, and personal biases of dominant coalitions and of the political personnel representing them in the highest levels of government are unimportant. It is the *public bureaucracy* that in fact "governs" in fundamental ways. Middle- and low-level actors in the public bureaucracy make current policies based on prior policy decisions. Coalition and elite goals and motivations may have little connection with what policies are made, who benefits from them, and who pays for them. Moreover, the replacement of one dominant coalition by another should produce no profound changes in public policies.

Although each of these approaches is useful only in certain contexts, my strategy is to synthesize them into a single model. Such an integrated formulation attempts to specify when asking "who governs" is or is not important for understanding public policies. It predicts when shifts between dominant coalitions will or will not produce major policy change.

Argentina provides an excellent context for my analysis for three reasons. First, three distinct types of authoritarian political systems existed there from 1930 through 1970. Each regime was supported by a unique array of forces constituted by different classes and sectors of society. Their policy goals and priorities were widely divergent. No two consecutively ruling coalitions shared a consensus on fundamental issues. If dominant coalitions and changes between them were ever important for determining public policies, they should have been influential in Argentina during the 1930–1970 period.

Second, four important developments in Argentina in the late 1940s and early 1950s form the basis on which the authoritarian and bureaucratic arguments are integrated: (1) the public bureaucracy became large and extensively unionized; (2) the ostensible leaders at the highest levels of government began to demonstrate a chronic inability to retain their position for more than brief intervals; (3) a shortage of previously unallocated government resources began to develop; and (4) a pervasive social stalemate and general crisis of authority began to grip the nation.

Third, and perhaps most importantly, Argentina provides an appropriate context for this analysis because its post-1966 governments were the archetypical examples (or paradigmatic cases) of O'Donnell's original bureaucratic–authoritarian regime type. If there exists any testing ground on which this version of O'Donnell's thesis is truly safe—any area in which it should be in the least danger of rejection or modification—it should be in Argentina.

This research adds to the scholarship on Latin America in several ways. It is one of the first efforts to test the hypothesized linkages between types of authoritarian rule and public policies rigorously (see also the essays in Collier 1979). While such relationships have been specified by other analysts, most discussions have dealt at abstract theoretical or simple definitional levels. In addition, this work has a number of possible implications for researchers who are concerned with the state and various forms of corporatist interest representation in Latin America. These analysts often appear to assume that the Latin American state can be usefully regarded as a unified rational actor that formulates and executes public policies in order to maximize the gains of dominant coalitions and political elites.

The *integrated formulation* developed here, in contrast, predicts the possible fragmentation of the state in Latin America. It envisions political elites in conflict with the low- and middle-level public bureaucrats and argues that under certain conditions public policies may cease to reflect the interests and motivations of the dominant coalitions and the elites who represent them in the highest levels of government. Policy outputs may, instead, increasingly become the outcomes of intrastate bargaining and conflict. If so, a new explanation will have been provided to account for the economic and social problems that face the Latin American nations. Scholars typically explain those difficulties on the basis of "external" determinants such as the problems created by delayed dependent development, U.S. imperialism, multinational corporations, and so on. The integrated formulation does not seek to minimize the importance of such factors. It does suggest, however, that simple government mismanagement, poor planning, and faulty policy execution may in some cases be major contributing factors to the social and economic problems that beset the nations in the region.

This research also aims at the heart of an increasingly important theoretical problem in public policy research. A confusing variety of elite, class, interest group, rational actor, organizational process, bureaucratic politics, pluralist–democratic, and state–centered approaches to public policy analysis currently exist in the literature. Each constitutes an island of theory. Each is apparently useful in some policy areas and in some settings. None of the existing approaches seems in and of itself to hold much potential for emerging as a general, grand theory. The problem is how to take the next step toward linking the islands of theory. The strategy employed here attempts to translate apparently "competing" arguments into common terms and link them together by specifying the conditions under which one or another approach is likely to be useful for explaining and predicting public policies. The result of this strategy is a formulation that has greater scope and generality than either of the currently existing authoritarian or bureaucratic/incremental arguments.

Accordingly, Chapter 3 sets out the theoretical framework of the competing arguments and the integrated formulation. Chapter 4 considers the comparative usefulness of the various explanations with respect to who has actually governed in Argentina since 1930. Chapter 5 continues that analysis, focusing on public policies concerning the state, the institutionalization of the military, and the depoliticization of the system. Chapters 6, 7, and 8 examine industrialization and foreign policy, labor policy, and expenditure and revenue policy, respectively. Finally, in Chapter 9 the merits of the three competing arguments are assessed; and the case for the integrated formulation is concluded to be the strongest.

Notes

1. The term is from Schmitter 1972b.
2. See, for example, Stepan 1966 and Nelson 1969.

THREE

The Theoretical Framework: Authoritarianism, Incrementalism, and Constraints on Decisionmakers

Research on the political evolution of the Latin American nations has argued that those countries are developing along a new path that is not leading them toward either democracy or totalitarianism but toward the development and elaboration of a variety of authoritarian and corporatist political systems in which there is generally (1) only limited and nonresponsible pluralism, (2) no elaborate or guiding ideology, (3) little extensive or intensive mobilization of the populace, and (4) a tendency toward small leadership groups that exercise power within poorly defined limits (Linz 1964, 1972, 1975). A number of scholars attribute such developments to the region's Hispanic heritage.[1] Other researchers cite the cases of Germany and France as they are analyzed by Karl Marx (1964), Friedrich Engels (1969), V. Trotsky (1961), Alexander Gerschenkron (1952, 1966), Barrington Moore, Jr. (1966), and Ralf Dahrendorf (1967). They argue that the emergence of authoritarian political systems in Latin America can be explained on the basis of such factors as the economically and politically dependent status of those nations,[2] the lateness of their socioeconomic modernization,[3] or the fact that the Latin American nations are passing through certain novel stages in their socioeconomic modernization.[4]

The implications of this trend toward "Bonapartist," "Bismarckian," or "corporatist-authoritarian" political systems (Schmitter 1972a, 90) are clear. At certain critical junctures, different coalitions tend to establish their economic and political hegemony. Knowledge of which coalition is dominant at any given point in time is therefore said to be critical for understanding public policies in Latin America. "Who governs" tends to determine what policies will be made, for whom, and at whose expense. Because coalitions hold sharply divergent views about what should be done for whom, the replacement of one ruling group by another should produce a fundamental redistribution of the costs and benefits of public policies. Because contrasting coalitions appear to supplant one another in more or less sequential fashion in the course of a nation's history, a country's public policy outputs should show a series of such basic policy shifts.

O'Donnell (1973, 1974, 1975) provides the most thorough treatment of this thesis, which is referred to here as the "who governs" authoritarian argument. In his original examination of authoritarianism, O'Donnell identifies successive stages of *traditional, populist,* and *bureaucratic* authoritarian rule, passed through by every Latin American nation.[5] Each type of authoritarian rule is associated with a particular stage of capital accumulation (O'Donnell 1975) and, as a consequence, with the economic and political domination of a particular coalition of forces.[6] *Traditional* systems are characterized by dominance of a politically inert populace by the foreign export sector. *Populist* systems are largely ruled by the interests of industrialization and expansion of domestic markets. *Bureaucratic* forms of rule are essentially technocratic and antipopular, concerned to expand basic industries. These dominant coalitions and the elite political personnel who represent the alliances in government determine what policies will be made, who will benefit from them, and who will pay for them.

A prime difficulty with this thesis is that coalitions and elites in Latin America do not always seem to determine the basic distribution of policy costs and benefits. In some contexts, essentially identical coalitions adopt different policies; in others, different coalitions enact similar measures. The expected policy distinctions are not always apparent in the empirical world.

Charles Anderson and Albert Hirschman take note of this problem and observe that in Latin America wide gaps frequently exist between policy proposals, plans, or statements and actual policy outputs; that swings in official ideology are often far greater and more dramatic than swings in actual policy outputs; that the motivation to solve a problem often outruns an understanding of it; that the effectiveness of decisionmakers is constrained or conditioned by the objective realities of their environment; and that policies are more prudential and pragmatic than ideological or doctrinaire (Anderson 1967, 68–86, 115–138; Hirschman 1968a, 227–246).[7]

The work of other researchers yields findings that appear to fall in between that of O'Donnell and Anderson and Hirschman. Authoritarianism and different types of authoritarian rule are important, but policy decisions are found to be nonideological and incremental during the existence of a particular type of authoritarian system (Purcell 1973b). Newly arriving political elites and coalitions are successful in altering policy outputs and processes only in the areas in which their goals are most intense and their technical expertise is most applicable (Schmitter 1971b; Ames 1973). Even in the Brazilian case, which is presumed to be one of the most important coalition changes recently occurring in Latin America, the new coalition was cautious when it came to power in 1964. Its members did not seek to destroy the old system and effect radical policy change. They sought instead to mesh the old with the new, modify previous policies rather than abandon them, and advance carefully in a number of policy areas (Schmitter 1973, 205).[8]

The implication of these analyses is that those who govern (and who thereby have de jure control over the policy process) do not always appear to be useful predictors of public policies. The replacement of one dominant ruling coalition by another does not invariably result in a fundamental or sweeping policy reorientation. The type of political system, the makeup of the dominant coalition, and the backgrounds and preferences of the actors who hold high-level government positions might be useful for predicting policy *plans or proposals;* but actual policy *outputs* do not invariably appear to be explained by the coalitional formulation.[9]

An obvious alternative approach to understanding patterns of policy outputs in Latin America is to assume that elites are irrelevant and to employ some incremental change, organizational process, prior decision, or bureaucratic formulation.[10] Despite the variations among such models, all entail an assumption that the detection of problems, the perception of the nature of problems, and the range of available policy responses are at least partially dependent on what the policymaking organization did in the past. These formulations therefore lead to the following basic expectations: (1) the best single predictor of current policy should be previous policy; (2) the interests and preferences of dominant coalitions and political elites do not determine what policies are made, for whom, or at whose expense; and (3) changes between sets of top-level governing groups should not produce major or nonincremental policy changes. These expectations appear to be congruent with much of the evidence discussed above.

The difficulty is that the conditions generally thought to contribute to the adoption of such styles or modes of decisionmaking are not observed in Latin America. In discussing their "disjointed incremental" model, for example, David Braybrooke and Charles Lindblom note that that mode of decisionmaking may be dominant only when power in society is diffused. Power in Latin America is frequently concentrated in the state and its various coalitional backers. Incremental change models are said to be adopted when there is a need to maintain an underlying consensus on fundamental issues (1963, 73–78). Latin American societies are frequently divided along class and sectoral lines. Their members appear to share no consensus on the issues that confront them. Hegemonic crises, or stalemates, frequently develop among the rival forces that contend for power.[11] Authoritarian policies are allegedly adopted in the first place as a means for imposing some semblance of consensus and unity (Linz 1972, 26).[12]

Incremental decisionmaking models should be appropriate when policies are made by middle- and low-level professional bureaucrats (Braybrooke and Lindblom 1963, 73–78). In Latin America, however, the decisionmakers at the highest levels are said to make even day-to-day decisions, not the bureaucracy (Anderson 1967; Purcell 1973b). Even the most minor and routine decisions are passed upward to persons situated at the highest levels of the bureaucratic hierarchy, and those leaders tend to deprecate and forget previous policy initiatives (Hirschman 1968a, 244). Each attack on a problem should therefore be a fresh and original effort. Prior decisions fail to serve as a basis for learning or as the core policy commitments from which incremental adjustments might be made.

Clearly, then, the authoritarian and various bureaucratic formulations each explain some policy outputs and outcomes but not others. My strategy is to confront the apparent inconsistencies in the authoritarian and bureaucratic/satisficing theses. First, I shall translate the two approaches into common terms so that their apparently competing aspects can be eliminated. Then I shall develop a formulation that synthesizes the two arguments. That *integrated thesis* will attempt to specify in advance and on theoretical, rather than empirical, grounds the conditions in which the predictions of the two currently distinct approaches should be supported. In that way, a formulation both wider in scope and more generalizable than either the "who governs" or "who cares who governs" theses is developed without any appreciable sacrifice in parsimony.

Construction of the integrated formulation, of course, rests on the argument that the authoritarian and bureaucratic theses are not really contradictory. I shall show that they are compatible. For the moment, I only note that the integrated formulation assumes that who governs is always important. It is cautious in not assuming, however, that the ostensible rulers at the top levels of government, who have de jure control, necessarily have de facto control that would allow them to act effectively to formulate, execute, and otherwise influence public policies. Under certain conditions, the apparent rulers may lose their control. Other actors may enter the policymaking arena and dominate it. Who these other actors are, the conditions that might enable them to gain control, and why their domination of the policymaking arena might be important are explored below.

The task of reconciling and eventually integrating the "who governs" authoritarian and bureaucratic theses entails a consideration of the logical structure of the authoritarian formulation. If the replacement of one coalition by another is to result in a fundamental policy change, the following three assumptions should hold true:

1. Dominant coalitions and the elite political personnel who represent them in the highest levels of government effectively formulate, execute, and otherwise influence public policies;
2. If knowledge about the constituency of the dominant coalition were available, such information would enable one to predict the basic distribution of goods and services, that is, what types of public policies would be made and who would benefit or suffer from them; and
3. The degree of consensus about what public policies should be made, who should benefit from them, and who should pay for them is rela-

tively greater within each of the dominant coalitions than across the coalitions existing at different points in time.

The fulfillment of these assumptions generates some difficulties, however. Even if dominant coalitions and the elite political personnel who represent them in government are important in determining policy goals and priorities, there is no guarantee that the elites will be successful in actually executing the policies they prefer. Motivations—what Anderson (1967, 134) and Harvey Starr (1978) call *willingness*—may often be frustrated so that the ruling coalition and elite political personnel at each stage of authoritarian rule fail to govern effectively. Even if one assumes that the leaders in each of the three authoritarian political systems formulate and attempt to execute public policies as if they were unified, "rational" actors utilizing a "synoptic" method of problem-solving,[13] such leaders still might not produce policies that would serve to maximize the gains of the members of the coalition at each stage (Allison 1971, 33).

The problems the leaders of each coalition face are complex. The problem detection and information feedback systems elites have at their control are limited. These systems may therefore give the elites only a partial view of the socioeconomic conditions surrounding them, the problems that may arise from that environment, the problems that actually arise, and the possible range of policy alternatives to deal with them.[14] In other words, the coalition leaders may seldom have the comprehensive understanding necessary to adopt a "rational" method of problem-solving.[15] For this reason alone dominant coalitions might not be able to translate their policy goals and priorities into actual policy outputs. Even if the coalition members and political elites do know exactly what they want and need to do, resource limitations and the difficulty in effecting rapid reallocations of resources from one sector of society to another may still constrain what the decisionmaking elites can actually do. Knowing what to do and how to do it may produce "rational" decisions, policy proposals, and plans; but knowing is different from doing. Decisions are distinct from actual policy outputs.

All of this suggests that dominant coalitions might not be able to convert their policy goals and priorities into actual policy outputs. To paraphrase Starr (1978), dominant coalitions may be *willing* to implement the policies they prefer, but the complexities of the problems they face and the limitations on the resources they have at their disposal may deny them the *opportunity* to govern effectively. If that is the case (if different coalitions acquire political control but many are limited in the extent to which they can actually apply their power), "who governs" at the top may not, after all, be a critical consideration for understanding public policies. The replacement of one ruling group by another may produce only marginal changes in policy outputs.

In summary, it appears that two different lines of argument might be developed to integrate the authoritarian/rational thesis with the various bureaucratic/satisficing theses. Dominant coalitions in Latin America and the elite political personnel representing each of them in the highest levels of government may be important considerations in public policy analyses; but the impact those coalitions (and changeovers between them) have on actual policy outputs may be minimized by two factors. First, the complexities of the problems that elite decisionmakers face and limitations on their time and analytical abilities may force even newly arriving elites to forego the formulation of radically new, utopian policies and instead utilize prior decisions as a means for reducing uncertainty. Second, the problem of mobilizing new resources and the difficulty of reallocating existing resources may constrain the effectiveness of policymakers and force them to adopt current policies that are much the same as previous policies.

Whether taken alone or in combination, both of these arguments could be used to integrate the theses and clarify why shifts between dominant ruling coalitions in Latin America only *sometimes* result in major policy changes. It is important to reemphasize, however, that elaborations along either line would, in effect, presume that the dominant coalitions and elite political personnel are in fact the key actors formulating and executing public policies. The goals, motivations, and policy priorities of those groups—the actors' *willingness*—should, ceteris paribus, be reflected in actual policy outputs. The integration effort would implicitly assume that actors with de jure and de facto control are one and the same and proceed to focus on the additional factors that constrain and limit the effectiveness of those who govern at the top.

A third, more general line along which to integrate the apparently competing formulations is suggested by the idea that the equation of changeovers in dominant coalitions and elite political personnel with shifts in the actors who actually control the policymaking arena is misleading. The decision to focus on dominant ruling coalitions and the elite political personnel who represent them in government may not have been wise because such actors are not the ones who actually formulate, execute, and otherwise influence public policies.

If different groups rule but many fail to govern effectively in Latin America—if coalitions acquire political control but many are limited in the extent to which they can actually apply their power—then perhaps bureaucratic organizations and the middle- and low-level professional employees who work in them are fundamentally important in most policymaking arenas. Whether they are postal workers, engineers on publicly owned railroads, machinists in public corporations, or individuals who are more generally classed as public bureaucrats, the professional public employees play critical roles in the policy formation and/or policy implementation stages of most decisionmaking processes. They are the bridges between society at large and the elite political personnel. Whether one focuses on coalitions, elites, interest groups, or the citizenry at large, the professional middle- and low-level public employees are very much the "hidden actors"—the common denominators—in the policymaking arenas of all but the least complex and most highly personalized political systems.

The professional public employees and the bureaucratic organizations in which they work collect information, process it, and pass it upward to the elite personnel. Thus, they at least partially determine what the elite political personnel perceive to be problems and possible responses. If the elites lack a comprehensive view of the problems that confront them and the range of policy options that exist to deal with those conditions, it may be partly because the bureaucratic problem detection and information feedback mechanisms fail to provide such information. If the elite political personnel are to act, in most cases they must act through the public bureaucracy. Bureaucratic organizations execute whatever policy statements or plans are adopted by the political elites. They enforce public laws and collect revenues. They disburse benefits and locate new resources. If the elite political personnel have difficulties in mobilizing new resources, it may be because the bureaucracy has only a limited ability to collect revenues. If the elite political personnel have difficulties in reallocating existing funds, it may be because the bureaucracy is resistant to efforts to shift monies to different agencies or programs.

The relevance of these points becomes apparent when one considers the nature of the bureaucratic establishments in Latin America.[16] Scholars cite different factors as possible explanations of why the bureaucracies in that region have developed as they have. Some mention an Iberic or colonial heritage (Henry 1958; Lambert 1971; Hanson 1974) and poor recruitment practices (Scott 1966; Petras 1967). Others cite the weakness of previously existing administrative structures (Anderson 1967), poor administrative practices, and the complexities of the developmental tasks confronting the public bureaucracies (Waterston 1964). However, all of these researchers perceive the bureaucracies in Latin America as being characterized by the following relevant features:

1. A marked tendency toward red tape or *papeleria*;
2. A tendency toward bureaucratic inertia;
3. General unwillingness to accept any responsibility for making even the most minor decisions;
4. A hesitancy to follow even direct orders, or a tendency to accept the principle *Se acata pero no se cumple* ("I obey but I do not execute");
5. Tendencies toward slackness, poor work, high absenteeism, low morale, and the retention of even the most incompetent employees;
6. Tendencies toward the expansion of the number of autonomous agencies, increases in the size and complexity of existing agencies, and increases in the number of public employees, which lead to
    a. an increasing inability on the part of the elite political personnel to

coordinate and control the bureaucracy;

b. an increasing number of situations in which individual bureaucratic organizations end up working at their own speeds, for their own ends, and without much consideration for the progress of related efforts by other units; and

c. an increasing trend toward overstaffing, especially at the lower levels of the public bureaucracy;

7. A tendency toward hiring practices which are based on personal or political considerations rather than on ability;

8. A tendency toward a bias in which the bureaucrats perceive that change, however minor, may lead to the loss of their privileges and status; and

9. A tendency toward a relatively low rate of turnover in the bureaucratic personnel at the middle and low levels—which, if accompanied by high rates of turnover in the elite personnel, may lead to a lack of congruence between the interests of the high-level actors and the professional public employees.

All this leads, therefore, to the recognition of four rather basic points. First, employees in the public sector are in a strategic position to deny the elites their opportunities to govern effectively; more pointedly, in many settings it may be the middle- and low-level professional employees in the public sector who effectively govern in the policymaking arena. Second, if left undisturbed, any stable configuration of actors in the policymaking arena whose members hold stable interests should at least attempt to make current policies that are only marginally different from previous policies that satisfy their basic interests.

Third, elites and dominant coalitions do not make public policies in a vacuum. If such actors are to effect policy changes, maximize their gains and rule more authoritatively in the policy areas that interest them, they may often need to penetrate the professional public employee dominance of the policymaking arena and overcome the apparently normal reluctance on the part of middle- and low-level public employees to accept changes that could result in loss of status and privilege. If public employees do successfully resist the elites and thus constitute an additional constraint on their efforts to implement the policies they prefer, it seems likely that a shift from one dominant coalition to another will not, after all, result in a fundamental change in public policies.

Finally, if the shift in the locus of authority in the policymaking arena actually occurs, "who governs" at the top may be important for understanding public policies prior to the shift, while factors more germane to the public employees may be useful for explaining postshift policy outputs.

The last conclusion is quite obviously the most interesting. If it is possible to specify the conditions in which those who govern at the top will and will not dominate the policymaking arena (or, conversely, when public employees and the bureaucratic organizations in which they work will and will not be dominant), the apparent inconsistencies between the authoritarian and bureaucratic theses will have been overcome.

Four factors appear to be particularly important for determining whether nonbureaucratic potential actors in general and political elites in particular will have the *opportunity* to govern effectively in the policymaking arena:

- The abilities of coalitions and elites to press their demands in clear and consistent fashion;
- The balance of opposing forces in the policymaking arena and the existence of a crisis of hegemony, or stalemate, in the struggle for authority in society;
- The sheer size and complexity of the public sector and its degree of entrenchment; and
- Limitations on the availability of previously uncommitted resources.

The first constraint concerns the ability of actors to press their demands in persistent and unambiguous fashion. Stanley Hoffman (1968, 243–252) and Morton Halperin (1974, 89) suggest that cabinet-level "in-and-outers" are more likely than professional public employees to look for quick results and to exhibit ideological behavior. A high level of cabinet instability would probably exaggerate such tendencies. If cabinet officers recognize that they may have only a very short time in which to formulate and execute public policies, it is likely that they will exhibit a predilection for the grand plan or the dramatic policy statement. If solutions are called for, solutions must be presented, even if only on paper. For this reason, it is probable that cabinet-level in-and-outers will tend to emphasize responses to the problems that confront them. They will tend to make their policies at least appear to be fundamentally distinct from those of their predecessors.

Gaps can be expected to develop, however, between the ideological policy statements and actual policy outputs if cabinet-level instability is so pervasive that what John Davies (1966, 175) calls a "gypsy encampment atmosphere" grips the highest levels of government. From the point of view of the political elites, it should be apparent that true policy innovation and creativity require time and stability. At the very least, some period of time is required before a new cabinet official can be expected to have learned his office. Formulating policy responses to complex problems requires careful thought and evaluation. Time and stability are exactly what the high-level political elites may not have, however, if their turnover rate is high. They may live in a crisis environment in which solutions are demanded but survival in office is dependent on their taking some (almost any) immediate action. Thus, it is likely that highly unstable political elites will reflect a predilection for the grand plan but may actually tend to respond in traditional ways to the problems that confront them. Short time horizons may require cabinet-level officials to reach back in their institutional memories to solutions that were tried by their predecessors.[17]

Elite instability may produce gaps between ideological policy statements and actual policy outputs for a second reason. If the elites are constantly being shuffled, it is unlikely that they will be able to mobilize their subordinates. The professional middle- and low-level public employees who retain their positions when the leadership is altered will recognize that their superiors will have only very short tenures in office. The permanent staffs may feel threatened by the elites' ideologically based proposals for massive policy changes. They will be unwilling to risk their positions for a cabinet-level superior who probably will not be in office when the plans made today are executed tomorrow. The normal bureaucratic tendency to hold back and to resist change may therefore be exacerbated by the fact that a cabinet officer is viewed as a lame duck on the very day he is appointed.

The second important factor, related to the first, concerns the balance of forces in the arena. If two or more nonbureaucratic actors participate in the policy process but their efforts cancel each other out or result in a pluralist counterbalance, the middle- and low-level public employees may have considerable latitude in making new policy decisions and in simply continuing to execute old policies. The same outcome may pertain if two or more other opposing actors are participating and the bureaucracy acts as the "swing man," enabling one or another side to dominate.

The third critical consideration that may serve to deprive nonbureaucratic potential actors of the chance to participate effectively in the policy-making arena concerns the size of the public sector and its degree of entrenchment. In general, it appears that the greater the level of employment in the public sector and the greater the extent to which middle- and low-level professional public employees are protected from disciplinary acts by their superiors (as a result of public unions, some civil service programs, and so on), the more difficult it will be for elite political personnel to control and manage the public sector effectively. In other words, public bureaucracies are notoriously unresponsive, and increasing employment and unionization, for example, may decrease the likelihood that nonbureaucratic actors will be able to dominate the policymaking arena.

The size of the bureaucratic establishment is related to a series of complex factors, however. Bureaucracies do not simply spring into being. They are created as responses to some need or demand that may originate either from civil society or from within the state. Each bureaucracy has some governmental or extragovernmental actor or actors for which it provides some benefit or service. Thus, the creation of a bureaucratic agency represents a commitment on the part of the state to initiate some action and allocate some resource in behalf of those actors. The establishment of an agency is also a commitment to the bureaucrats and lesser-level employees who are hired to staff the organization.

Such commitments have a clear implication. An organization's standard operating procedures serve the interests of the agency's employees, but they may also serve the interests of the agency's clienteles. If that is the case, the public employees and their clienteles can both be expected to resist efforts by political elites to withhold or constrain responsibilities, goods, and services that have been provided in the past. In other words, once middle- and low-level public employees and their clienteles have received some benefit, they may be mobilized to ensure that the policy that serves their mutual advantage is at least maintained. To that extent, the initial commitments may constrain the subsequent decisionmaking latitude of the political elites.

For example, it should be easier, from the point of view of elite political personnel, to expand welfare and pension benefits than to contract them; easier to create publicly owned corporations than to dissolve them; easier to expand the state's role in the economy than to retreat from an already-high level of penetration and control—in a phrase, easier to start something than to stop something.

This implies, of course, that elites and other actors could overcome the limitations imposed by the public sector if they could simply expand existing programs and create new ones.[18] This raises the fourth critical consideration. The more policies elites start, the more policies will exist for elites to stop in the future. Each new program or program expansion entails new commitments. More clienteles are created. More resources are allocated. More bureaucracies are established, and more existing agencies are expanded. Such developments will exacerbate command-and-control problems within the state. They will lead to the formation of more and more groups and interests in civil society with a stake in the political game and, as a result, increase the likelihood of a pluralist balance or stalemate in both the policy arena and society at large. Most important, however, these developments will lead to an even greater problem if and when the creation of a new program or the expansion of an old one requires the political elites to effect cutbacks in other areas. Such reversals will be difficult if prior commitments are old and well established or if the public employees are well entrenched. On the other hand, if the shift to a zero-sum game can be avoided—if the elites can control or acquire previously unallocated resources—the elites may be able to retain a high degree of effectiveness not by reversing old policies or by cutting back on existing programs but by creating new programs, moving into new policy areas, and adding yet another layer to the government.

Once previously unallocated resources cease to be available, however, political elites and other nonbureaucratic actors may lose even that *opportu-*

nity to govern effectively. It is noteworthy that a growth in the size and complexity of the public sector tends to occur during periods of populist rule. Like the leaders of liberal democratic governments in the United States, populist leaders in Latin America sometimes have a genuine interest in improving the well-being of the low- and middle-income sectors of society. In other instances, the motivations of the populist leaders in Latin America may be purely cynical. They may adopt certain policies only because they wish to control the populace and forestall revolutionary upheaval. In either event, the populists appeal to the masses for support. They tend to create new programs and to expand old ones that channel benefits and services to low- and middle-income groups (O'Donnell 1973; Di Tella 1968b). Populist governments in Latin America also tend to nationalize foreign-owned enterprises and replace them with publicly owned corporations and autonomous agencies. Finally, populist systems tend to expand the role of the public sector in managing and guiding the national economy.

All of these policies result in an increased pluralization of society at large and an increased bureaucratization of the political system. That factor alone may be sufficient to initiate the shift of effective control out of the hands of the political elites and perhaps move real authority downward into the hands of the professional public employees. Populist expansion of the public sector may create only the potential for such a shift, however. Whether the political elites can prevent such a relocation of authority or retrieve control once they have lost it, appears to depend on their stability, the balance in the arena, and the availability of previously unallocated resources.

The expansion of the size and complexity of the public sector by populist regimes should make life difficult for postpopulist leaders. Dominant political coalitions and elite political personnel that come to power after the era of bureaucratization may be unable to set basic policies or reallocate policy costs and benefits. The policymaking arena may be dominated by middle- and low-level professional public employees.

Coalitions and elites will not necessarily lose as a result of the growth of the public sector, of course; control of the policymaking arena will not necessarily shift away from them. To the extent that their domination begins to be eroded, they can be expected to respond. They may attempt to overwhelm the bureaucracies by persistently pressing unambiguous demands. Elites may reduce the number of public employees, attempt to return publicly owned corporations to the private sector, and try to disrupt unions in the public sector. They may attempt to demobilize and suppress the clienteles that support the existing bureaucratic agencies and programs, tinker with civil service reforms, and so on.

There is at present no way to predict with precision the ultimate resolution of the struggle for control. In some instances, coalitions and leaders will succeed in their attempts to establish or reestablish their hegemony; on other occasions, they are likely to fail. It seems reasonable to speculate that tactics such as those outlined above will have a high probability of being successful only if elites are stable, capable of being dominant or sufficiently coercive in the arena, and/or are able to acquire the necessary resources to enact the policies that the postpopulist leaders prefer. If, however, two or more of the four factors develop more or less concomitantly, effective control of the policy-making arena will almost certainly shift away from the coalitions and leaders. If that occurs, direct attacks on the bureaucracy will likely fail.

Even if control of the arena does shift into the hands of the public employees, postpopulist political leaders and coalitions may not be completely incapacitated. A number of means exist through which elites can partially overcome or circumvent the constraints on their capacities to formulate and implement the public policies they prefer. They may, for example, be able to act effectively at a symbolic level. They may be able to retain a degree of actual authority if they act in areas in which policy pronouncements are tantamount to policy executions (that is, areas in which they do not need to rely on bureaucratic compliance with their demands). They may be able to create "new" resources to enact the policies they prefer. Postpopulist elites may be effective if they create new bureaucratic agencies embodying interests and values congruent with their own or if they act in areas in which no policies have been made previously. Finally, elites in the postpopulist period may attempt to retain some control by centralizing and restructuring the bureaucracy itself.

Policies that share these characteristics are clearly not insignificant. They are not, however, the types of measures that appear likely to effect fundamental redistributions of the costs and benefits of public policies. At least in the short run, such policies seem more likely to have the potential for resulting in only marginal cost–benefit changes. Indeed, if effective control of the policymaking arena has shifted to the professional middle- and low-level public employees, these are precisely the types of measures to which successful policymaking by the political elites and dominant coalitions should be restricted during the postpopulist period.

With the foregoing in mind, it is relatively easy to integrate the authoritarian and bureaucratic theses. First, it is important to note that both approaches are similar insofar as they both assume the importance of the actors with de facto, or actual, control of the policymaking arena. The two formulations make distinct assumptions about just who those actors are and how they decide. The authoritarian thesis focuses on coalitions and high-level governmental leaders who are (at least implicitly) thought to formulate and implement public policies in rational, value-maximizing, or synoptic fashion. The bureaucratic theses, in contrast, assume that public sector organizations have effective control and that they either satisfice or follow a pattern of partisan mutual adjustment.

Next, it is important to underscore the genuine importance of the "who" assumption. The interests and concerns that are brought to the public arena and given serious attention (the public agenda) tell one a great deal about "preferred policies"—what governments are *willing* to do. Change the actors—bring in new ones with very different preferences, perceptions, and goals—and governments may be *willing* to undertake very different policies and programs. That said, however, it seems clear that actors' *willingness* to adopt a policy does not ensure its actual or perfect adoption; actors must also have the capacity or *opportunity* to implement. To the extent that actors lack such *opportunities* or are in some way constrained, they will be unable to translate preferred policies into actual policies.

Specifically, the integrated thesis says that when (1) elites are able to press their demands in persistent and unambiguous fashion in the policymaking arena; (2) a balance does not exist in the arena between opposing, non-bureaucratic forces; (3) the public sector is neither large nor extensively unionized; and (4) the elites possess previously unallocated resources—then those who govern at the top (dominant coalitions and political elites) should be important for understanding public policies. The makeup of the dominant coalition should predict what policies are made, for whom, and at whose expense. Transitions between dominant coalitions with different perspectives should produce major policy shifts. As these conditions cease to exist, effective control of the policymaking arena should *pass out* of the hands of the elite political personnel and may move downward into the hands of the public employees. This conception of the four conditions—as *constraints* on elite influence—will be reflected in the analyses below. Under these conditions, the authoritarian thesis will cease to be relevant for understanding public policies. The ability of the elites to direct and redirect public policies toward their preferences will be decreased. Bureaucracies and the clienteles they represent will constitute a constraint—a drag—on elite efforts. What policies are made, who benefits from them, and who pays for them will be determined by what has been done in the past and what can be done in the future. Who governs at the top will cease to be fundamentally important for understanding public policies.

The integrated formulation thus succeeds in merging two arguments that appear on the surface to be inconsistent. A comparison of the authoritarian, bureaucratic, and integrated formulations will determine which provides the most accurate predictions and whether the integrated thesis offers an improved understanding of public policies.

It is, of course, premature to say whether or not the integrated formulation has any empirical value for understanding public policies. It is not too early, however, to point out three of the argument's immediate implications. One contribution is seen in the formulation's attempt to link what Forward (1971) calls "islands of theory" in a crude hypotheticodeductive network. The effort here is designed to retain the apparently competing approaches so that their individual advantages may be salvaged. The integration effort goes beyond this point, however, to consider why certain formulations work in different policy contexts. It then proceeds to link the arguments in a common web. Certain concepts—de facto control, actors' *willingness* to adopt certain policies, their *opportunities* to do so—are assumed to be invariably important. Because which actors have control, what they prefer, and the extent of their implementation capacities can logically be expected to vary from case to case and through time within cases; however, the argument suggests that neither universal nor even very general relationships should hold at the empirical level. Under different conditions one would expect to discover different associations, different ways of making public policy, and different explanations of what is done.

The four prior conditions—what Boynton (1982) would call *auxiliary conditions*—then, are developed as an initial basis for predicting which types of actors should have what capabilities. If that prediction is valid, there is some common theoretical ground for predicting which submodel should be useful. Regardless of whether the integrated formulation is empirically supported or not, this strategy for synthesizing existing explanations appears to have a variety of implications for future research.

The integrated formulation also has a number of implications for scholars interested in the political state and the development of corporatist systems of interest representation in Latin America. The new argument suggests that the state may not always be a unified rational actor as many researchers in these areas in effect assume. Instead, the state may become fundamentally fragmented, with the elite political personnel playing a role like any other "interest group" in intrastate bargaining and conflict.

Perhaps the most important aspect of the integrated formulation is its pessimistic implication for political change. If low- and middle-level public employees do take control of the policymaking arena so that political elites are reduced to being mere interest groups, even in pluralist democratic settings, the prospects for fundamental policy change seem slim. Because the power of the elites may be constrained by the public employees, whose strategic position enables them to dominate the policymaking arena, the replacement of political elites either through elections or coups d'état and shifts in constituency attitudes can realistically be expected to have only marginal impacts on policy established in the past. The integrated formulation is not deterministic, of course. Power may not, after all, shift to the public employees and, as has been said, a variety of steps may be taken in an attempt to stop the shift. If and when such a relocation occurs, however, little short of a revolutionary destruction of the bureaucracy is likely to succeed in returning authority to the political elites. The new formulation is therefore quite clearly a thesis one would prefer to reject. The very real fear is that rejection will not be possible and that under certain fairly common conditions, professional public employees may resist the political elites.

Before concluding this chapter, several caveats should be mentioned with respect to the integrated thesis. First, like any "good" or "useful" model, the formulation here greatly simplifies reality. An effort to specify the conditions under which elite or public employee dominance is more or less likely can be tremendously complicated. In any complex political system, it is probable that different sets of actors will dominate different policymaking arenas. In such settings, elites or public employees may sometimes be dominant; but additional types of actors may also play important roles in different arenas. The dominant configuration of actors in a policymaking arena may change at different stages in the decisionmaking process.[19] Finally, newly arriving elites might have partial success in penetrating public employee control of the policymaking arena. If that occurs, both elites and the low- and middle-level public employees might be important for understanding public policies. The newly arriving elites might produce policy realignments that are neither fundamental nor marginal.

A number of additional points should be understood. The integrated argument predicts that elites will be generally unable to influence public policies when the four conditions are present and that professional public employee dominance of the policymaking arena will tend to result in a pattern of incremental adjustment in policy outputs. Those two expectations are distinct and mutually independent because there is no assurance that public employees will universally accept the operational priorities, standard operating procedures, and long-range goals of their agencies. Public employees may not, in other words, conceive themselves to be members of the types of large-scale governmental organizations that are known to adjust outputs incrementally in some contexts. As a result, even though the professional public employees may successfully resist elite pressures for policy change, there is no assurance on these grounds that they will prefer to base current policies on prior decisions. Professional public employees, like the elites and coalitions, may have some specific policy goals that lead them to promote sharp policy shifts. Professional public employees might therefore resist the policy changes sought by the elites and simultaneously promote important policy changes that they themselves desire. I predict, however, that the public employees will not desire major policy changes and that they will be content with only marginal adjustments of previous outputs. The rationale for this prediction is based less on the argument that permanent government employees have some professionalized identity with their agencies than on the contention that low- and middle-level public employees generally tend to avoid uncertainty, seek continuity, and resist changes that might eventually work to their disadvantage.

Even if it is plausible to begin with a prediction that permanent public employees will prefer to adjust policies incrementally it should be understood that such actors may frequently lack the capacity to effect such adjustments. Neither elites nor public employees may actually be in full control of the policymaking apparatus. Low- and middle-level professional public employees, like the political elites, may face difficulties in formulating and implementing public policies. Like the elites, they, too, may be frustrated in their efforts to implement the policies that are congruent with their goals. It may therefore not be a question of elites or professional public employees; the integrated argument uses permanent government staffs as a default option. If elites are not effective and do not control the arena, the public employees do. This is a great simplification, of course, made plausible by the fact that public employees almost invariably play key roles in policy formulation and implementation processes. However, other additional actors may also be important or it may be possible that no one controls the arena—that no one is dominant and that no one really decides.

If policymaking does not invariably follow a pattern of incremental adjustment once the elites become ineffective, it should also be emphasized that marginal changes in policy outputs do not imply that public employees have actually taken control of the policymaking arena. If one assumes, for example, that the interests and policy goals of decisionmakers remain stable between time t and time $t + 1$, it would be plausible to expect that policy decisions at time $t + 1$ should be based on prior decisions made at time t in situations in which policymakers are

1. Sensitive to the interests of all (or many) sectors of society, but those "competing" sectors share a fundamental consensus that does not change between time t and time $t + 1$;
2. Sensitive to the demands of all (or many) sectors of society, but the policymakers perceive that those competing demands have counterbalanced each other between time t and time $t + 1$;
3. Sensitive to the interests of some particular sector(s) and the interests of the sectors do not change between time t and time $t + 1$; or
4. Insensitive to the demands of all sectors of society.

If the set of decisionmakers is stable (if the decisionmakers share a stable consensus about what is to be done and how), then regardless of the identities, backgrounds, and motivations of the decisionmakers, it seems reasonable to expect that implemented policies will remain basically unchanged. Incremental change patterns may also develop for another reason. While the integrated argument focuses attention on four factors that may limit the policymaking effectiveness of top-level governmental personnel and dominant coalitions, those four conditions clearly do not exhaust the range of possible constraints. Political elites may fail to execute their desired policies in the presence of the four conditions, and an incremental style of policymaking may be adopted; but such results might actually be attributable to such other factors as the international environment or balances that result from agency infighting.

This means that one cannot work backward by examining policy trends and concluding something about who made them and why. This point will be discussed extensively in Chapter 4, but it should be noted here that a test of the integrated argument requires one to work forward. Assumptions are made about (1) what elites, coalitions, and permanent low- and middle-level public employees desire, or are *willing* to promote in the way of public policies and (2) the conditions in which elites or public employees should be effective. These postulates lead to empirical predictions about what policies should look like through time.

Evidence of successful elite policy implementation and/or the lack of a pattern of incremental change in the presence of the four conditions will be sufficient for rejection (or at least revision) of the argument. At the same time, however, it should be recognized that satisfaction of the empirical predictions will not conclusively demonstrate, or confirm the validity of, the thesis; such findings would support or be consistent with it. This is the nature of the enterprise. As long as alternative explanations of the observed policy patterns exist—and they almost always will—progress is made by rejecting or disconfirming arguments that do not work.

For this reason questions of timing become important in the analysis. Shifts between dominant coalitions occurred in Argentina both in the absence of, and in the presence of, the four conditions. If elites implemented the policies that they preferred when the constraints were absent but failed to do so when they were present, the evidence will be regarded as supporting the integrated argument. The thesis will not be "proven," but neither will it be rejected.

Notes

1. Scholars who have argued that the patterns of political evolution in Latin America are explained on the basis of the region's Hispanic heritage include: Hartz 1964; Morse 1964; Sarfatti 1966; Lipset 1967; Wiarda 1973, 1974a, 1974b; and Veliz 1972.

2. See, for example, Hirschman 1961; Baer 1961–1962; Kling 1968; Dos Santos 1968a, 1970; Furtado 1969; and Cardoso and Faletto 1969.

3. See, for example, Kenworthy 1967, Cardoso and Reyna 1968, Hirschman 1968a, Soares 1968, Schmitter 1971a, Collier 1975, and Collier and Messick 1976.

4. See, for example, Bodenheimer 1971, O'Donnell 1973, and W. Smith 1976.

The citations in this and the two foregoing notes barely begin to tap the literature on the causes and consequences of authoritarian political development in Latin America. Other sources would include R. Collier and Collier 1979; Cardoso 1973; Chalmers 1969; Cotler 1972, 1975; Kaufman et al. 1975; Purcell 1973a, 1973b; Putnam 1967; Ray 1973; Schmitter 1974b; Erickson 1972; Gramsci 1957; Poulantzas 1973; Di Tella 1965, 1968); Trotsky 1961; Merkx 1969; Mamalakis 1969; Newton 1974; Pike 1974; Malloy 1974, 1977; Collier 1979; the January 1974 issue of the *Review of Politics;* and the April 1977 issue of *Comparative Political Studies.*

5. Unless otherwise noted, all references are to O'Donnell 1973. The interested reader may wish to consult O'Donnell's other works for more extensive treatments of the third, or bureaucratic, stage of authoritarian rule. Alternative typologies and discussions of subtypes of authoritarian and corporatist systems are available in Linz 1964, 1972; Schmitter 1974a; and Collier, Spencer, and Waters 1975.

6. In O'Donnell's formulation, each type of authoritarian system is associated with a number of additional factors. In his extensive treatment of changes and developments occurring within bureaucratic–authoritarian systems (1975), for example, O'Donnell argues that such systems display the following defining characteristics: (1) they appear as a consequence of the political activation of the popular (urban) sector; (2) they correspond to an important transformation in the stage of capital accumulation; (3) they are excluding types of economic systems; (4) they are excluding political systems; (5) they are depoliticizing political systems; and (6) in each of them, high government positions are held by persons who have risen through successful careers in complex and highly bureaucratized organizations such as the armed forces, the state itself, and private enterprise.

7. Similar observations have been made by Beechert 1965, Waterston 1964, Anderson 1965, Lambert 1971, and Valenzuela 1976.

8. Schmitter (1973, 205) labels this style of leadership as "defensive modernization." Moore (1966) calls it "revolution from above," but it is designed to effect evolutionary, rather than radical, change. Whether the outcome was intentional or simply the consequence of the limited effectiveness of the new Brazilian leaders, the result of the 1964 coup in Brazil is analogous to the following description of similar changes in Germany and Japan: "As they proceeded with conservative modernization, these semiparliamentary governments tried to preserve as much of the original social structure as they could, fitting large sections into the new building wherever possible. The results had some resemblance to present-day Victorian houses with modern electrical kitchens but inefficient bathrooms and leaky pipes hidden decorously behind newly plastered walls" (Moore 1966, 438).

9. Perhaps Anderson says it most succinctly: "No political ideology or political movement proved to be a 'cure-all' for the problems of development and post-war Latin America. Furthermore, few policy styles had the clear-cut distinctiveness that is generally attributed to them. Military governments tended to engage in large-scale public works projects, and so did other types of regimes. In some cases, political stability and 'no nonsense' government contributed to economic growth, and in other cases it did not. Large-scale public enterprise was generated by regimes espousing nationalism and social reform, but just as frequently by military conservative regimes" (1967, 352).

10. Such models have been proposed by Cyert and March (1963), Wildavsky

(1964), and Thompson (1967). Wildavsky, for example, notes that "Budgeting turns out to be an incremental process proceeding from an historical base, guided by notions of fair shares, in which decisions are fragmented, made in sequence by specialized bodies, and coordinated by repeated attacks on problems through multiple feedback mechanisms" (1964, 62). Davis, Dempster, and Wildavsky (1966a, 1966b); Crecine (1967, 1970); Sharkansky (1968, 1970a, 1970b); Anton (1970); Sullivan (1972); Tucker (1975); and Hoole (1976)—all these apply incremental models in a series of budgetary analyses. Models that focus on the impact of prior behaviors and decisions are also developed and applied in research on nonfiscal policies. Alker and Greenberg (1971) and Alker and Christensen (1972), for example, develop a model of decisionmaking in the United Nations that draws directly on the work of Cyert and March (1963). Jones (1964), Allison (1971), Halperin and Kanter (1973), and Halperin (1974) develop similar formulations. Finally, a series of related bureaucratic politics, internal process, prior decision, or organizational models are developed and/or discussed by Deutsch (1966), Lovell (1970), Starr (1972), Tanter and Ullman (1972), Neustadt (1970), Art (1973), Axelrod (1973), Rose (1973), and Brady (1974).

11. The body of literature on social stalemates and hegemonic crises is extensive and includes Gramsci (1957), Trotsky (1961), Di Tella (1968), Nun (1969), and Poulantzas (1973).

12. As Linz puts it, "Authoritarian regimes are fundamentally born as the result of the incapacity or fear of sustaining the unity of a society under conditions of freedom. . . . Authoritarian regimes have as a basic purpose . . . to maintain the unity of a polity threatened, really or in their imagination, by deep divisions. . . . Authoritarian rule is based on the denial of the existence of such divisions . . . and the need to build a secular community that would bridge or obliterate the loyalty to communities other than the state" (1972, 26).

13. According to Braybrooke and Lindblom, rational actors who utilize the "synoptic" method of problemsolving "choose among alternatives after careful and complete study of all possible courses of action and all their possible consequences and after an evaluation of those consequences in the light of [their] values" (1963, 40). This mode of decisionmaking is thus distinct from Braybrooke and Lindblom's "disjointed incremental" style in which decisions are made "through small or incremental moves on particular programs rather than through a comprehensive reform program. It is also endless; it takes the form of an indefinite sequence of policy moves. Moreover, it is exploratory in that the goals of policymaking continue to change as new experience with policy throws new light on what is possible and desirable. In this sense, it is also better described as moving *away* from known social ills rather than moving *toward* a known and relatively stable goal. In any case, it is policymaking that chooses those goals that draw policies forward in the light of what recent policy steps have shown to be realizable; the utopian goal, chosen for its attractiveness without thought of its feasibility, is not a heavy influence on this kind of policy making" (1963, 71), emphasis in original.

14. Scholars who make this argument include Sprout and Sprout (1956, 1957, 1965), Snyder, Bruck, and Sapin (1962), Robinson and Snyder (1966), Farrell (1966), Anderson (1967), Hirschman (1968a), Paige (1968), Jervis (1968), Kissinger and Brodie (1968), Kissinger (1969), Boulding (1969), Deutsch (1970), Lovell (1970), Rakoff and Schaefer (1970), and Zinnes (1972).

15. A comprehensive understanding entails that decisionmakers have (1) a specified set of relevant values and objectives, (2) a set of perceived alternative courses of action, (3) evaluations of the likely consequences of each alternative, and (4) a net evaluation of each set of consequences (Allison 1971, (34).

16. A review of the existing research on public administration and bureaucracies in Latin America is available in Hopkins (1974).

17. The reader may recall Paige's hypothesis that "The greater the crisis, the greater the propensity for decisionmakers to supplement information about the objective state of affairs with information drawn from their own past experience" (1968, 295), Lovell 1970,133–203) offers much the same proposition in his discussion of what he calls "historical dynamics," but he goes a step further and appears to hypothesize that the institutional memory of the decisionmaker's organization is also important.

18. To the extent that nonincremental expansions of policies do occasionally occur in situations in which the public sector is large and entrenched, one might expect them to be characterized by "learning curves."

19. This possibility is implicit in the work of Frankel (1963), Schilling (1962), Hilsman (1964), Cohen (1971), Tucker (1975), and Hoole (1976).

FOUR

Who Governed When in Argentina? Coalitions, Presidents, Cabinet Officers, and Public Employees

I shall assess the usefulness of the integrated thesis, compared with the two more conventional explanations, in understanding Argentine policymaking since 1930. First, according to the authoritarian/rational model, I shall look at the political coalitions that have dominated since that time. Then, following the predictions of the bureaucratic/satisficing model, I shall focus on Argentina's cabinet ministers and public employees. Finally, I shall examine the development of the four factors that the integrated thesis claims are critical for understanding policy in Argentina: the ability of government leaders to press their demands in a persistent and unambiguous fashion; the existence of a balance, or stalemate, between opposing nonbureaucratic forces; the expansion and unionization of public employment; and the resources available to elites.

The thrust of the integrated formulation is the postulating of a set of conditions that should help predict where the authoritarian argument or some bureaucratic thesis should be useful for understanding public policies. To the extent that the four *auxiliary conditions* sometimes exist but do not always exist, it suggests that the authoritarian and bureaucratic theses both have specific and particular domains to which they are applicable but that neither is likely to provide a general model isolating universal relationships.

Presidents and Coalitions

On September 9, 1930, the constitutionally elected government of Hipolito Yrigoyen was overthrown in a military coup d'état. The insurgents, led by General José E. Uriburu, thus ended fourteen years of legally elected middle-class, Radical party rule. Between Uriburu's 1930 uprising and 1970, fifteen men sat in the Casa Rosada, the seat of the Argentine government. Nine came to power as a result of military coups. One ascended from the vice-presidency when the sitting president became ill and resigned. Only five of the fifteen succeeded in governing for the constitutional six-year period. One president lasted only three days in office. Three more governed for less than a year. Yet another remained in office for slightly more than a year.

This pattern of presidential instability masks what is generally seen as having been a basic underlying stability in who actually governed in Argentina. Although the identities at the top shifted repeatedly, the literature on Argentina's political history argues that only three coalitions dominated the life of the nation during the 1930–1970 interval. Guillermo O'Donnell (1973), for example, argues that his three forms of authoritarian rule existed in Argentina as follows:[1]

- (1930–1943) *traditional authoritarian rule.*[2] Dominant coalition: foreign export sector and export-related industrialists;
- (1943–1952) *populist authoritarian rule.* Dominant coalition: domestic industrialists, the military, urban workers, and producers of nonexportable agricultural goods;
- (1952–1966) *period of hegemonic crisis.* No dominant coalition;
- (1966–1973) *bureaucratic–authoritarian rule.* Dominant coalition: a segment of the military, large and efficient industrialists, foreign capitalists, and technocrats.

While it will be pointed out below that there are serious reasons for remaining skeptical of O'Donnell's characterization of Argentina's coalitional history, his description is generally supported by the work of other researchers. Thus, it can be said that Argentine specialists share a surprisingly high degree of consensus about which coalitions maintained political control in which periods between 1930 and 1970. Uriburu's overthrow of Yrigoyen on September 9, 1930, ended middle-class rule in Argentina and reestablished the political domination of Argentina's conservative, export-oriented landed elites and their allies among the export-related industrialists. At some point between 1940 and 1943, the members of the traditional authoritarian coalition were themselves ousted from power. The end of their rule probably came on June 4, 1943, when the government of Ramon S. Castillo was toppled in a second military uprising. The rebellious officers were led by General Arturo Rawson; but less than forty-eight hours after Castillo's overthrow, Rawson himself was removed to be replaced by General Pedro Pablo Ramirez. The era in which a coalition of small- and middle-sized industrialists, labor, the military, and the producers of nonexportable agricultural goods would govern Argentina had thus begun. This populist coalition, which Juan Domingo Perón mobilized and dominated, maintained its control until some point during the 1950–1955 interval. Whether it was as early as the droughts of 1950–1951, the death of Eva Perón (the president's wife and key political advisor) and the beginning of Perón's second term in 1952, or as late as the eventual overthrow of Perón by the military in September 1955, the populist coalition lost control. From that point until the overthrow of President Arturo Illia by the military on June 28, 1966, no group emerged to establish even the appearance of having a firm control of the course of events. Argentina appeared to be entering a new era with the 1966 coup, however. The military had intervened in Argentine politics on numerous occasions since the overthrow of Perón in 1955; but in 1966 it appeared that the military had taken control and intended to keep it. The officers named retired General Juan Carlos Ongania as president of the new government and moved with him to form a new, antipopulist coalition of large and efficient industrialists, foreign capitalists, and technocrats in the public bureaucracy. If the authoritarian thesis is valid and dominant coalitions are crucial for understanding policies, these dates should be important. Fundamental realignments in what policies were made, who benefited from them, and who paid for them should have occurred in 1943 when the shift from traditional to populist authoritarian rule was made; 1952, when the shift from populist rule to the era of the hegemonic crisis took place; and 1966, when the hegemonic crisis appeared to come to an end and the military under General Ongania began to establish the bureaucratic form of authoritarian rule.

Despite the scholarly consensus and evidence supporting the standard interpretation of Argentina's coalitional history a central difficulty arises. This is in the assumption, frequently made by scholars, that a group that benefited from a policy decision must have been a part of the ruling coalition. The enactment of the policy in question is "explained" by arguing that the group that benefited from it was influential in its formulation and execution. The reasoning is clearly tautological. As Kenworthy correctly observes, "the *output* of politics is simply too thin a reed on which to build an interpretation of the *input*, namely, who influenced whom when policy was being formulated" (1972, 16; emphasis original). This argument casts doubt on such accepted beliefs of the standard interpretation as that

- The export-related industrialists played a role in the traditional authoritarian coalition;
- Light industrialists were an important component of the populist authoritarian alliance;
- The bureaucratic–authoritarian coalition included a unified military and excluded labor.

Thus, the import substitution industrialization (ISI) policies of the 1930–1943 period are generally seen as having been made by and for the export-related industrialists who benefited from them and who were allied with the export sector in the traditional authoritarian coalition. Both Merkx (1969) and Diaz Alejandro (1970, 218) suggest a slightly different motivation for the ISI policies of the 1930–1943 era. Industrialization may have been promoted not to benefit the export-related industrialists but to advance the interests of the export sector and facilitate the adjustment to the new socioeconomic conditions of the post-1929 depression era.[3]

This is an important possibility, suggesting that ISI policies of this period might have been undertaken unilaterally by the export sector. If the agriculturalists were engaging in defensive modernization to protect their own interests, the export-related industrialists need not have been involved in the policy formulation and execution process. They need not have been included in the traditional authoritarian coalition. The same industrial promotion policies might still have been enacted.

Similarly, the standard interpretation argues that the promotion of light consumer goods was intensified after 1943 because light-consumer-goods industrialists were allied with labor, the military, and the producers of non-exportable agricultural goods in the populist coalition. Industrialization policies benefited the light industrialists; therefore, they must have pushed for their enactment.

The problem, of course, is that there is little concrete evidence that the light industrialists played an important role in the populist movement during the early stages (1943–1945), when the major ISI promotion measures were enacted. Miguel Miranda and Rolando Lagomarsino, Perón's two key advisors who are most commonly associated with the promotion of ISI under Perón, may not even have known Perón until after the initial set of ISI promotion policies had been adopted (Kenworthy 1972, 18).[4] Whether this was the case or not, it is true that Miranda was not appointed to the presidency of the Argentine Central Bank until it was nationalized in March 1946. He did not become the president of the National Economic Council until he resigned from his bank position on July 17, 1947. Lagomarsino was not appointed secretary of industry and commerce until Perón named his first cabinet on June 6, 1946.

In lieu of direct evidence that the light industrialists were involved in the early stages of the populist movement, at least four alternative explanations of the post-1943 ISI promotion policies can be noted. First, a very few light industrialists may have enlisted with Perón as a means for furthering their own personal and financial interests, and such individuals may have had important impacts on public policies; but they may also have been acting as mavericks rather than true representatives of the light industrial sector. Di Tella's observations appear to support this possibility. Although he notes that "newly risen industrialists" from the consumer goods sector strongly supported the populist coalition (1965, 71), he observes in another place that "most industrialists were against [Perón], as were the more traditional industrialists" (1968a, 255–256). This seems to imply that light industrialists were important in the populist movement, but that they participated on their own, not as sectoral representatives. A second possible explanation of the post-1943 ISI promotion policies is that the leaders of the 1943 coup may have come to power with a view toward mobilizing labor support. Measures to promote the labor-intensive consumer goods industries might have been enacted not to enhance the interests of the light industrialists but as a means of attracting support to the populist movement. As Diaz Alejandro observes, "Light manufacturing, construction, government and nationalized railroads came to be viewed more as sources of jobs than as activities for producing goods and services" (1970, 113). Put more simply, more jobs for Argentina's urban workers might have meant greater support for Perón's populist movement.

A third explanation of the 1943–1952 consumer goods industrial promotion policies is that they were the inadvertent result of basic industrial development. Beginning as early as the 1920s, the military began to promote the expansion and modernization of Argentina's basic industries and infrastructure as a means for safeguarding the nation's security in the face of perceived threats from the United States and Brazil. The 1929 depression and events surrounding the outbreak of World War II could only have increased such preoccupations;[5] and policies after 1943 may have been designed to encourage basic industrial development. The fact that the consumer goods industries expanded instead may be attributable less to conscious, rational design than to simple mismanagement and misapplication (Treber 1969; Diaz Alejandro 1970; Kenworthy 1972). A fourth potential explanation combines elements of the first three. It draws heavily on the so-called revisionist interpretations of the Peronist movement (S. Baily 1967; Snow 1969; P. Smith 1969, 1972; and Kenworthy 1972, 1973, 1975) and assigns a dynamic quality to the populist coalition. This argument yields the following three tentative conclusions: (1) the initial post-1943 ISI measures[6] were adopted by the conservative military leaders of the coup, who were attempting to safeguard national security; (2) the initial set of post-1943 ISI policies were probably executed and enforced during the July 7, 1944–February 24, 1946 period with a view toward attracting the support of labor; and (3) the two important ISI measures which were enacted shortly after the 1946 election—the nationalization of the Argentine Central Bank and the creation of the Argentine Overseas Trade Corporation (IAPI)—probably resulted from the pressure of a few of Argentina's light industrialists.

All three conclusions are based on an analysis of the timing of events during the 1943–1947 period. The enactment of the initial set of ISI policies came in the first half of 1944 at a point when official government policy was still harshly antilabor and before Perón had emerged as the dominant figure in the government. The timing places the adoption of these measures before the arrival of the light industrialists in the governing circle. It therefore seems unlikely that these particular policies were enacted by and for that sector, more plausibly, they were motivated by the military's desire to modernize for defense.

This does not explain, however, why the initial set of post-1943 ISI policies was enforced so extensively during the July 7, 1944–February 24, 1946 interval. Although severe problems would be encountered in October 1945, Perón completed the first major stage of consolidating his position on July 7, 1944, when he was named to the vice-presidency. President Farrell announced on February 1, 1945 that the nation was in a phase of preelectoral organization.

If Perón was to win the upcoming election, he would need to broaden his base of support. The old, established unions, which he already controlled, would provide him with organizational assistance; but Perón would also need the support of rural workers and the new urban immigrants. It was at this point, therefore, that Perón began to appeal to a mass rather than a strictly unionized audience. The Statute of the Peon, which greatly improved the conditions for Argentina's rural workers, was announced, perhaps not coincidentally, on November 18, 1944. On December 4, the first mass rally in support of Perón took place as two hundred thousand workers paraded to thank him for a recent decree on pensions (Stickell 1972). On February 27, 1945, the "Rights of the Worker" was made public (S. Baily 1967, 101). Perón's promotion of consumer goods industries may well have been yet another example of his efforts to broaden the base of the populist movement. A rapid expansion of such labor-intensive operations meant jobs. If properly handled, jobs could be translated into votes among the new urban immigrants. A small number of light industrialists, such as Miranda and Lagomarsino, had finally been recruited to government service by 1946. Their arrival marked the first documented point at which light industrialists could have been responsible for the adoption of ISI measures. This evidence casts considerable doubt on the standard interpretation of industrialization policy between 1943 and 1952. Just because light industries expanded after 1943, it does not follow that light industrialists were included in the populist coalition.

In another element of the standard interpretation, O'Donnell (1973) originally argued that a unified military came to power in the bureaucratic–authoritarian coalition with a view toward repressing the Argentine popular sectors and excluding them from the political and economic life of the nation. In later discussions, however, O'Donnell maintained that the bureaucratic–authoritarian coalition actually evolved in a number of significant ways during the tenures of Presidents Ongania and Levingston. The coalition was still unique and important, but it was neither as coherent nor as enduring as he originally believed.

This new perspective on the bureaucratic-authoritarian coalition is reinforced by a review of events in two areas. First, there is evidence that both the coalition itself and the bureaucratic–authoritarian policy alignment evolved after the June 28, 1966 coup. Second, Ongania and Levingston recruited high-level decisionmakers who had originally risen to positions of authority during prior, nonbureaucratic–authoritarian administrations. Such recycling of cabinet officers should not have been common if Ongania and Levingston intended to break with the past. I shall examine both of these points briefly.

The bureaucratic-authoritarian coalition came to power on June 28, 1966. During the next six months, Congress was disbanded, political parties were dissolved, the Supreme Court was reconstituted, the universities were *intervened*, and plans were announced to modernize and reorganize the nation's port facilities and railroads. (Federal government *intervention*, in

Argentine usage, means that the freedom and autonomy of the *intervened* unit are suspended and the unit placed under the direct supervision of a governmental appointee.) Despite all of these actions, both S. Baily (1966, 303) and Rowe (1970, 476) conclude that the first six months of the Ongania administration were characterized by policy drift and ideological vagueness. The basis for this assessment is clear. Although these actions were repressive and authoritarian, they were not unique.[7] All of these steps had been taken before by nontechnocratic, nonbureaucratic-authoritarian governments of the pre-1966 era.

A positive sense of direction, therefore, may not have begun to develop until the January 4, 1967 appointment of Adalbert Krieger Vasena as the minister of the economy and labor. Krieger Vasena is generally credited with having initiated the post-1966 influx of technocrats and the Krieger Vasena team developed the economic policies of the post-1966 period (Braun 1973; Portantiero 1971). The government did not intervene in union wage negotiations, for example, until March 1967 when Krieger Vasena broke workers collective agreements and gave the state the power to set wages.

The arrival of the Krieger Vasena economic team may have produced an immediate effect on state–labor relations. Sharp popular protests had erupted in reaction to the new government's policies during the August 18, 1966–March 1, 1967 period. Following the General Confederation of Labor's (CGT) call for a strike on March 1, 1967 and the government's use of the Civil Defense Law, however, a period of labor calm developed. The number of strikes and of strikers and workers' days lost to strikes in the federal capital fell to levels below those reported in any year since 1907.

Proponents of the authoritarian thesis maintain that this Pax Obrera developed because workers had been effectively suppressed. At least one other explanation is possible. For reasons which had little to do with the policies of the Ongania administration, a considerable portion of the labor movement did not consider itself excluded from the government. The Argentine labor movement was sharply divided between those who wanted to resist the government and those who wished to cooperate with it.[8] At the time of the first general work stoppage under Ongania in October 1966, two major factions existed within the CGT. One group (headed by José Alonso and variously known as the "62 a pie de Perón," the Alonsoistas, or the Isabelistas) was loyal to Perón and against the Ongania regime. The other major group was headed by Augusto Vandor. It favored a program of "Peronism without Perón" and cooperation with the Ongania administration. At the October 1966 congress of the CGT, one of Vandor's independent Peronists was elected secretary-general of the confederation; other Vandoristas captured half of the seats on the executive council (Jordan 1970). Thus, the CGT was dominated by Augusto Vandor throughout the period of labor calm that began in March 1967.

Perhaps of equal importance, the period of labor peace ended when Vandor and his supporters began to lose their control of the labor movement. On March 28, 1968 the unions most opposed to the Ongania administration organized as the CGT of Paseo Colon under the leadership of Raimundo Ongaro (head of the Peronist-dominated printers' union). Vandor's group, the CGT of Azopardo, continued to favor cooperation with the government. (Jordan 1970, 89–90; Iscaro 1973, 382ff).[9] On August 23, 1968 the automobile workers in Cordoba went on strike. On September 25 the employees of the state-owned oil corporation (Yacimientos Petroliferos Fiscales) in La Plata and Ensenada initiated a fifty four-day strike in protest over government efforts to increase the working day from six to eight hours. The CGT of Paseo Colon announced support of the oil workers, but Ongaro's efforts to turn it into a general nationwide work stoppage on October 17 failed to attract support.

The Ongania adminstration did not have to respond effectively to a unified labor movement. A considerable portion of the Argentine labor movement was united behind Vandor in the CGT, the CGT of Azopardo, and later in the "participationist" and "dialogist" factions of the CGT of Azopardo. For a considerable period, these groups were willing to cooperate—or at least communicate—with the government.

All of these considerations imply that the bureaucratic–authoritarian period was not actually initiated in Argentina until some time after March 1968 when sustained labor opposition began to develop. The alliance was already beginning to dissolve, however, by August 20, 1968. The move to oust Illia in 1966 had been led by the heads of Argentina's three military branches: Lieutenant General Pascual Angel Pistarini (army), Rear Admiral Benigno Ignacio Varela (navy), and Brigadier General Adolfo Teodoro Alvarez (air force). This classic military junta persuaded Ongania to accept the presidency; issued the Statute of the Revolution on June 29, 1966 and thereby dissolved Congress and all provincial legislatures; disbanded all political parties; reconstituted the Supreme Court; and granted legislative power to the Revolution. This group of soldiers epitomized the military of the bureaucratic–authoritarian period according to most accounts; but by October, 1968 they had all been removed from their cabinet positions, and the departure of Economic Minister Krieger Vasena had been assured. Thus, some ten months before the beginning of the popular uprisings of the Cordobazo which led to the eventual overthrow of Ongania and his replacement by General Levingston,[10] the leaders of the 1966 coup had lost their government positions.

Julio Alsogaray's replacement as secretary of the army was Lieutenant General Alejandro A. Lanusse. During the conflicts between the Colorado and Azul factions of the military in 1962,[11] Lanusse had fought against the officers who wished to establish a more or less permanent military dictatorship. Ongania had taken the same position, of course, at the time of the 1962 fighting; he had clearly shifted his views after coming to power in 1966. The point to be noted, therefore, is that it was Lanusse who eventually toppled the Levingston administration and ended the permanency of the bureaucratic-authoritarian Revolucion Argentina by allowing the election of Hector Campora and the final return of Perón. Finally, it should be recalled that in October 1968 Krieger Vasena's departure was assured when he was designated the next president of the International Monetary Fund.

The removal of the three military leaders of the June 28, 1966 coup and the appointments of Alsogaray and later Lanusse quite clearly raise questions about the actual extent of military unity during even the first stages of the bureaucratic-authoritarian period in Argentina. Combined with the announced departure of Krieger Vasena and the shift in state–labor relations in March 1968, all of this evidence tentatively suggests that a "true" bureaucratic-authoritarian coalition may have existed for only an extremely short period in Argentina.[12]

Further support for revising the standard interpretation of Argentine history is found in the fact that both Ongania and Levingston recruited decision-makers who had served in previous administrations. Two examples of these "old faces" who returned to government service after 1966 were Dr. José Astiqueta and Maria de Pablo Pardo. Following the June 28, 1966 coup, General Ongania placed right-wing, Catholic nationalists such as Dr. Carlos Gelly y Obes in charge of the nation's educational system (S. Baily 1966; Rowe 1970; W. Smith 1976). The inclusion of right-wing, Catholic nationalists is thought to have marked a departure from previous policies in Argentina and is taken as one of the indications that Ongania intended to exclude and repress labor. Less than a year after the coup, however, on June 8, 1967, Ongania replaced Gelly y Obes with Astiqueta. Astiqueta had served as the minister of education and justice during the last days of the Perón-dominated, generally prolabor administration of General Farrell. On June 17, 1970 Levingston named Maria de Pablo Pardo to the Foreign Ministry. Pablo Pardo had served for one day as the minister of the interior under Lonardi in 1955 when the latter was attempting to remove the hard-line anti-Peronist, Dr. Eduardo Busso, and effect a conciliation with labor and Perón's followers. Both of these reappointments by Ongania and Levingston may therefore have signaled at least a limited retreat from harsh antilabor, anti-Peronist policy positions.

It is in the economic area, however, that reappointments by Ongania and Levingston are most interesting. Their key economic advisors—Aldo Ferrer and Krieger Vasena—had served during the administrations of Frondizi and Aramburu, respectively. Ongania's ambassador to the United States, who played a key role in attracting foreign capital to Argentina during the bureaucratic–authoritarian period, had served as a principal economic policy-maker under Frondizi and Guido. One of Ongania's secretaries of finance had served as the minister of trade under Lonardi. One of Levingston's secretaries of finance was the head of a combined finance and treasury ministry under Lonardi. With the exception of these last two individuals, all of these policymakers had served in nonbureaucratic–authoritarian administrations that apparently sought, at different points in their existence (much like the bureaucratic–authoritarian governments of Ongania and Levingston), to exclude labor and attract foreign capital.

It is possible, of course, that these individuals had altered their views by the time they were incorporated by Ongania and Levingston. For that reason, one should be cautious not to overstate the importance of these reappointments. Nevertheless, they should not be overlooked. If the military and government technocrats gained new importance when the bureaucratic–authoritarian coalition came to power in 1966 (as O'Donnell still maintains), there was also a resurgence of old leaders who may have carried with them biases toward policies that had been tried before. In any event, the reappointments raise questions about the contention that the bureaucratic–authoritarian coalition of Ongania and Levingston constituted a sharp philosophical break with the past.

The possibility that the standard interpretation of who governed in Argentina is misleading or erroneous suggests the need for a healthy skepticism toward the existing analyses. Other hypotheses might be used to explain the policies that were enacted in the different periods of authoritarian rule in Argentina. One should not be overly hasty in rejecting the existing work, however. As I shall show, there is still some evidence that the traditional, populist, and bureaucratic–authoritarian coalitions did exist, although not in the forms in which they have been conventionally understood.

The Cabinet Officers

Different coalitions and presidents may have ruled in Argentina, but important policy innovations and shifts have frequently been associated with specific individuals who held cabinet or high-level advisory positions in the government. These were the elite political personnel, the "in-and-outers" (Halperin 1974, 89), who actually formulated and implemented public policies. The authoritarian formulation predicts that as different dominant coalitions gained political control, they would have recruited high-level policymakers whose backgrounds and interests were congruent with those of the alliance members. This in fact, tends to be the case, providing additional, direct support for the authoritarian argument.

Such support is counterbalanced, however, by the high levels of instability in the Argentine cabinets, an important concern of the integrated formulation. Although Argentina's chronic economic problems are frequently attributed to structural bottlenecks and the difficulty of developing in a delayed dependent setting, it seems likely that no small portion of that nation's problems may be explained by simple bad government, mismanagement, and cabinet-level instability (Salera 1966). True policy innovation and creativity require time and stability. If elites are constantly being shuffled, it is likely that they will be forced to rely heavily on plans and programs developed by their predecessors. They will be unable to press their demands in persistent and unambiguous fashion. When a chronic crisis of authority exists within the cabinet, middle- and low-level public employees will be encouraged to resist or even ignore their constantly changing leaders. If the Argentine cabinet became wildly unstable at a particular time, it seems probable that effective policymaking authority might have begun to shift out of the hands of those who governed at the top.

A considerable body of evidence is available on the class and occupational backgrounds of Argentina's political elites, although it is infrequently cited. It is generally supportive of the authoritarian formulation. As each coalition came to power, it apparently tended to recruit policymakers whose backgrounds were congruent with those of the alliance members. An examination of the backgrounds of the elite political personnel thus reveals a series of shifts in the sectors and classes represented in Argentina's various governing teams, cabinet officers and high-level advisors since 1930.

Lawyers were predominant in the traditional authoritarian teams of 1936 and 1941. As José Luiz de Imaz notes, "almost all of the ruling teams [between 1930 and 1943] came from within the ranks of the upper class" (1970, 15). Recruitment was primarily ascriptive. The inclusion of other groups and sectors was minimal. The populist authoritarian teams of 1946 and 1951 were thus dramatically different from those of the pre-1943 period. Lawyers still constituted the single largest group, but their representation was reduced. The role of professional politicians and entrepreneurs also declined. Only the importance of the military and other groups not classified by Imaz increased since the traditional and populist authoritarian periods.

The direct role of the military was reduced under the bureaucratic–authoritarian government of General Ongania (1966–1969). This decline presents a mild paradox. The governments of Frondizi, Guido, and Illia were ostensibly civilian administrations; but the direct role of the military was greater under those leaders than during the military dictatorship of General Ongania.[13]

The changes in the roles of the entrepreneurs and the professional politicians and union leaders after 1966 accords more closely with the standard interpretation and the authoritarian thesis. Although Frondizi and Guido included greater absolute numbers of entrepreneurs, industrialists constituted a greater proportion of the Ongania governing team. These were apparently the technocrats of the bureaucratic–authoritarian coalition. Before 1943, most of the entrepreneurs who participated in government were attorneys who represented the corporations that controlled Argentina's meat and cereal export operations (Imaz 1970, 28). The entrepreneurs who served during the populist period were small- and middle-size industrialists who actually owned their own enterprises. The entrepreneurs of the post-1966 period differed sharply from those who had preceded them in government service. These were the corporate executives who managed the largest national and multinational conglomerates. The elimination of professional politicians and union leaders from the Ongania administration should also be noted. This, too, appears to accord with the authoritarian thesis that the bureaucratic–authoritarian coalition moved to depoliticize the system and exclude labor from the government.

It appears, then, that there is at least some similarity between the shifts from one dominant coalition to the next and the changing patterns in the recruitment of Argentina's elite political personnel. If that is the case, however, it should be noted that certain aspects of the evidence on Argentina's cabinet members are clearly not consistent with what one might expect under the authoritarian thesis. Because these problems are almost entirely overlooked, I shall examine them in detail.

A number of scholars supplement the data on the backgrounds of Argentina's political elites by emphasizing the roles that key cabinet officers played in influencing particular economic policies since 1930 (e.g., Murmis and Portantiero 1971; Eshag and Thorp 1974; Zuvekas 1968; Braun 1973). The point, however, is that there have been far too many of them. Too few of Argentina's economic policymakers have retained their positions long enough to have had impacts of major significance. Under Perón, for example, it is possible to identify three different economic teams. Between 1941 and 1970, thirty-four different individuals held the principal position in Argentina's economic policymaking establishment.[14] Those officers averaged only .88 years, or approximately 321 days, in power each. In each of five different years (1943, 1945, 1955, 1962, and 1963) three different leaders were named to head the economic establishment; it had two leaders in each of two additional years (1957 and 1970). In a nation that since at least 1946 has developed successive five-year plans to chart its economic development, the planners have seldom been in office when the time came for actually implementing their projects.

Cabinet instability has not been limited to the economic policy area, however. The thirty-three individuals who served as foreign minister between 1941 and 1970 averaged only .91 years (332 days) in office each. The nation had two foreign ministers in 1941, three in 1943, three in 1944, four in 1945, and a total of ten during the five years, eight months between January 30, 1958 and October 10, 1963. Only six men survived as foreign minister for periods of three years or more during the 1941–1970 interval. Of those six, four served in the period that predated the overthrow of Perón in 1955.

It has been impossible to trace the changeovers in all of Argentina's cabinet positions, but the evidence shows the general instability. In none of eight areas—the Economy, Foreign Affairs, the Interior, the Army, the Navy, Public Works, and Labor and Welfare—did the cabinet officers manage to retain their positions for more than an average of 1.88 years (686 days) each. In comparison, the various presidents from Lonardi through Ongania averaged 2.46 years (897 days) in office.

Cabinet shifts should be expected, of course, at the beginning of a new administration. A number of others should be expected as a result of deaths, illnesses, personal and financial problems, and so on. But even when such factors are considered, the image of Argentina's cabinets is one of only barely controlled chaos and confusion. Multiple changeovers in the same year were so frequent that a minister (or secretary) could not even be certain that he would survive long enough to spend the annual budget that he was proposing. On at least one occasion, a cabinet officer was replaced on the same day he was appointed. The replacement served less than four months before he was removed; his replacement held office for only two days.[15]

Even the shape of the cabinet was repeatedly altered. In most cases, these reorganizations either resulted in the creation of entirely new, increasingly specialized ministries or secretariats or established a two-tiered cabinet system with an inner and an outer circle. As such, those reorganizations appear to have been efforts to gain administrative control over a political state that had grown increasingly complex in the period after the overthrow of Ramon Castillo in 1943.[16]

Certain periods of relative stability can be identified in the Argentine cabinet. The 1933–1936, 1946–1949, 1949–1952, and 1952–1955 periods stand out most notably. The more general pattern, however, is one of almost continuous fluctuation within the cabinet. To the extent that such shifting can be taken as an indicator of a crisis of authority within the government itself, it would appear that Argentina passed through such phases in the following periods: 1931–1933, 1937, 1939, 1941, 1943–1946, 1949, 1952, 1955–1959, 1961–1964, 1966–1967, and 1969–1971.

As has been said, some of these personnel changes were undoubtedly insignificant. Some occurred for nonpolitical reasons. In other instances, individuals with virtually identical class and occupational backgrounds, policy preferences, and priorities probably succeeded one another. It is likely, however, that the majority of ministers and secretaries left their positions either because they were under pressure to do so or because they wished to protest some government action or policy. It is probable, therefore, that individuals with divergent outlooks and goals may have replaced one another in at least the more important cabinet positions.

To focus exclusively on the similarities and differences between successive ministers or secretaries is to miss the point, however. That a shift occurs in the leadership of an administrative unit may be of consequence in and of itself. As Diaz Alejandro puts it, even though different administrations and ministers of the economy have attempted to execute major policy changes,

> much time and effort are wasted by public and government officials waiting
> to see who the next president or minister of the economy is going to be. The

time horizons of policymaking have become extremely short, as survival takes precedence over other considerations. Public opinion, on the other hand, expects new ministers to perform economic miracles in a few months; grumbling begins punctually two or three months after a new minister is installed. (1970, 134)

Chronic instability may have induced Argentina's cabinet-level political elites to adopt strong ideological positions. It may also have forced them to reach back to modify previous policies in only marginal ways. At the same time, the rapid elite turnovers and the fact that Argentina's public employees remained leaderless for long periods may have encouraged the professional employees to hold back and resist. Thus, to the extent that an ongoing crisis of authority existed within the government itself during much of the period since 1930, control of the Argentine policymaking arena may have shifted to the public employees who remained in office while presidents, cabinet officers, and coalitions came and went. Because the cabinet officers were constantly being shuffled, it seems unlikely that they could have pressed their demands in persistent fashion and thereby overcome the resistance of the permanent public employees. If that is true, it may in fact be the case that Argentina's public employees (and through them their clienteles) came to govern effectively in Argentina.

The Public Employees

A shift in the location of effective policymaking authority might have been likely even if the Argentine public sector had remained small and weak. If elite instability developed in a context in which the public sector was large and highly unionized, the transfer of authority would have been even more probable.

As the state's economic activities increased, the number of public employees also grew. Between 1935 and 1942, 82,300 new positions were created within the Argentine government. That number represented a 48 percent increase (or an average of 11,760 positions per year) over the seven-year period. Bunge implies that this influx of public employees raised the cost of government by 138 percent in the years between 1933 and 1939 (1940, 404).

The expansion of public employment was most dramatic, however, during the populist era in Argentina. A decrease in the number of employees between 1942 and 1943 is probably attributable to the purging of the public sector in the period immediately following the overthrow of Castillo. Between 1943 and 1952, however, there was a 144.4 percent increase as 349,900 new employees were added to the public payrolls. Under Farrell (1944–1946), the majority of the growth was in public and semipublic corporations. Thus, the expansion in public employment may have been an unintended consequence of nationalizing foreign companies. Workers who had once been employed by domestic or foreign concerns were quickly transformed into public employees. Under Perón, the greatest immediate expansion was in the central administration. By 1948–1949, however, a recession had set in. The traditional authoritarian governments of the pre-1943 period had reacted to a similar downswing in the economy in the 1938–1939 interval by slowing the rate of increase in public employment. Perón's response was in the opposite direction. When the rate of economic expansion began to slow in the late 1940s, employment in both the central administration and the decentralized agencies rose sharply.

By 1951, the number of national government employees had reached an all-time high. The economy recovered somewhat in 1950–1951, but severe droughts in 1951–1952 reduced agricultural production. As a consequence, negative trade balances developed in those years, and the economy entered another recession. As has been said, these factors combined with the slowing down of import-substituting activities to bring an end to the populist coalition. They also combined to bring about a pause in the steady expansion of public employment in Argentina. Gold reserves from World War II had been sufficient to support increased government employment during the 1948–1949 recession, but such reserves were not available during the early 1950s. Thus, the number of public employees was reduced by 55,000 in 1953 and 1954. That reversal perhaps marks the end of Argentina's populist period as well as any other single factor. Two points of immediate interest should be noted. First, the "wrong" governments succeeded in reducing the size of the public sector in the post-1952 period. The relatively weak governments of Aramburu, Frondizi, Guido, and Illia during the era of the hegemonic crisis managed to reduce the number of national government employees by 61,900 between 1956 and 1963.[17] In contrast, public employment actually increased by 14,300 during the bureaucratic–authoritarian government of General Ongania (1966–1969). This difference in the direction of change in the 1956–1963 and 1966–1969 periods is surprising. One of the factors that led to the 1966 deposition of Illia was the costly and inefficient public bureaucracy (Rowe 1970, 475). A major goal of the 1966 coup makers was to centralize Argentina's bureaucratic establishment and increase its efficiency (O'Donnell 1973; W. Smith 1976). However, the actual result of Ongania's administration was a net increase in the number of employees. Employment never again returned to its 1952 peak of 592,300; but employment in 1969 was only 3.5 percent below that level.

The second interesting aspect of the post-1952 patterns in public employment concerns the areas in which the governments were and were not able to reduce the employment levels. The decreases were concentrated in the central administrative agencies, that is, in the areas most likely to be under the close control of the elite political personnel. Decentralized agencies (public and semipublic corporations) showed only minor fluctuations except in 1959 when Frondizi apparently responded to a severe depression by allowing the number of employees in such units to rise sharply. This contrast should not be overlooked. It is generally conceded that the large deficits of the public and semipublic corporations created the need to reduce public sector employment (Eshag and Thorp 1974, 96). Unfortunately, these public and semipublic corporations are also the least likely to be controlled by cabinet-level officials. As Jordan (1972) describes them, these "bureaucratic oligarchies" are sufficiently autonomous that the public and semipublic corporations constitute a major independent interest group in Argentine politics.

It is well recognized that the Argentine bureaucratic structure is massive and inefficient (Rottin 1949; Owen 1957; Whitaker 1964b, 126; Garcia-Zamor 1968; U.S. Department of Labor, Bureau of Labor Statistics 1968 17). Overstaffing and featherbedding undoubtedly vary from agency to agency, but two observations should be sufficient to make the point. The first is Aizcorbe's comment that "the state oil company, Yacinientos Petroliferos Fiscales, employs approximately twice the personnel that private oil companies do. In 1966, the state-owned Aerolineas Argentinas had about 115 employees per plane. For such private airlines as ALA and Austral, the rate was only 39 employees per plane. Squandering is evident" (1975, 23–24).

The second observation develops from a search of the records of Argentina's Office of Governmental Coordination and Control. The role of this agency is to organize government operations and maximize interagency cooperation; yet it had no information on what subministerial agencies existed, where they were located, or what their responsibilities were.

If the Argentine public sector is cumbersome and inefficient, it also seems likely that the public employees are cautious, reluctant to accept change, and—if Scott (1966, 306) is correct—unresponsive even to the presidents and ministers who hire them. That situation would be difficult for Argentina's elite political personnel to overcome.

Their command-and-control problems may be exacerbated, however, by the fact that public employees in Argentina are union members. The number of union members in Argentina increased sharply under the populist governments, and it is highly probable that this pattern of expansion was extended to include public employees. A listing of the Argentine unions with more than thirty-five members as of August 23, 1957 includes the following public employee organizations:[18]

• Railway workers	208,406
• National civil employees	190,000
• State workers	124,679
• Municipal workers	74,000
• Light and power workers	38,000
Total	635,085

This list may exclude a number of additional public employee unions in fields such as oil, mining, bank, port, meatpacking, and the postal service.

However, these unions alone account for 63.5 percent of the 987 thousand employees who held positions at all levels of government in 1957 according to Salvador Treber (1971). Thus, even though the evidence seems inconclusive, it is at least suggestive that a significant portion of Argentina's public employees are union members.

The relationship between the government and the employees of Argentina's state-owned railroads is an extreme—but nevertheless useful—example of the problems that may arise when political elites are forced to deal with public employee unions. According to S. Baily (1967, 62–63), 100 thousand workers were organized in three different transport unions (Union Ferroviaria, La Fraternidad, and Union Tranviaria) in 1935. By 1940 they included 115 thousand members. Thus, these unions were reasonably large and well established by the time the Ramirez regime came to power. As such, they were the targets of the repressive policies of the populist governments but were never brought firmly under government control.[19] Resistance by the railway unions was not important, however, until December 1946 and February 1947 when the Perón government announced the purchase of the French and British railroad networks in Argentina. By those acts, large numbers of highly organized and reasonably independent workers became employees of the state. Deterioration of the rail lines increased rapidly (Whitaker 1964b, 126). By the time President Illia took office in 1963, the annual operating deficit of the railroads was approaching a third of a billion U.S. dollars. Quite clearly, some reorganization or revitalization of the state-owned railway system was needed.

Perón is commonly criticized for having neglected the nation's infrastructure, but he initiated the reform efforts in 1951. Similar railroad reorganization plans were proposed by Frondizi (in 1958 and 1961), Illia (in 1963), and Ongania (in 1966). In each case, the presidents and the political elites were resisted by the most powerful railway unions. In each case a confrontation developed. More often than not, it was the elite political personnel who were forced to yield and postpone their plans.[20]

Perón's effort led to a strike by La Fraternidad in January 1951. On January 24, 1951, the populist leader threatened to invoke a national civil defense law that would draft striking workers into the military if they did not return to their jobs. In May La Fraternidad was intervened by the government. In July that union renewed its strike; workers sabotaged the equipment. Finally, in September 1951, the government was forced to declare a national state of siege.[21]

In 1961 Frondizi announced the initiation of a new government plan (Decree 4061) to dismiss eighty thousand railroad employees, speed up the retirement of twenty thousand others, close eleven railroad equipment factories, and abandon some kilometers of track.[22] The railroad workers reacted by calling strikes on May 15 (twenty-four hours), July 18 (twenty-four hours), and August 21 (forty-eight hours). Finally on October 30, a strike was begun that would last until December 12, when Frondizi announced that the government had yielded to the workers' demands. In Decree 11.578 of that date, all workers were allowed to return to their jobs without danger of reprisals, all imprisoned workers were released, the railroad equipment factories were reopened, previous work rules and retirement policies were reestablished, the government agreed to pay strikers 80 percent of their lost wages, a 20 percent pay increase was granted, and, finally, the government agreed to postpone all railroad-related questions for an indefinite period (Iscaro 1973, 361–363).

In 1963 it was Illia's turn to attempt to revitalize the railroads. His Four-Year Railroad Development Plan was designed to reduce the number of railroad employees gradually and trim the operating deficit of the railways by 42 percent. The unions once again opposed the plan. Once again, the government backed down and postponed its efforts. Once again, also, Illia's alleged "derationalization" of the public bureaucracy was apparently a contributing factor to his overthrow on June 28, 1966 and his replacement by General Ongania of the bureaucratic–authoritarian Revolucion Argentina (Rowe 1970, 475).

In December 1966 yet another railroad reorganization plan was announced. Both La Fraternidad and the Union Ferroviaria announced strikes and called on the General Confederation of Labor to issue a plan of resistance to the new government's policies. The government took advantage of the internal divisions that then existed within the labor movement. It revoked the legal status of the Union Ferroviaria, blocked union funds, dismissed striking workers, and invoked the old Peronist national Civil Defense Law under which striking workers could be drafted into the military and thereby placed under the threat of military justice.

The point should be clear. Having developed a vast array of public enterprises and a massive, highly unionized public bureaucracy, the Argentine elite political personnel had deprived themselves of certain policy options. The middle- and low-level public employees—individuals who retained their positions while presidents and cabinet officers came and went—had vested interests in maintaining at least the existing distribution of policy benefits. When the cabinet instability began to become chronic, permanent government staffs became the only actors who held stable positions in the nation's policymaking apparatus. The establishment in which the public employees were enmeshed was cumbersome and inefficient. Bureaucratic operations constituted a massive drain on national resources. Elites may have wished to alter these conditions, but they frequently discovered that the large and extensively unionized Argentine public sector was difficult to administer. Thus, the Argentine state—like the Argentine society—began to become increasingly divided against itself after 1950. Many of the post-1950 governments attempted to exclude, repress, or otherwise control labor; but by 1950 labor had already assumed the guise of unionized public employees and taken at least partial control of the state.

Conclusion

According to the authoritarian thesis, three distinct types of authoritarian political systems existed in Argentina during the 1930–1970 period, and each adjusted previous policy outputs on the basis of its own interests. A number of questions have been raised in this chapter, however, about the actual constituency of the traditional and populist authoritarian coalitions and about whether the bureaucratic–authoritarian alliance actually succeeded in establishing its control.

The bureaucratic formulation, on the other hand, expects the departure of old leaders and the arrival of new coalitions and elite political personnel to have only marginal impact on what policies are made, for whom, and at whose expense. The integrated formulation attempts to synthesize the authoritarian/rational and bureaucratic/satisficing arguments. It argues that coalitions and political elites are unlikely to be dominant in the policymaking arena if

- The elites are unable to press their demands in persistent and unambiguous fashion;
- A balance exists between opposing nonbureaucratic actors in the arena;
- The public sector is large and extensively unionized;
- The elites possess no previously unallocated resources.

To the extent that these conditions are absent, the predictions of the authoritarian thesis will hold. Coalitions and transitions between coalitions should be important for understanding public policies. The more the four constraining conditions prevail, the more likely it is that some bureaucratic formulation should be useful for understanding policies, because the policymaking effectiveness of the elite political personnel is limited.

All four of these constraining conditions had developed by the end of the populist authoritarian period in Argentina. It was at that point, according to the integrated formulation, that control of the policymaking arena should have shifted out of the hands of the elite political personnel and the dominant coalitions they represented.

Under the populist governments that ruled Argentina between 1943 and 1952 the Argentine state increased its penetration of the economy. The number of public employees was greatly expanded. They became unionized and enmeshed in a complex and inefficient bureaucratic establishment. The public bureaucracies created a massive drain on the state. By the end of the populist period, tendencies toward elite instability and failure developed. In the postpopulist period those tendencies became chronic. As the consumer goods stage of ISI came to an end, a general hegemonic crisis began to develop. That, too, became chronic.

In the pre-1950 period, before these trends and tendencies developed, who governed at the top may indeed have been crucial for determining what policies were made, who benefited from them, who paid for them, and what factors covaried with the fluctuations in policy outputs through time. In the period of the hegemonic crisis, however, the bureaucrats and the lower-level public employees alone held stable positions in the policymaking arena. They alone had policy inertia in their favor. The large and generally inefficient public corporations in which many of the public employees were situated drained resources and thereby reduced the capacities of new leaders to expand into new areas.

If the public employees have become increasingly important for determining what policies could be made in the postpopulist period, the importance of coalitions and political elites should have been reduced. The expectation of the integrated formulation is that the transitions from populist authoritarian system to the era of the hegemonic crisis (1952) and from the era of the hegemonic crisis to bureaucratic–authoritarianism (1966) should have had less dramatic impacts on public policies than the shift around 1943.

Notes

1. The precise dates of these transitions have been supplied by O'Donnell in personal communications with the author.

2. It is important to emphasize that the export and export-related industrial coalition did not maintain its hegemony over a scarcely differentiated population in Argentina. By 1930, a middle class had developed that was sufficiently large to have supported the fourteen years of Radical party rule. Labor organization movements were also well underway.

3. According to Merkx, most of the industrial promotion measures of the 1930s "were not undertaken for the *specific* purpose of aiding the industrial sector, but rather were intended to safeguard the export market, aid agricultural production, and maintain Argentina's ability to meet her international obligations. Nevertheless, when the government policies of the thirties are summarized, they sound like a checklist of import-substitution techniques: expansionary fiscal policy, investment in the infrastructure, tariff increases, currency devaluations, negative terms of trade movement for rural goods, exchange discrimination, and artificially imposed bilateral trade patterns" (1969, 89–90; emphasis original).

4. Miguel Miranda was Perón's chief economic advisor during the period between 1946 and 1949. He is alleged to have been the embodiment of the light industrialists who supported Perón (Abelardo Ramos 1973, 191), and a self-made man whose tin- and chromeplating, food, and canning concerns had expanded during the 1930s and early 1940s (Kenworthy 1972, 17).

5. These points are pursued in some detail in Chapter 6.

6. The specific 1944 actions referred to here are (1) Decree 4316 of February 12, which authorized the Directorate of Military Manufacturers (DGFM) to form mixed

companies for the production of chemicals and metals; (2) Decree 7595 of March 28, which authorized the DGFM to form mixed companies for the production of chemicals and metals; (3) establishment of the Argentine Industrial Credit Bank for the purpose of granting long-term loans to Argentine industry; and (4) Decree 14.630 of June, which authorized subsidies and protection for ISI activities.

7. The discussion in Chapter 5 is largely dedicated to demonstrating this point.

8. Useful surveys of the history of the Argentine union movement are available in: Alexander 1962, 1965, 1968; Troncoso and Burnett 1960; S. Baily 1967; Jordan 1970; Peralta Ramos 1972; Iscaro 1973; and Zorrilla 1974.

9. Two additional points of interest might be noted. The first is that union opposition to the government originally began to coalesce in 1967 around the leadership of Amado Almos, head of the sanitation workers' union. Ongaro (head of the printers' union) assumed the leadership of the antigovernment unions and formed the CGT of Paseo Colon in 1968 after Olmos's death (Peralta Ramos 1972, 176). The second point is that after 1968 the CGT of Azopardo became divided between the "participationists" (who favored actual cooperation with the government) and the "dialogists" (who were willing to maintain communications with the government and to refrain from actually opposing it). Vandor himself was included in this latter group (Jordan 1970).

10. The name Cordobazo is generally used for a series of major popular uprisings that occurred between April and June of 1969. The government responded successfully to this crisis, but the Cordobazo is generally credited with having broken the back of the Ongania administration (Portantiero 1971, 94).

11. For a useful review of the Colorado–Azul conflicts, including a precise statement of the positions of both sides, see Millington 1964.

12. These issues are raised again in Chapters 7 and 8.

13. Under Ongania, the military participated in government primarily through the National Security Council (Consejo Nacional de Seguridad, CONASE). This point is discussed in greater detail in Chapter 5.

14. Leadership changeovers in the Treasury and Finance Secretariats are not included here, but they were equally as rapid as those in the Ministry of the Economy.

15. The text only hints at the chaos in the Secretariat of the Army in 1962. The full known sequence of changes (which may still be incomplete) was as follows: on April 2, 1962 General (ret.) Martino Bartolome Carrera; early on the 21st, General Enrique Rauch; late the same day, General (ret.) Juan Batista Loza; August 10, General Eduardo Senorans; on the 12th, General José Octavio Cornejo Saravia; on September 24, Lieutenant General Benjamin Rattenbach; on May 15, 1963, General Hector Alberto Repetto; and on October 16, General (ret.) Ignacio Avalos.

16. I would like to thank Luis Zone for making his own unpublished research on the structural changes in the Argentine government available to me. Although a number of additional sources have been utilized in assembling the information which is presented, Zone's work has been invaluable in making a chaotic and confusing series of changes somewhat intelligible.

17. Illia did not assume the presidency until October 12, 1963. It is possible, therefore, that he should not be included in this list of presidents who reduced public employment.

18. U.S Department of Labor 1959.

19. Shortly after assuming power in 1943, Pedro Pablo Ramirez promulgated a new Law of Professional Associations (Decree 2669) under which only unions legal-

ly recognized by the government could represent their members in collective bargaining. The railroad unions protested the new policy and were therefore intervened on August 23, 1943 (S. Baily 1967, 72–73; Iscaro 1973, 344). In October and November, labor opposition to government policies increased so that in December 1943, Perón effected the repeal of the hated Decree 2669. In January 1945 a new decree was issued making strikes illegal and declaring that which occurred without government permission to be crimes against the state. The February 27 announcement of the "Rights of the Worker," which was later incorporated into the 1949 constitution, did not include the right to strike. Once again, the railroad unions led the protest against government encroachment on union rights. In May 1945 the executive committee of La Fraternidad passed a series of resolutions condemning the government's limitations on the right to strike and its interventions of the municipal and textile workers' unions. On July 7, 1945 Farrell lifted the state of siege that had been in effect since 1943; and in the following months the "liberal" unions (La Fraternidad, shoemakers, textile workers, and commercial employees) increased their attacks on the *government* (S. Baily 1967, 84–85). In September La Fraternidad and the textile and shoemakers' unions withdrew from the CGT and formed the Argentine Committee of Independent Unions (COASI). The Union Tranviaria and commercial employees' unions supported these actions with wildcat strikes (S. Baily 1967, 86). In 1948 La Fraternidad protested against Perón's application of the 1902 Residence Law, under which aliens could be deported if they constituted a threat to the state (Alexander 1965, 37). Alexander summarizes the situation: "Although Perón was successful in gaining control of the top union leadership of the labor movement, he could never completely destroy the opposition in the rank and file, and there were numerous instances during his tenure in office when the lower-echelon leadership of the unions defied the President" (1968, 187).

20. Several other instances in which the railway workers struck in protest against government policies might also be mentioned. On February 1, 1956 the Aramburu government announced that wages would be frozen until March 1958. The following month, the government imposed new legal restrictions on the unions (Iscaro 1973, 322–323). In October and November of 1956, therefore, the railroad workers joined with the commercial, bank, and telephone employees in a series of strikes for higher wages. In October 1957 the railroad workers struck again. This time the protest was against the government's wage freeze and its elimination of the right to strike (Decree 10.596). Troops were brought in to run the rail lines during the forty-eight-hour strike on October 22 and 23. In 1958 yet another important railroad strike occurred. Nearly 240 thousand workers walked off their jobs for six days in a demand for higher wages. The dispute was not ended until November 28 when Frondizi declared the strike to be illegal and drafted all of the striking workers into the military.

21. The connection between the railroad strike and the declaration of a state of siege may have been only indirect. On September 28, 1951 dissident military officers led by General Benjamin Menendez attempted to topple Perón. The turmoil surrounding the strike may have encouraged that action, but the abortive coup may also have been stimulated by Perón's announcement on August 22 that his wife Eva would run as his vice-presidential candidate in the upcoming elections. (Eva was ultimately withdrawn and Quijano was named to the number-two spot on the ticket.)

22. For discussions of Frondizi's 1958 railroad reorganization plans, see Eshag and Thorp 1974, 96 and Zuvekas 1968.

FIVE

Policies Toward the State, the Military, and Society

A further breakdown in the predictions of the "who governs" authoritarian thesis is apparent when changes in policies toward the organization of the state, attempts to institutionalize the role of the military in government, and efforts to depoliticize the system in Argentina are examined. The "who-governs" thesis predicts that sharp contrasts should be identifiable in all three of these areas, in particular when comparing the populist and bureaucratic authoritarian periods. The populist authoritarian governments of Ramirez, Farrell, and Perón should have mobilized the popular sector and included it for the first time in the political life of the nation. The military's role in government should have been largely provisional and ad hoc. The size and complexity of the government should have increased as a result of the initiation and expansion of a variety of welfare and public works programs during the populist period without any concerted efforts to reorganize or control the growing bureaucracy. Following in the wake of these developments, the bureaucractic–authoritarian coalition of the post-1966 period should have attempted to establish an exclusionary and depoliticized system. The military members of the bureaucractic–authoritarian coalition should have unified themselves and taken control of the government with a view to establishing a more or less permanent military dictatorship. The technocrats of the bureaucratic–authoritarian coalition should have rejected the political bargaining, electioneering, and pressure group politics that distorted earlier efforts at objective policymaking. The technocrats should therefore have sought to *reorganize the state, increase its operating efficiency,* and *"rationalize" policymaking.*

The integrated formulation predicts that the shift from populist authoritarian rule (1952) and to bureaucratic–authoritarian rule (1966) should not have produced fundamental policy changes in these three areas. Cabinet instability had become chronic by the early 1950s; a large, highly unionized public bureaucracy had developed; cyclical balance-of-payments, foreign exchange, and inflation problems combined with the cumbersome and inefficient public bureaucracy to drain the resources elites had at their command;

67

and the completion of the consumer goods phase of import substitution industrialization in the late 1940s or early 1950s had eroded the populist coalition, but no new bloc of actors had evolved to establish firm political control.

All four of these conditions should have shifted control of the policy-making arena. From about 1952 onward, public bureaucrats rather than coalitions and political elites should, by the integrated formulation, have in fact governed the nation. The ability of different ruling coalitions to make basic policy changes should have been reduced. The military and the technocrats in the bureaucratic–authoritarian coalition might have tried to establish a permanent antilabor, depoliticized regime in which policymaking was based on rational criteria; but it is unlikely that they could have succeeded. All of the newly arriving political elites after about 1952 should have been able to extend, intensify, and even marginally reverse existing policies but should have failed in their efforts at fundamentally remaking and dramatically reversing what had been done before. Unable to go ahead, they should, by the theory, have built on what had been done before. This is apparently just what happened.

Policies Toward the Organization of the State Itself

The authoritarian thesis predicts that reform efforts to centralize and "rationalize" the policymaking process should be restricted exclusively to the post-1966 period, when the technocrats of the bureaucratic–authoritarian coalition were dominant actors in the Argentine policymaking arena. The impact of these "Harvard-trained" administrators (Abelardo Ramos 1973, 286) in the post-1966 period is allegedly apparent in their efforts to (1) restructure the public bureaucracy, (2) create the Office of the President, and (3) establish the National Development Council (Consejo Nacional de Desarrollo, CONADE) (W. Smith 1976).

The evidence supports the integrated formulation, however. The formal organization of the Argentine state remained largely unchanged between 1898 and 1943. With the arrival of the populist authoritarian coalition, however, the number of cabinet-level positions increased from eight to fifteen. A second set of new, increasingly specialized ministries and secretaries was created in 1949 with the adoption of the Peronist Justicialista Constitution.

The first major structural reform measures were adopted in 1954. The new organization called for the retention of most of the previously existing cabinet positions, but it also established four superministries[1] constituting an inner cabinet designed to guide and manage the operation of the remaining ministries. The Frondizi reorganization of 1958 reinstituted this two-tier arrangement. In this plan, eight ministries that closely paralleled the eight established by the 1898 constitution were to oversee the operations of a varying number of secretaries. Rather than being unique or innovative, the 1966 reorganization was a simple reinstitution of a hierarchical arrangement within the cabinet. In this instance, five ministries were designated to direct the operations of the remaining agencies.

Three points might be noted in connection with these three efforts to restructure the Argentine government. First, none of the plans actually reduced the number of cabinet-level positions. The trend since 1945 was toward increasingly specialized cabinet agencies. Units were frequently renamed or combined with other agencies, but they were seldom abolished. The second point is that the evidence from the 1954, 1958, and 1966 government reorganizations is consistent with the expectations of the integrated formulation. All three reforms appear to have been efforts by the political elites to regain administrative control by centralizing decisionmaking authority at the highest levels of government. As expected, the first effort at reform was made in the early 1950s. The 1958 and 1966 reorganizations appear to indicate the predicted failure of the preceding efforts. Finally, the technocratically inspired bureaucratic–authoritarian reorganization of 1966, which created an inner and an outer cabinet appears to have been little more than a replication of the 1954 and 1958 reforms. Regardless of whether Argentina's elites have been technocrats or simple politicos, since 1954 they have frequently attempted to reorder the state so that they could govern effectively. Government reorganization is almost an established tradition in Argentina; and more often than not, the leaders have gone about effecting their administrative reforms in similar, rather than distinctive, ways.

Reforms within the office of the president provide additional, if somewhat weaker, support for the integrated formulation. Contrary to what one proponent of the "who governs" thesis believes, the technocrats of the bureaucratic–authoritarian period did not create the office of the president (W. Smith, 1976). That office was in fact created in 1948 during the first Perón administration and originally included the National Defense Council; the National Bureau of Research, Statistics, and Censuses; the Economic and Social Council; the Council for Interministerial Coordination; the Subsecretariat for Information; and the president's personal assistants and secretaries. The following year, the Bureau of Coordination of State Information was added.

The creation of the Office of the President may thus have been a very early attempt to centralize policymaking authority. The timing and early constitution of the office suggest that that may not have been its exclusive purpose, however. Coming, as it did, at a point when Perón was attempting to consolidate labor support and shift to providing workers with symbolic, instead of material, benefits, the Office of the President may also have been conceived as a base from which to direct the massive propaganda campaign that Perón launched to retain labor support and suppress his opposition. The creation of the Subsecretariat for Information and the Bureau of Coordination of State Information in 1948 and 1949 thus both coincide roughly with the initiation of Perón's systematic antipress campaign in 1947.

Whatever the original reasons for creating the Office of the President, however, the point to be noted is that it remained in existence throughout the 1948–1970 period. The apparent downgrading in the importance of the office during the Frondizi-to-Illia interval (1958-1965) is difficult to account for under the integrated formulation. The proliferation of entirely new agencies and the establishment of a tiered system of agencies within the Office of the President in 1968 seem to provide some support for the authoritarian formulation. Nevertheless, the office of the president in Argentina was created and sustained by the political elites of the 1948–1966 period. It was not an original, technocratically inspired policy innovation of the bureaucratic–authoritarian era.

Similar observations can be made in regard to agencies that have been charged with the tasks of planning and coordinating national development and collecting and analyzing statistics. From 1945 on, it is possible to trace the evolution of units that bore similar duties and responsibilities: the National Postwar Council (Consejo Nacional de Postguerra), which was headed by Perón himself; the National Economic Council, which was led by Miguel Miranda and later by Dr. Alfredo Gomez Morales; the Economic and Social Council and the National Bureau of Research, Statistics, and Censuses, which formed part of the newly created Office of the President in 1948; the Secretariat for Administrative Research and the Secretariat for Statistics; and the National Development Council (Consejo Nacional de Desarrollo, CONADE), which was created in 1964 by Illia in response to requirements of the Alliance for Progress. The technocrats of the bureaucratic–authoritarian coalition may have upgraded these agencies in the period after 1966; but it seems clear that their efforts to improve the nation's planning and analysis capabilities were not true policy innovations. Rather than breaking sharply from previous policies, the efforts of the technocrats in these areas appear to have been simple extensions and intensifications of steps that had been taken originally by previous, nontechnocratic, nonbureaucratic–authoritarian policymakers.

Two central points emerge from this discussion. First, administrative reform efforts developed on time in the early 1950s. Since then, efforts to restructure the Argentine state and to centralize policymaking have almost become a part of the Argentine political tradition. The fact that successive reform efforts were required appears to indicate the predicted failure to bring the public bureaucracy under control. Second, the changes discussed here have been incremental. There is little evidence that the technocrats of the post-1966 bureaucratic–authoritarian period had any special or particular impact in these areas. Rather than providing any new or particularly innovative solutions to the problems of managing the public bureaucracy, the governments of the post-1950 period tended simply to redo what had been done before.

The Institutionalization of the
Military Role in Government

Similarly, the integrated formulation is more useful in understanding the role of the military in Argentina. According to the authoritarian thesis, military efforts to establish a dictatorship and to institutionalize its role in the policy-making process should have been unique to the post-1966 bureaucratic–authoritarian administrations of Ongania and Levingston. Sharply divided over questions of how to deal with the nation's socioeconomic problems and over the appropriate nature of the military's role in resolving those difficulties, the military kept its intervention in politics prior to 1966 temporary and ad hoc. With the arrival of the bureaucratic–authoritarian coalition in 1966, however, the military had finally developed a unified view on the need to repress labor and foster the development of the nation's infrastructure and capital or basic industries. The imposition of a permanent military dictatorship and the institutionalization of a military role in decisionmaking were designed to accomplish those ends.

The difficulty is that this description of the post-1966 changes in military attitudes and behaviors is misleading. When viewed from a long-term perspective, the coup d'état of June 28, 1966, which toppled Illia and established the bureaucratic–authoritarian dominance of General Ongania, does not appear to have constituted a radical or fundamental departure from previous military interventions. Questions about the degree of unity of the bureaucratic–authoritarian military have been raised by the facts that (1) one of the members of the original junta lasted less than six months in office and (2) none of the junta members remained in their positions after August 20, 1968. Doubts about the military's (as opposed perhaps to Ongania's personal) intent to establish a more or less permanent military government were also raised by the appointment of Lieutenant General Julio Alsogaray and later Lieutenant General Alejandro A. Lanusse, two figures who may have favored a return to civilian rule, as secretaries of the army.

Additional considerations suggest that analysts have tended to overstate the uniqueness of the post-1966 governments. The military did not, for example, come to see itself for the first time as the force of light in a messianic struggle against the forces of darkness when it deposed Illia in 1966. The military interventions by Uriburu, Lonardi, and Aramburu clearly seem to have been regarded as only temporary interruptions of civilian rule that were launched with the negative intention of simply removing the existing leaders from power. As such, those brief interludes do seem distinguishable from the Revolucion Argentina of 1966.

On at least one other occasion, however, the officers deposed a sitting president and established a permanent military dictatorship so that they could complete their perceived mission. That was in 1943 when a group of pro-Axis military officers deposed President Castillo. Although the military was unified on few other points, as Robert Potash observes, "The one point on which all seemed to agree was that theirs was a strictly military movement: civilians would take no part and the military would run the future government" (1969, 197). The sense of mission of the 1943 coupmakers is apparent in the words of an anonymous document circulated among high-ranking officers shortly before the uprising:

> A harsh dictatorship was necessary [in Germany] to impose on the populace the sacrifices which were necessary for a formidable program [of national development and unification]. Such shall be the case in Argentina. Our government will be an inflexible dictatorship. . . . It will attract the support of the populace, but the people will have to work, to sacrifice and obey. To work more and to sacrifice more than any other people. Our generation sacrificed on the altars of a higher good: The Argentine fatherland, which later will shine with unequalled light for the good of the continent and for all mankind. (cited in Romero 1969, 133)

Thus, the Revolucion Argentina was not the first military government that took control in Argentina and intended to keep it. Neither were the leaders of the 1966 coup the first to have the support of a united military. Internal disunity and fractionalization have been characteristic of the Argentine military; but at least a superficial consensus and a sense of mission or destiny did not originate in the bureaucratic–authoritarian era.

William Smith, in particular, alleges that the institutionalization of a military role in the policymaking process was a unique characteristic of the post-1966 period (1976, 36–37). Nevertheless, the National Security Council (Consejo Nacional de Seguridad, CONASE), which was designed to formalize military access, has its own precedents. As Potash observes, the military played no regularized role in the policymaking arena from the beginning of Perón's first term in 1946 to the early days of Aramburu's administration in 1955 (1972, 49–54). Aramburu changed that situation, however, on the very night that he became president, when he signed Decree–Law 2908. That measure created a revolutionary council, which was

> to consist of the Vice President and the ministers of each of the three armed services and was to countersign every decree–law issued by the government in exercise of legislative functions. It was also to countersign the appointment of all cabinet members and provincial intervenors and to give its consent to all important plans, declarations, and measures designed to implement the goals of the Revolucion. . . . For almost two and one-half years the military, through a legally recognized body, shared authority with the President. (Potash 1972, 54)[2]

Even the duty of controlling internal unrest and subversion, formalized in CONASE, had precedents. A special police agency had been established by Castillo within the Interior Ministry on January 31, 1942, for example. Its mission was to exercise "vigilance over and suppression of anti-Argentine activities." A Comision Nacional de Investigaciones had been established following the overthrow of Perón in 1955. The mission of this agency was to organize and direct the repression of the Peronist elements.

Efforts to Depoliticize the System

Efforts of the bureaucratic–authoritarian coalition to depoliticize the system also echoed past measures by previous nontechnocratic, nonbureaucratic–authoritarian governments. This is clear in terms of (1) policies toward elections, political parties, and the national Congress; (2) policies toward the Supreme Court and the national universities; (3) policies toward the press; and (4) policies toward labor. These will be dealt with in turn.

Guillermo O'Donnell asserts that efforts to minimize bargaining and politics developed after 1966 because technocrats had gained increased policymaking authority in the Ongania administration, and they viewed such practices as hindrances to the rationalization of the policymaking process that they sought to effect (1973, 84). W. Smith makes much the same point (1976, 37). Both of these researchers find supporting evidence for their claim in the fact that the military moved in 1966 and thereby forestalled the scheduled 1967 elections, in which half of the Congress would have been up for election along with several crucial provincial governorships. The backers of the 1966 coup had good reason to expect that the Peronists might win significant electoral gains.[3] Rather than face that risk, they decided to "change the rules of the game" (O'Donnell 1973) and move in preemptive fashion to topple the Illia administration, dissolve the political parties, and disband the national Congress.

These steps may in fact have been the result of technocratic desires to depoliticize the system. The difficulty, however, is that similar measures had been adopted by other nontechnocratic, nonbureaucratic–authoritarian governments of the pre-1966 era. The military had acted at least once before, for example, to forestall an election that seemed likely to produce an unfavorable outcome. That was in 1943 when the officers deposed Castillo in order to prevent the election of Patron Costas (Potash 1969, 183), dissolved Congress, and officially repressed the Communist and Socialist parties. Lonardi disbanded the Congress in 1955 after the overthrow of Perón. Guido decreed the abolition of all parties and the closing of Congress on May 20, 1962.

Efforts to suppress the supporters of Perón were also not unique to the bureaucratic–authoritarian period. In 1956 Aramburu decreed the abolition of the Perónist (Justicialista) party and banned Peronist leaders from running as electoral candidates. On August 22, 1958 the Argentine Federal Court of Appeals rejected a petition by the Peronist party for legal recognition. The Peronist and Communist parties were abolished again in December 1960 as a result of their alleged participation in an antigovernment uprising. On July 24, 1962 Guido barred the Peronist and Communist parties from running presidential and vice-presidential candidates. On May 17, 1963 Guido decreed that candidates of the Peronist Popular Union party could field candidates only in congressional races. Even Guido's annulment of the Peronist victories in the elections of March 18, 1962 had a precedent. Uriburu had done much the same thing in 1931 when he annulled the results of the Buenos Aires provincial elections which had been swept by the Radical party candidates.

The picture that emerges from all of this is one of almost chronic intervention in Argentine electoral politics. Technocrats may have been unique to the post-1966 governments of Ongania and Levingston, but the desire to depoliticize the system was not. Silvert refers to a tendency toward "political absoluteness" or a "messianic view of politics" (1970, 436–437) as a consistent theme pervading Argentine history, apparent, he argues, in Rawson's 1943 statement, "Now there are no political parties, but only Argentines" and Aramburu's 1955 inaugural message, "We appeal to all inhabitants of the republic to postpone all tendentious and partisan interests to the higher interests of the collectivity" (p. 437).

Additional examples of the bureaucratic–authoritarian efforts to suppress dissent appear to be evident in Ongania's reconstitution of the Supreme Court and his July 29, 1966 intervention of the nation's universities. Here again, however, nonbureaucratic–authoritarian governments had done similar things. Perón, for example, attacked the Supreme Court in his first inaugural address on June 4, 1946 because it had ruled that two of his favored measures were unconstitutional. The following month, a Peronist representative in the Congress introduced a bill of impeachment of four of the five Supreme Court justices. Three justices and the attorney general were finally removed from office a year later.[4] The lower courts were purged in 1949, and under a provision of the new constitution all judicial appointments were subject to reconfirmation (Whitaker 1954). Finally, Lonardi dissolved the Peronist-dominated Supreme Court on October 5, 1955. A less biased, more progovernment court was sworn in two days later.

In October 1943 the government dismissed university professors who had signed a letter calling on the army to support "effective democracy and American solidarity" (Whitaker 1954). The forty-thousand-member student association was dissolved. A number of the professors were reinstated after the March 27, 1945 declaration of war on the Axis powers; but many of the pro-Axis rectors and deans were then imprisoned. On May 2, 1946, shortly after Perón's first election, all of the nation's universities were simultaneously intervened for the first time in Argentine history. Between October and December of that year, nearly 70 percent of the faculty were dismissed. On January 1, 1948 the government put into effect a new university plan which decreased the autonomy and administrative freedom of the universities. The removal of antigovernment professors continued. By 1953, nearly 90 percent of the 1945 faculty had been replaced. Another new university pact was announced in 1953. The measure gave Perón unlimited power to appoint the rectors and deans who were themselves responsible for all other appointments. A stipulation requiring rectors to have held a degree for ten years was removed and the prohibition against political activities was repealed. Finally, according to Arthur Whitaker, the entire educational system was converted into a Peronist propaganda machine (1954, 173). After the overthrow of Perón in 1955, Lonardi intervened the universities; and a program of "de-Peronization" was begun.

Efforts in the post-1966 period to censor and manipulate the mass media are apparently yet another indication of bureaucratic–authoritarian desires to depoliticize the system by stifling dissent. Such steps were taken by the Ongania and Levingston administrations, but harassment and censorship of the press by the bureaucratic–authoritarian governments may actually have been less extensive than it had been under previous administrations (S. Baily 1966, 303; Rowe 1970, 483).

Through 1930, the Argentine press was relatively free of control by the national government. After the military overthrow of the constitutionally elected Radical party government of President Yrigoyen, however, General Uriburu attempted to suppress two newspapers (*La Prensa* and *La Nacion*) that had remained hostile to the government. Under Justo, the Argentine Supreme Court reversed its position and sanctioned a measure of federal control over the press (Whitaker 1954, 158). Castillo took advantage of this new power. On May 6, 1942 a pro-Axis newspaper, *El Pampero*, was closed by government order. Control and censorship of the press continued after Castillo was ousted on June 4, 1943. On January 27, 1944, for example, Ramirez's successor, General Farrell, closed the internationally respected *La Prensa* for five days. Control of the media was intensified even further under Perón:

> First, a pattern to which all [newspapers] were expected to conform was set by the regime's own papers. Chief among these was *Democracia*, which was owned by the Eva Perón Foundation and which had a circulation of about 200,000. One of its features was a column signed "Descartes," which was generally believed to be the pen name of Perón himself, though he never avowed it publicly. When conformity was not forthcoming and pressure had to be applied, he used various combinations of measures which included harassment by government inspectors, reduction of supplies of newsprint (a government monopoly), inspired attacks by Peronist mobs and

strikes by Peronista employees, subsidies to persons willing to be corrupted, and purchase of controlling interests by his associates. (Whitaker 1954, 159)

These efforts to control the opposition press and mount a propaganda campaign were directed after 1948 from the already-mentioned agencies within the office of the president. The government thus took control of the privately owned radio stations, for example, and linked them with a newly created agency in the office of the president. New legislation in 1949 made it illegal to offend the dignity of any public official. If the author of any offending article could not be found, the editor of the publication in which it appeared could be imprisoned. A new congressional committee was established in January 1950 to oversee "anti-Argentine" activities. Its operation eventually led to the suspension of more than sixty newspapers. In October 1950 the supply of newsprint to *La Prensa* was reduced. Vendors went on strike against the newspaper the following January and picketed the plant. The owner of *La Prensa* was indicted for anti-Argentine activities. On March 20, 1951, the government finally expropriated *La Prensa*. This newspaper, which had detailed the worst violations of civil rights by the Peronists, reappeared on November 19, 1951 as an official voice of the Peronist-dominated General Confederation of Labor (CGT). The nation's radio broadcasting system was reorganized once again toward the latter part of 1953, when all existing licenses were abruptly canceled. New regulations requiring at least 70 percent native Argentine ownership were enforced. Finally, the number of broadcasting companies was reduced to three, all supervised or operated by the government.

Press controls were relaxed somewhat, shortly before Perón's downfall in 1955. On July 6 Perón announced the end of the revolutionary stage of his movement and called on his critics to engage in a dialogue with him. Arturo Frondizi, then the head of the opposition Radical party, obliged the president and on July 27 made the first opposition broadcast to be heard in the nation for ten years. The relaxation of controls continued after the September 1955 coup d'état. Lonardi decreed on October 19 that all Argentine newspapers would receive a uniform allotment of fifteen tons of newsprint per day, for example. On December 7, 1955 *La Prensa* was removed from the control of the CGT and returned to its former owner.

Government control of the press began to intensify once again, however, once Lonardi had been replaced by General Aramburu. Lonardi had attempted to chart a course toward reconciliation with the Peronists; under Aramburu, the supporters of the ousted dictator were repressed on nearly every front. While anti-Peronist publications had thus been repressed during the 1945–1955 interval, Aramburu put the shoe on the other foot and moved quickly to suppress the pro-Peronist media between 1955 and 1958.

The image that emerges from all of this is therefore quite similar to the one noted above in connection with Argentina's electoral history. Censorship and control of the media were common both before and after 1966. Whenever any government came under attack, the tendency was to react by attempting to suppress the critics. There was no sudden constriction of the freedom of the press by the bureaucratic–authoritarian administrations of Ongania and Levingston.

Efforts to stifle dissent seem to be an integral element of the Argentine political tradition. It may be that if elites consistently fail to resolve the fundamental problems which they confront, a consistent pattern of repression develops as they attempt to buy time for themselves by acting in one of the few areas in which they can still be effective. All repression does not result from elite failure, of course. Nevertheless, much of the suppression that does occur may, in a sense, be explained if a pattern of chronic failure in other policy areas can be detected.

Efforts to depoliticize the system by excluding labor from the political life of the nation are alleged to have been particularly important defining attributes of the post-1966 bureaucratic–authoritarian administrations of Ongania and Levingston (O'Donnell 1973; W. Smith 1976). Labor policies are the core of the authoritarian thesis. All of the governments in Argentina may have attempted to limit dissent by intervening in electoral politics, subverting the courts, disrupting the universities, and controlling the press. Only the bureaucratic–authoritarian governments, however, should have been strongly antilabor if the "who governs" authoritarian thesis is valid. In light of this prediction, it is rather curious that the repressive measures adopted by Argentina's most strongly antilabor governments were not substantially distinct from the policies pursued by the nation's least antilabor, most strongly populist regime. To be sure, there were differences in the labor policies of the populist and bureaucratic–authoritarian governments; but the distinctions have not been as clear-cut as is commonly believed.

A national Civil Defense Law (17.192) and a compulsory Arbitration Act (Law 16.636) are a case in point. William Smith (1976) regards these repressive measures as unique to the post-1966 bureaucratic–authoritarian period in Argentina. The former threatened the drafting of dissident workers who refused to return to their jobs. The latter effectively eliminated the right of the workers to strike. The difficulty, of course, is that Perón himself invoked a civil defense law in order to quell a railway workers' strike on January 24, 1951. The Compulsory Arbitration Act was similar in substance (if not in precise form) to measures enacted in 1943 (Decree 2669), 1945 (Decree 23.852 as ratified by Law 12.921), 1956 (Decree–Law 9270), 1957 (Decree 10.596), and 1962 (Decree 8946). Even the Illia government, which Ongania toppled, had decreed a new regulation of the Law of Professional Associations. Under that measure, political activity by unions was prohibited, open shops were legalized, the government was given control over union funds, more than one union was permitted to exist in a given field, new rules for union elections were imposed, increased autonomy was granted to local unions, and strikes were made permissible only after a vote of the full union membership (S. Baily 1966, 303). Even the "Rights of the Worker," which was made public by Perón himself on February 27, 1945 and was later incorporated into the 1949 constitution, failed to include the right to strike.

Efforts to constrain, and later freeze, wages, announced in 1967 and 1968 were also not unique to the post-1966 period. Even the ostensibly pro-labor government of Perón had adopted similar policies. Workers' salaries increased sharply after 1943, when the populist coalition came to power. By 1949, however, the government was already enacting measures calling for an increase in foreign investments, the stimulation of the long-neglected agricultural sector, a reduction in public expenditures, the restriction of new investment credits for Argentina's consumer goods manufacturers, an increase in labor productivity, and finally, the containment of real-wage increases (Cafiero 1961, 329–346; Ferrer 1967, 197). In 1950 the "prolabor" Perón government implemented a new program that compelled labor unions to sign new wage agreements at two-year intervals rather than the usual one-year intervals. In 1951 Perón asked the CGT and the principal manufacturer's association, the General Economic Confederation, to help stabilize wages and prices. The CGT itself helped launch a program in 1952 to control inflation by increasing production and decreasing spending. Limitations on the domestic consumption of beef were imposed the same year in order to increase Argentina's potential meat exports.[5]

These points can be carried a step further. Perón himself, the leader of the populist coalition and the mobilizer of the Argentine masses, had begun to abandon labor at a point no later than 1948–1949. He had clearly sought to include labor in the political life of the nation by providing workers with tangible benefits during his rise to power within the populist coalition in the 1943–1945 or 1946 period. In the interval following his election, however, Perón consolidated his movement. The CGT was finally brought under his direct control. The Laborista party, which had provided the organizational backing for Perón's election and sought to retain some independence from Perón, was effectively destroyed and replaced by the Partido Unico. The CGT and the Secretariat of Labor and Welfare increasingly sought to discourage unapproved labor strikes. When workers walked out without permission, the government showed little hesitation in forcibly breaking the strikes.

Conclusions

The weight of the evidence reviewed in this chapter is clearly in favor of the integrated formulation. The arrival of the bureaucratic–authoritarian coalition in 1966 did not result in any major policy changes in the direction of re-organizing the state, institutionalizing the military's role in government, or depoliticizing the system. Efforts in these areas are among the defining char-acteristics of bureaucratic–authoritarian systems. I have demonstrated that the post-1966 governments of Ongania and Levingston generally met this definition.

As I have also showed, however, the steps taken by the post-1966 gov-ernments were often little more than extensions or intensified versions of policies adopted by previous, nontechnocratic, nonbureaucratic–authoritarian administrations. The fact that evolutionary or incremental patterns of devel-opment were identified in the sections on administrative reform and the mili-tary's role in government is also consistent with the integrated thesis. Finally, the discussion demonstrated that the policy preferences and even the exclu-sionary/depoliticizing means for achieving those goals were part of the nor-mal pattern in Argentina since at least the early 1950s. The Ongania and Levingston administrations may indeed have been of the bureaucratic–authoritarian type, as a number of researchers suggest; but they were not really new beginnings. In these areas at least, the shift to bureaucratic–authoritarian rule did not fundamentally change policies.

At least two other, somewhat surprising points should be noted. The first is that the post-1966 and immediate post-1943 governments were remarkably similar. Like the bureaucratic–authoritarians, the leaders of the 1943 coup that toppled Castillo (1) came to power with a view toward retaining it for a considerable period; (2) came to power with a positive, messianic sense of mission about how to solve the nation's problems; (3) moved immediately to depoliticize the system by closing the Congress, dissolving political parties and imposing controls on the press; and (4) acted to repress labor. This point will be carried a step further in Chapter 6.

The second point of interest is the gradual shift by Perón from a pro-labor, inclusionary stance to an antilabor position in the 1947–1949 period. This shift will be explored more systematically in Chapter 7. It is important because it roughly coincided with the adoption of a number of other policies that are generally associated with only the post-1966 bureaucratic–authoritarian period. It was in 1946, for example, that Perón launched his first attacks on the Supreme Court and the nation's university system. Those efforts were intensified in 1948 and 1949. The systematic campaign against the press was begun in 1947. In 1948 the office of the president was orga-nized as a base for conducting the extensive propaganda campaign that masked the fact that labor was receiving less and less in the way of tangible benefits from the government. The upward trends in workers' real incomes and share of the GDP received were abruptly halted in 1949. The nationalis-tic bias of the early stages of the populist movement was abandoned. A U.S. military aid mission arrived in Buenos Aires in 1945. A small loan was accepted from the Export–Import Bank in 1946. By June of 1947, Argentina had been included in President Truman's post–World War II rearmament program. The apparent early populist support for Argentina's consumer goods import-substituting industrialists also began to slacken. The nation's first integrated iron-and-steel plan was approved, and all bans on foreign loans were lifted in 1947. By 1949, the shift to bureaucratic–authoritarian socioeconomic policies was nearly complete. A year of productivity was proclaimed. Investment credits for the nation's light industrialists were restricted. New plans were made to stimulate the nation's agricultural sector. Finally, efforts were launched to decrease government spending. All of these considerations raise questions, of course, about the standard interpretation of the 1943–1952 period in Argentina as homogeneously populist.

Notes

1. The reorganization under Perón in 1954 created the supercabinet positions Political Affairs, Economic Affairs, Technical Affairs, and National Defense. Some listings include the Ministry of Foreign Affairs and Culture and the newly recombined Ministry of Interior and Justice in the inner circle.

2. As Potash notes, the vice-president at the time was Admiral Rojas, so the navy actually had two seats on the revolutionary military council. He also observes that over time, General Aramburu managed to free himself of the control of the council and designate it (Decree-Law 3440 of November 22, 1955) as only an advisory body (1972, 54–56). Nevertheless, while the CONASE under Ongania may have been the first successful attempt to institutionalize the role of the military in the policy-making process, it was not the first effort taken in that direction.

3. In the elections of March 18, 1962 neo-Peronist parties had won in four provinces. They had also backed a Christian Democrat who won in Jujuy. Under pressures from the military, Frondizi moved the next day to annul the results. He announced the intervention of the provinces in which the neo-Peronists had scored victories. Only nine days later, President Frondizi was removed from office. Guido reannulled the elections on April 28, 1962. On April 21, 1964 Illia submitted a bill to Congress rescinding the absolute restrictions on the Peronist and Communist parties that had been imposed by Guido. Henceforth, both would be allowed to run candidates as long as the Peronists did not use the name of Perón and the Communists were not subject to the interests of other nations. (Only a little over a year earlier, on March 27, 1963, Guido's minister of the interior, Rodolfo Martinez, Jr., had been forced out of office by the military for proposing a similar plan for reincorporating the working class into the electoral process.) As a result of Illia's legislation, Perónists gained control of thirty-five seats in the Chamber of Deputies in the March 14, 1965 elections. In April 1966, the Peronist candidate for governor in Mendoza won 41 percent of the vote.

4. One of the justices was simply allowed to resign, so that four of the five justices on the Supreme Court were actually replaced.

5. The government also attempted to limit wage increases at several points during the 1952–1966 interval.

SIX

Industrialization and Foreign Policies

The authoritarian thesis predicts that the three types of authoritarian coalitions should have pursued different types of industrialization and foreign policies. Thus, the traditional authoritarian leaders of the 1930–1943 period should have promoted the expansion of the export-related industries because such activities benefited certain elements of the dominant ruling coalition. The populist administrations of the 1943–1952 interval should have had a nationalistic bias and encouraged the development of the consumer goods import substitution industries (ISI) because industrialization policies were made by and for light industrialists. Finally, the bureaucratic–authoritarian governments of the post-1966 period should have welcomed foreign capital and fostered the expansion of the nation's infrastructural and basic industrial sectors, because foreign and domestic monopoly capitalists were members of the bureaucratic–authoritarian alliance.

However, by examining Argentina's changing industrialization and foreign policies during the 1930–1970 period, I shall provide general support for the integrated formulation. Dominant coalitions did make a difference in setting such policies in the period before the development of the four constraining factors, while changing sets of political elites failed to alter policies in the subsequent interval. Those who governed at the top in Argentina were important during the first half of the 1930–1970 interval; but from then on, the dominant coalitions ceased to have major impact. The development of a bureaucratized political system reduced the capacity of political elites to direct and redirect public policies according to their preferences. They may have been *willing* to alter previous industrialization and foreign policies, in other words, but they may not have had the capacity or the *opportunity* to do so. Changes in Argentina's industrialization and foreign policies became more evolutionary than abrupt or dramatic.

The discussion in this chapter also yields two unanticipated findings. First, it seems clear that different types of industrialization were often promoted simultaneously and that actual patterns of industrialization frequently had little to do with the motivations of the policymakers. As a result, dominant and subordinate patterns of actual outcomes and policy goals can be identified throughout almost the entire 1930–1970 period. The neat stages or periods of industrial development implied by the "who governs" authoritarian thesis did not always exist. Different coalitions may have attempted to promote the expansion of different industrial sectors; but poor planning, mismanagement, and faulty policy execution often produced totally unanticipated outcomes.

The second, somewhat surprising finding concerns the impact that the Argentine military and a variety of changing international and foreign policy factors had on the nation's industrialization efforts. For example, the military began to perceive the need for basic industrial development and modernization of the nation's infrastructure as early as 1930; and factors such as the 1929 depression, the outbreak of World War II, and the initiation of U.S. plans to modernize the Latin American militaries helped to create that perception. The military attempted to promote the nation's basic industries in the period after the 1943 coup that toppled Castillo; but their efforts failed and served only to produce a largely unintended expansion of the consumer goods sector of the economy. Concern for industrial development and modernization of the military forced the abandonment of Perón's nationalistic, anti-U.S. policies in the late 1940s. Newly available foreign capital and new national security threats served to stimulate at least an incremental expansion of the basic industrial sector from 1954 on.

All of this leads me to the tentative conclusion that basic industrial development in Argentina may have followed an evolutionary pattern. Expansion of this sector was not retarded until the arrival of the bureaucratic–authoritarian coalition in 1966. The Argentine military has promoted basic industrial development since at least 1930. Special efforts to promote that sector were made when national security was most threatened. Progress was made when new capital became available from foreign sources. Faulty policy administration in the pre-1950 era and bureaucratic resistance thereafter delayed, misdirected, and eventually masked this consistent trend. Neither policy outputs nor policy outcomes had any necessary or direct correspondence to what elements were included in the ruling coalitions or what they wanted to do.

First, I shall review the factors that contributed to the military's perception of the need for basic industrial development and modernization of the infrastructure. Next, I shall focus on the military's efforts to promote basic industrialization during the age of populism. Finally, I shall review the growth in basic industrial development in the post-1954 era. All three sections will link this developing emphasis on basic industrial development to the actual outcomes of the industrialization process. They will trace the factors that contributed to the perception of the need (that is, to the *willingness*) to expand the nation's basic industries and modernize its infrastructure and the considerations that denied the political elites the opportunity to move ahead to accomplish those tasks.

Initial Incentives for Basic Industrial Development

Industrialization policies during the 1930s and early 1940s resulted in the expansion of Argentina's consumer goods industries. Under Uriburu and during the first part of the Justo administration, economic policies focused on balancing finances, paying off foreign debts, and hoping that the economy would eventually return to the boom conditions of the 1924–1929 period (Dalto 1967, 132). An important shift occurred in 1933 when Justo appointed Federico Pinedo as his finance minister. In December of that year, Pinedo proposed the Plan de Restructuracion–Plan de Sanchez Sorondo. The legislation called for the imposition of exchange controls, the creation of committees for the regulation of meat and cereal production, a new public works program, monetary devaluations, controls on imports, new controls on dumping and drawbacks, and the creation of a national central bank (Murmis and Portantiero 1971, 19–24).

The 1933 plan itself was never formally approved by the Congress. Nevertheless, the plan appears in many ways to have summarized the basic framework of the economic policies that were enacted in piecemeal fashion by the Argentine governments through the end of the 1930s. For example, by 1935 three key agencies had been created to regulate and control the agricultural export sector: the elevator board, the meat board, and the cereal board.

The governments of this period were also moving in other areas that had a more direct bearing on Argentina's industrial development. Differential exchange rate and import exchange permit systems were established in 1933. Measures were adopted in 1934 that unified the nation's internal taxes and thereby ended the erection of protective tariff walls between the provinces. In 1935 the Argentine Central Bank (Banco Central de la Republic Argentina, BCRA) was established.

In the summer of 1937–1938, poor harvests decreased agricultural production. The resulting lower export volume was combined with a reduction in the prices that Argentine agriculturalists were receiving on the world market. Those two developments produced Argentina's first negative trade balances since 1930. In responding to the 1929 depression, Argentina's policymakers had enacted a series of differential exchange rates, trade permits, and trade barriers. In November of 1938 the official exchange rate for the Argentine peso was devalued. Exchange permits were made a requirement for the importation of all goods. The type of product to be imported became a criteria for determining whether the purchase could be made at the free or official exchange rate. In August 1939 Ortiz took yet another protectionist step when he abolished the free market exchange rate for all merchandise imports.

The economy recovered somewhat in 1939, but by 1940 World War II had begun in Europe. Deprived of its traditional export markets, Argentina once again suffered a negative balance of payments; and once again, Argentina's policymakers responded in predictable ways to the developing crisis. Federico Pinedo was recalled to serve once again as finance minister; and on December 17, 1940 he introduced the Plan de Reactivacion-Plan de Pinedo in the Argentine Senate. This legislation included proposals for new drawback and antidumping regulations, the adjustment of the tariff system, the state purchase of excess agricultural produce, long-term industrial credits, and the "nationalization"[1] of the British railroads (Murmis and Portantiero 1971, 35; Rofman and Romero 1973, 145; Abelardo Ramos 1973, 68–71).[2] In 1941 a Trade Promotion Corporation was established to encourage the export of nontraditional products (Diaz Alejandro 1970, 100). There is some disagreement over what motivated the adoption of these measures and in whose behalf they were enacted (Murmis and Portantiero 1971; Merkx 1969). Nevertheless, the dominant theme was clearly the expansion of Argentina's consumer goods import substitution sectors.

This was not the only pattern that was developing during the 1930s and early 1940s, however. Since the early 1920s there had been an interest, primarily on the part of the military, in developing Argentina's basic industrial sector in order to strengthen Argentina's economic independence and military defense. In 1922 the state petroleum corporation (Yacimientos Petroliferos Fiscales, YPF) was created, with General Enrique Mosconi as its first director. According to Robert Potash (1969, 24), the purpose of the agency was to demonstrate that Argentina had the capacity to develop its petroleum resources without foreign assistance. Following the overthrow of Yrigoyen by the military on September 6, 1930, a second critical step was taken toward the development of Argentina's infrastructure and basic industries. On November 8 the Superior Technical School was established and placed under the command of Lieutenant Colonel Manuel Savio. Its purpose was to undertake the study of problems related to basic industrial development (Potash 1969, 77).

In the late 1930s, three factors began to develop that appear to have increased the military's emphasis on basic industrialization and modernization of the infrastructure. The first was the already-mentioned deterioration of the economy in 1938. The military had intervened in 1930 at least in part because of the 1929 depression. The economy had recovered steadily after the implementation of Pinedo's trade controls in 1933. The abrupt reversal of the trend toward an improving economic situation in 1938 could only have served to reemphasize Argentina's continuing vulnerability to world economic conditions.

The second factor that encouraged the Argentine military to favor basic industrial development was the deterioration of Argentina's national security in the late 1930s. Both Brazil and the United States seemed to pose increasing threats to Argentine dominance of the southern cone of South America, at the least. The Brazilians were apparently spending considerably more for defense than the Argentines. Production of iron and steel, two goods of extremely high strategic value, had been initiated in Brazil in 1925. By 1939, production was sufficiently high to reduce Brazil's dependence on imported iron and steel significantly. In comparison, Argentine iron and steel production was not begun until 1938. Output was expanded at a much slower rate than had been the case in Brazil. Argentina's dependence on imported iron and steel consequently remained high through the early years of World War II.

As the potential Brazilian threat to Argentine national security and regional hegemony began to become more ominous in the late 1930s, a third factor encouraging Argentine military support of industrialization arose in increasing U.S. pressures for a hemispheric security pact. A special Inter-American Conference for the Maintenance of Peace was convened by President Franklin Roosevelt, who personally journeyed to the meeting in Buenos Aires. Together with the U.S. Secretary of State Cordell Hull, Roosevelt offered proposals for

- A binding commitment for reciprocal assistance in the event that any nation in the hemisphere were attacked by a non-American nation
- The creation of a new commission to implement that pledge
- Acceptance by all of the nations of the hemisphere of the neutrality measures just adopted by the U.S. Congress in an effort to avoid the coming war in Europe (Whitaker 1954, 106)

The third proposal was rejected entirely by the conference and the United States was forced to accept the adoption of watered-down versions of the first two. As Arthur Whitaker notes:

Hull found Saavedra Lamas [the Argentine Foreign Minister] not cooperative . . . but hostile. He could hardly have been otherwise, for Hull's first two proposals ran counter to Argentine foreign policies, current and past, and his third proposal, an isolationist neutrality, would have exposed Argentina to greater economic losses than any other American nation in case of war in Europe, for Argentina was dependent in an exceptionally high degree upon her trade with Europe. (1954, 106–107; see also T. Bailey, 1969, 684; and Scenna 1970, 156).

Argentine relations with the United States continued to fluctuate in the following years and proved central to Argentina's efforts to establish itself as an independent nation.

In the face of Argentina's continuing economic vulnerability and increasing pressure from Brazil and the United States, the emergence of the Hitler and Mussolini regimes in Germany and Italy was probably significant. Their early successes following the outbreak of World War II in March 1939 provided striking evidence of the potential for a military-led program of industrial development. The 1938 recession, the apparently growing threat from Brazil, and U.S. promotion of a hemispheric security pact may have underlined the need for an expansion of the basic industries. At least a portion of the Argentine military believed that the Axis powers demonstrated how such developments could be undertaken.

Argentine–U.S. relations remained relatively cordial, however, as these factors developed during the first two years of the Ortiz administration. In 1939 Argentina accepted a neutrality proposal in return for a U.S. pledge of assistance if Argentine trade with Europe were interrupted. In 1940 the Act of Havana stipulated (1) that the transfer of the American possessions of any European power was prohibited unless they were transferred to, and administered by, a commission of the American republics and (2) that the signatories would regard an attack on one nation as an attack on all of them. Ortiz was clearly interested in the agreement. If England fell, Argentina might be able to acquire control of the Malvinas (Falkland) Islands and thereby end the Anglo–Argentine dispute over their possession. Argentina initialed the Act of Havana, and Argentine–U.S. relations reached a new level of cordiality.

When Paris fell to the German troops on July 20, 1940, however, Argentina took another equally significant step. Four days after, the government requested a record defense appropriation measure from the Argentine Congress. At the same time, Ortiz submitted a bill calling for the creation of the General Directorate of Military Manufacturers (DGFM) "to manage existing and future military factories and to promote the development of industries related to the needs of the armed forces" (Potash 1969, 123). By August 1940, Ortiz had been forced by his ill health to withdraw from active duty as the president. His departure allowed the ultraconservative, proisolationist Castillo to serve as the acting president. Relations with the United States immediately deteriorated.

Another turning point in Argentine–U.S. relations came in March 1941, with the passage of the Lend Lease Act. Ruiz Guinazu, Castillo's foreign minister, rejected the U.S. secretary of state's offer of a one-million-dollar loan on the grounds that it would increase U.S. influence in Argentina. In September the DGFM was formally established; and Colonel Manuel Savio, former commander of the Superior Technical School, was named as its head. For the time being, at least, it appeared that Argentina would refuse Lend Lease aid and attempt to modernize its own military.

Argentine–U.S. relations, however, were not totally disrupted. The Castillo government responded to a request from the Inter-American Financial and Economic Advisory Committee and began to nationalize foreign flagships that were docked in its ports (Hazard 1951). Argentina and the United States completed a new trade pact and agreed to lower tariffs on each other's exports. On December 10, 1941 all Japanese funds in Argentina were frozen. On December 29 Argentina recalled its ambassador from Germany.

Thus, by the end of 1941, the U.S. use of the carrot and the stick seemed to be pushing Argentina off its neutrality position. From the U.S. point of view, however, Argentina had still not gone far enough. Castillo had still not broken relations with the Axis. For that reason, the United States continued to push and prod Argentina into disavowing its neutral position. By the beginning of 1943, Argentina was completely surrounded by nations whose militaries were being modernized with U.S. assistance. Such developments had apparently exacerbated an important division within the Argentine military. One faction favored the Allies and hoped to receive Lend Lease funds to modernize the military. It may have been this group that promoted the warming of Argentine–U.S. relations in the latter part of 1941. The other faction was pro-Axis. Its members sought to maintain relations with Germany, Japan, and Italy; receive assistance from those nations; and resist U.S. pressures for the establishment of a hemispheric security pact. Despite these important divisions, the two factions appear to have been in full agreement on at least two points. First, they were opposed to Castillo and the continued rule of the traditional sectors of the economy. The president had attempted to manipulate divisions within the military for his own political ends. He failed to obtain military assistance from either the United States or Germany. Second, the two factions recognized that the establishment of Argentine hegemony in a Latin America free of U.S. and Brazilian domination would require the industrial development of the nation. These sentiments appear to have contributed to the overthrow of Castillo on June 4, 1943.

The post-1943 governments clearly intended to promote Argentina's industrial development. The critical question was whether they would do it on the basis of their own resources, seek U.S. assistance, or attempt to obtain aid from Germany. Argentina's military might have been willing to move in the direction of the United States. Foreign Minister Storni, in a letter to U.S. Secretary of State Cordell Hull, insisted that the Ramirez government was really pro-Ally but that it would take time for the new president to control the pro-Axis segments of the military. In the meantime, Storni inquired about the availability of Lend Lease aid such as Brazil was then receiving. Hull's public response to Storni's note forced the latter to resign on September 9, 1943; but the Ramirez government did move on January 26, 1944 to break relations with the Axis powers. As events developed, however, Ramirez's breaking with the Axis led to his overthrow on March 9, 1944. When the Ramirez-to-Farrell shift produced no real changes in Argentina's relations with the Axis, the United States withdrew its ambassador and persuaded England to do likewise. The United States attempted to block the renegotiation of a new Argentine–English trade agreement. In September U.S. merchant vessels were ordered to avoid Argentine ports. In October 1944 Hull moved to prevent Argentina from presenting its case for neutrality to a meeting of the hemisphere foreign ministers.

These actions by the United States may have pushed Argentina in the direction of the Axis powers. In January 1944 the Ramirez government sent one "Alberto Hellmuth" to Spain in a secret effort to negotiate an arms agreement with Germany. As late as September 1944, Argentine diplomats in Spain were negotiating with German armaments officials (Potash 1969, 252).

In the midst of this international intrigue, Argentina's military was moving on its own to develop defense-related industries. The pattern had been set by the actions of Ortiz and Castillo vis-à-vis the General Directorate of Military Manufacturers (DGFM) in 1940 and 1941. Two decrees in 1944 established DGFM responsibilities for producing strategic metals and chemicals. An industrial credit bank was established to finance domestic industrial development. The War (Army) and Navy Secretariats were given permanent seats on the board of directors (Potash 1969, 252). General Savio was retained as the head of the DGFM. A graduate of Savio's school, General Julio Checchi, was appointed as the first secretary of industry and commerce. In June 1944 what Eldon Kenworthy (1972, 18) describes as Argentina's first integrated industrial promotion law was enacted (Decree 14.630). The outcome of these actions was the expansion of Argentina's light-consumer-goods import-substituting industries. Such activities had been protected since 1933, when systems of differential exchange rates and import permits were instituted, but the Ramirez and Farrell administrations are commonly thought to have extended the protection of ISI industries in what Carlos Diaz Alejandro refers to as a "delayed response to the great depression" (1970, 106).

It is often overlooked that this acceleration in the growth of consumer goods ISI activities may have been an *unintended* policy outcome. A very different real goal may have motivated the establishment of the Superior Technical School in 1930; the military pressure for the development of a steel production capability in 1937 (Diaz Alejandro 1970, 247); the lobbying for U.S. basic industrial development assistance in 1942; and the establishment and expansion of the DGFM in 1940, 1941, and 1944. Even the continual reappearance of General Savio, General Checchi's appointment to the Industry and Commerce Secretariat, and the assignment of extra military positions on the directorate of the industrial credit bank are consistent with the trend. The real goal may have been the development of the basic industrial base that would ensure the adequate defense of the nation in the face of threats from the United States and Brazil. In other words, despite the contention that basic industrial development was neglected until the advent of bureaucratic-authoritarian rule in 1966, national security concerns stimulated at least some elements of the military to perceive the need for such developments during the 1930–1944 interval. Recessions in 1929 and 1938, the emergence of the Axis governments, and U.S. and Brazilian pressures may have encouraged the military to take some actions. Sincere wishes to expand the nation's basic industries may have been frustrated, however. Perhaps more by chance than by choice, light-consumer-goods industries grew instead.

Basic Industrial Development
in the Age of Populism

According to the standard interpretation of Argentine history, the political and economic life of the nation was dominated during the 1943–1952 period by a coalition of domestic (light) industrialists, urban workers, producers of nonexportable agricultural goods, and the military. This populist coalition allegedly promoted nationalistic policies and measures designed to expand the consumer goods import-substituting sector of the economy. The completion of the consumer goods phase of ISI in the late 1940s or early 1950s eroded the dominance of this coalition. At that point, according to the standard interpretation, nationalistic and ISI policies were abandoned.

The existing evidence raises doubts about this interpretation. Between 1946 and 1954, Argentine public policies were steering the nation in two opposite, apparently contradictory directions. This was especially true during the 1947–1949 interval. During these years, the nationalistic policies of the early populist period were both extended and abandoned. Policies that had effectively supported consumer goods production were intensified while consumer goods expansion was being rejected in favor of basic industrial development.

Consider, for example, the contradictions in Perón's position vis-à-vis the United States and foreign capital. As a result of negotiations under the hand of U.S. Secretary of State Edward R. Stettinius, in February 1945 it was agreed that the United States would sponsor Argentina's admission to the United Nations and provide the Farrell government with military assistance if Argentina would (1) declare war on the Axis nations and (2) ratify the Act of Chapultepec, which multilateralized the Monroe Doctrine and established a Pan-American defense pact (T. Bailey 1969, 755). The results of this agreement were immediately apparent. For instance, Argentina finally declared war on the Axis powers, German-owned industries in Argentina were nationalized, and the United States finally recognized the Farrell government. When the United Nations conference opened in San Francisco, Stettinius argued for Argentina's admission to the organization.

In the course of the San Francisco conference, however, Stettinius was forced to resign as a result of disputes over whether Argentina, Belorussia, and the Ukraine would be included in the United Nations. Stettinius's replacement, James F. Byrnes, dispatched Spruille Braden as the new U.S. ambassador to Argentina in May 1945. Braden advised the suspension of the economic and military aid agreements that had been negotiated by Stettinius in February 1945. When Farrell announced the scheduling of elections on July 7, 1945, the U.S. ambassador proceeded immediately to interfere in Argentina's domestic politics in an effort to block the election of Perón.

Argentine–U.S. relations reached a new low when the U.S. Department of State published the famous "Blue Book"[3] on the eve of Perón's electoral victory on February 24, 1946. The new president-elect did little to ease tensions. Two days after his inauguration on June 4, Argentina established diplomatic relations with the Soviet Union. Perón began an extensive program of nationalizing industry and in a speech on July 9, 1947 declared Argentina's economic independence. At a meeting of the U.N. Conference on Trade and Employment in Havana (November 1947–March 1948), Argentine delegates denounced U.S. imperialism and offered financial support to assist other Latin American nations with their development efforts. In April 1949 Perón outlined his now-famous "Third World" position for the first time. In the face of the developing cold war between the Eastern- and Western-bloc nations, Argentina would follow its own nationalistic course between laissez-faire capitalism and communist totalitarianism.

All of these points are well-recognized by Argentine specialists, of course. They are among the actions and occurrences that buttress the standard interpretation of Argentina's nationalistic populist period. It is often overlooked, however, that Perón's nationalistic actions may have been largely symbolic. Immediately following his election in February 1946, the president-elect dispatched representatives to Washington to negotiate a new arms agreement (Scenna 1970, 208). On June 26 Perón took the first steps toward ratification of the Act of Chapultepec. On September 19, 1946 the Export–Import Bank (EIB) agreed to loan the Argentine government 210 thousand U.S. dollars for the revitalization of its ports.

The timing, rather than the size, of the 1946 EIB credit is significant. Argentina had had previous loan and credit agreements with the EIB. Up to the beginning of 1940, seven loans had been approved for the purchase of trucks, oil refinery equipment, railway cars and engines, and other equipment (Elasser 1955, 88). In 1940 the Ortiz government completed three agreements for a total of 82.42 million U.S. dollars with the EIB. Of the pre-1940 agreements, however, only 120 thousand dollars was actually disbursed. All three of the 1940 agreements were canceled as Argentina's improving balance-of-payments situation in the early 1940s eased the need for assistance. Despite the relatively small amount involved, the 1946 EIB credit is therefore of interest because the assistance was actually disbursed. Just like Farrell when he negotiated with Stettinius's representatives for U.S. economic and military aid in February 1945, Perón may have been willing, by 1946, to abandon ideology for pragmatic politics.

An important turning point in Argentine–U.S. relations thus occurred by 1947. By June of that year, for example, President Truman had agreed to include Argentina in U.S. postwar military assistance programs. On July 8, the day before Perón's declaration of Argentine economic independence, all bans on foreign investments in Argentina were lifted. In 1948, when Argentina was promoting its own Marshall Plan for the rest of Latin America at the foreign ministers' meetings in Havana and Bogota, Miguel Miranda was optimistically noting that Argentina could expect to receive at least one billion dollars in economic assistance from the United States (Weil 1950, 31).

The picture of nationalistic policies that emerges from this evidence is thus a pragmatic one. Having come to power with the support of a popular coalition, Farrell and Perón took a number of steps that carried economic nationalism to new extremes between 1945 and 1949. In less obvious (but nevertheless important) ways, however, both Farrell and Perón moved simultaneously to make peace with the United States. Despite the traditional ideological interpretations of the populist period, the policies of the 1945–1949 interval were less nationalistic than is generally assumed. While nationalistic policies were being intensified in areas that were salient to the working-class sector of the populist coalition, they were being abandoned in areas that were of particular interest to the Argentine military.[4]

A similar contradiction developed in Argentina's industrialization policies during the populist period. On three previous occasions—1933, 1938–1939, and 1940—Argentina's conservative leadership, in the face of deteriorating economic conditions, had decreased the nation's import bill by artificially raising the price of imported goods. The result (if not the intent) of those previous measures had been the expansion of Argentina's ISI activities. Thus, when negative overall balances of payments developed between 1947 and 1949, Perón responded in traditional fashion. New tariff, exchange rate, and monetary devaluation measures were enacted in 1947, 1949, and 1950.[5] Those actions, as much as any others, caused Perón to become identified with consumer goods import substitution industrialization.

It is not often understood that the Argentine government was also trying to promote basic industrial development and the modernization of the infrastructure during the late 1940s. Here, again, the actions taken were typical of steps taken previously. As early as the 1880s, Argentina's leaders recognized that it was the responsibility of the state to promote the expansion of the sectors of the economy that benefited the nation in general and were unlikely to be promoted by private capital (Treber 1969, 26). In general, the state assumed its responsibilities by creating public or mixed-public-and-private corporations. Two enterprises created by the prepopulist governments, the YPF and the DGFM, have already been mentioned. Prior to the 1943 coup, other state-owned corporations were established in the areas of transportation (Ferrocariles Argentinas), energy production (Gas del Estado and Agua y Energia Electrica), trade (Lineas Maritimas Argentinas and Flota Fluvial), and aviation development (Fabrica Militar de Aviones).

The populist governments extended this trend toward the creation of new public and mixed-public-and-private corporations in the period after 1943. A number of those enterprises resulted from highly political considerations of the nationalistic populist governments. Subterraneos de Buenos Aires, the Empresa Nacional de Telecomunicaciones, and Aerolineas Argentinas should probably be classed in that category.

A number of other state corporations were apparently created as a result of more objective considerations, however. The Direccion Nacional de Fabricaciones e Investigaciones (DINIE), for example, resulted from the nationalization of the German-owned industries in 1945. As it was formally constituted on January 24, 1947 (Decree 1.921), DINIE included thirty-one separate enterprises operating in the construction, chemical, metallurgical, and electrical sectors of the economy. Operations were later added in the areas of textile, cement, plastic, and pharmaceutical production. By the time DINIE was granted its institutional autonomy in 1948 (Decree 8.230/48), it was responsible for such diverse projects as dike construction, irrigation, hydroelectric power generation, a distillery, petrochemical plants, and the production of oil transport tankers (Treber 1969, 33).

In June of 1947 the first step toward the establishment of another important state corporation was taken when Perón approved the Savio Iron and Steel Development Plan. The formal approval of the plan and the eventual creation of the SOMISA (Sociedad Mixta Siderurgica Argentina) corporation are significant. As was noted in the previous section, the Argentine military had a long history of concern for developing the industrial base that would ensure the adequate defense of the nation. That concern led to the formation of the Superior Technical School under the command of Lieutenant Colonel Manuel Savio in 1930 and to the creation of the DGFM under his command in 1941. The Savio Plan of 1947 carried the military's concern yet another step.

Measures such as the creation of DINIE and the approval of the 1947 Savio Plan are important indications of newly developing policy goals, even though the state corporations had few positive impacts on the Argentine economy. In general, the state enterprises were notoriously inefficient, costly, and overstaffed. As a rule, they failed to raise production levels in the basic industrial and high-technology sectors of the economy. For that reason, the major economic expansion during this period continued to develop in the consumer goods ISI activities. That result may have been largely unintended, however. DINIE, SOMISA, and later corporations such as Direccion Nacional de Fabricaciones e Investigaciones Aeronauticas (DINFIA) and

Astilleros y Fabricaciones Navales del Estado (AFNE) may reflect the actual policy preferences of the leaders of this period.

The conclusions to be drawn are obvious. The promotion of consumer goods ISI activities by the governments of the populist period does not imply that these governments were not simultaneously attempting to develop capital- and technology-intensive industries. The creation of DINIE and the approval of the Savio Plan in 1947 indicate that the populist governments recognized the limits of consumer goods import substitution industrialization by at least that date. The problem then became one of execution. In general, the domestic industrialists responded efficiently to the incentives that were offered through the state's tariff, trade, and exchange rate policies. It was the public sector that foundered. Publicly owned capital and technology-intensive industries failed to develop along with the consumer goods industries in the private sector because the state failed. The interest was there; the need was apparently recognized. The problem was putting the public corporations into motion.

It was in the execution phase that delays developed. By 1947, the populist policy of economic nationalism had been effectively abandoned; and Perón was taking the first concrete steps toward developing Argentina's heavy industries. Despite those important policy changes, however, the shifts to openly relying on foreign capital and to developing heavy industry were retarded. In 1950, for example, Perón was reluctant to publicize the fact that the EIB had granted Argentina a 125 million-U.S.-dollar monetary support credit. Execution of the Savio Plan was delayed until Perón obtained EIB support for the project in 1955.

The fact that such delays developed does not negate the fundamental importance of the 1947 policy shifts, however. Instead, the lags between the changes in policy goals and changes in policy outputs suggest two interesting questions. The first focuses on the problem of explaining why the goals changed when they did, the second on the reasons for the delays.

At least two factors may explain why the shifts in policy goals—from nationalism to effective cooperation with the United States and foreign investors and from exclusive ISI promotion to a balanced program of industrialization favoring both consumer goods ISI and basic industries—began to occur by at least 1947. On the one hand, it is reasonable to argue that at least two groups in the populist coalition were no longer willing to support a continued linking of consumer goods ISI with Argentine nationalism after 1947. Argentina's consumer goods light industrialists could not afford an extremely nationalistic government. While they benefited from the high tariffs and exchange restrictions of the Ramirez, Farrell, and Perón administrations, the light industrialists could not risk antagonizing the suppliers of the imported inputs on which their operations were dependent. During World War II, the United States had ordered its merchant ships to avoid Argentine ports. United States leaders had attempted to persuade the British to do the same. It could hardly have escaped the notice of the light industrialists that the United States might be willing to adopt similar measures in the future if Perón's nationalistic course became too extreme.

Portions of the military may also have been anxious to abandon both nationalism and the promotion of consumer goods industries by 1947. Argentine defense expenditures exceeded those of Brazil during the 1944–1946 period; but the Brazilians received U.S. Lend Lease assistance during that interval, while Argentina did not. In the postwar era, Brazil could expect to continue to receive the latest in weaponry and advanced training from the United States. Argentina could not expect to provide such improvements for its own armed forces. Assistance would have to come from abroad; and the United States had made it perfectly clear that the price for its military aid was the abandonment of the nationalistic and anti-U.S. policies of the Ramirez, Farrell, and Perón governments.

As has been said, this problem may have been recognized by at least some portions of the Argentine military during the 1930s. A key difference was that in 1947 there was no equivalent to the Axis to balance against U.S. and Brazilian pressures. The U.S.–Soviet dispute over Iran had begun to develop at the end of 1946. The Truman Doctrine was announced in the middle of the Greek–Turkish crisis, on March 12, 1947. However, these were only the opening rounds in what would become the Cold War. The Soviet Union did not explode its first nuclear bomb until September 23, 1949. The People's Republic of China was not established until the same month. The Argentine military, therefore, had few choices in 1947. If it could not modernize on its own, it might be forced to abandon the nationalistic policies and accept assistance from the United States.

Another factor may have influenced the thinking of the Argentine military in 1947. It had tried and failed to modernize itself without foreign assistance. Since the establishment of the DGFM in 1941, the military had made significant progress in a number of areas. In addition to armaments, the DGFM produced liquid gas piping, agricultural equipment, and oil-drilling machinery. It operated railroad equipment and maintenance facilities. The DGFM produced petrochemical products. Together with the YPF which was also dominated by the military, the DGFM exploited the nation's gas, oil, coal, iron ore, and sulphur deposits.

Despite these developments, the establishment of the DGFM and the effective (if unintended) promotion of ISI activities during the 1944–1946 interval had not succeeded in developing the domestic, industrial base that would ensure the adequate defense of the nation. While iron and steel production climbed sharply between 1943 and 1944, for example, output had remained relatively static from that point. As a consequence, iron and steel imports increased sharply after the end of World War II. In the meantime, iron and steel production in Brazil had surpassed Argentine output in both levels and rates of increase.

Both the light industrialists and a portion of the Argentine military may have been willing, therefore, to withdraw their support for a continued linking of consumer goods industrial promotion and Argentine nationalism in 1947. The light industrialists may have favored even further promotion of consumer goods industries. By this time they might have seen Perón's nationalism as a threat to their interests. The military may have wished to abandon both nationalism and consumer goods ISI and instead rely on foreign capital to promote the expansion of the nation's basic industrial and infrastructure sectors.

In any case, the deterioration of the economic situation in 1947 may have been the second factor that prompted the policy shifts. The war years had been beneficial to Argentina. The balance of trade had been positive in every year between 1940 and 1946. By 1947, however, the situation had begun to shift to Argentina's disadvantage. With the recovery of Europe under the stimulus of the Marshall Plan, the demand for, and price of, Argentina's exports began to fall. The nationalization of foreign investments and Perón's foreign purchase of surplus trucks and buses in 1946 and 1947 exacerbated the situation. As a result, Argentina suffered a negative overall balance of payments in three successive years between 1947 and 1949. Gold reserves fell. The cost of living rose. Real gross domestic product at factor costs actually declined between 1948 and 1949. In 1949 all payments to the exterior were halted, and Miranda's economic team was replaced. By 1950, Perón was forced to apply to the EIB for a monetary support credit.

Not all of these trends were apparent in 1947, of course. The onset of the recession in that year may have been sufficient, however, to convince at least some Argentines that consumer goods ISI could not be relied on to maintain an adequate rate of economic expansion. Sustained growth and adequate national defense would ultimately require the types of developments that the military had been promoting since at least the 1930s. In theory, it might have been possible to utilize the massive gold reserves to finance the development of the nation's capital and high technology industries, but by 1947 that chance had already been lost. Once the recession began, Argentina no longer possessed the extensive capital inputs that were necessary to underwrite basic industrial development projects. If such works were to be undertaken, assistance would have to come from abroad. Unfortunately, such aid was not likely to be available if Argentina maintained its nationalistic course.

The paradox in this should not be overlooked. From the beginning, nationalistic considerations had prompted the military's promotion of basic (capital-intensive, high-technology) industrialization. That had been true in 1930; it had been true of both the pro-Axis and pro-Allied elements of the military during the immediate pre–World War II era. By the time the military succeeded in convincing others of the need for such developments, however, events had progressed to the point that basic industrial development required the abandonment of the nationalistic course. In other words, if Argentina was to develop the capacity to defend itself against U.S. and Brazilian pressures over the long term, it would have to rely on U.S. assistance during the short term.

Thus, it is perhaps for these reasons that important shifts in the goals of Argentina's foreign and industrialization policies are detectable in 1947. From that point up to at least 1970, with only minor breaks, the Argentine governments showed a pragmatic and generally increasing willingness to rely on foreign capital to promote the nation's basic industries and modernize its infrastructure.

Given that important changes in policy goals can be detected in 1947, why was there a lag in their execution? Why did Argentina's leadership continue to espouse nationalism and support ISI after 1947? The who-governs authoritarian thesis would imply that nationalism and ISI were maintained through the late 1940s because the governing coalition supported such policies. That conclusion may be only partially valid. If one can distinguish between the sectors included in the coalition and the elite political personnel who actually held policymaking positions in the government, one can argue that coalitional pressures forced the political elites to maintain policies even after the leadership had recognized the limitations and unfortunate implications of such measures. Issues of economic nationalism had been used to mobilize labor by the Ramirez, Farrell, and Perón governments. Light domestic industrialists may not have actually belonged to the populist coalition, as both Kenworthy (1972) and Torgnato Di Tella (1968a) suggest; but they certainly enjoyed at least some benefits of the policies of the populist governments. For those reasons, neither the labor class nor the light industrial sector would have supported a rapid retreat from both economic nationalism and the promotion of consumer goods ISI. The labor class and the light industrial sector may have "trapped" the coalition's leadership. Abrupt and well-publicized changes in the foreign and industrialization policies that had been used to organize the movement would probably have caused major erosions in the support for the populist coalition. It would have been harder for the elites to go back than to go forward.

Thus, a pattern of policy "dualism" should have characterized the immediate post-1947 period. Economic nationalism should have been both extended and abandoned. Support for consumer goods industries should have been intensified while the leadership attempted to utilize the public sector to promote the development of Argentina's capital and high-technology industries. Highly public disbursements of symbolic benefits to the popular sector should have continued at a time when the leadership was moving toward a secret rapprochement with the United States and foreign capital. Of course, this is precisely the pattern that occurs during this interval. The post-1947 pattern is consistent with the integrated formulation.

The populist leadership failed in its apparent bid to expand rapidly into new areas of industrialization for several reasons. On the one hand, the governments elected to promote basic industrial and infrastructural development by establishing public and mixed-public-and-private corporations. In general, those enterprises proved to be counterproductive. They increased the number of public employees and thereby exacerbated the nation's fiscal problems but failed to increase production. As I have said, the problem may have been one of organization and execution.

Development via public corporations had another important implication, however. Even though the public enterprises were failures, the leadership could not abandon them. The creation of the public corporations brought labor—particularly unionized labor—inside the state. The popular sector may have been able to press its demands even from positions outside the state; but once workers had actually become part of the state, they were in a much stronger position to force the political elites to maintain even the most outmoded and counterproductive policies. The fact that the public employees had been hired in the first place constituted both a political and a financial commitment on the part of the elite political personnel. The leaders could not simply abandon those commitments by destroying the bureaucratic agencies and public corporations. Thus, even though the new units in the public sector may often have been created for sound economic reasons such as the expansion of the nation's basic industries, the public corporations may have become political "albatrosses" that the elites could neither destroy nor manage effectively. In the meantime, the state enterprises continued to drain off resources.

This situation began to change around 1950, when new resources became available from foreign sources.[6] A three-dimensional policy mix began to evolve in which the leadership acted simultaneously to (1) maintain supports for consumer goods production, (2) retain the "failed" state corporations, and (3) obtain new foreign capital and channel it into the basic industrial and infrastructure sectors either by creating yet another set of public corporations or by providing direct inducements to the private sector. Thus, for example, Argentina's retreat from consumer goods ISI policies proceeded only incrementally. The last vestiges of the 1944 measures were not eliminated until 1959. Existing, notoriously inefficient public corporations such as Ferrocariles Argentinos and the YPF were seldom abandoned. More commonly, they were simply bypassed. It was difficult to dissolve existing commitments; but with new, previously unallocated resources from abroad the leadership could maintain many of the existing policies and agencies and yet move ahead into new policy areas.

Perón therefore opened negotiations with California Argentina (a branch of Standard Oil) for a petroleum prospecting agreement in August 1953 (Villanueva 1966, 14). On February 11, 1954 an EIB credit for 2.52 million U.S. dollars, later canceled, was extended to the government for the purchase of railroad locomotives. In January 1955, the government approved a pact with Kaiser Industries for the construction of an automobile plant in Cordoba. Finally, on March 10, 1955, six months before Perón was overthrown and seven months before Raul Prebisch arrived in Argentina to act as Lonardi's economic advisor, the EIB extended a sixty-million-U.S.-dollar credit for the purchase of steel mill equipment. After years of delay, the 1947 Savio Iron and Steel Plan was about to be implemented with the assistance of foreign capital.

These events in the early 1950s were milestones in Argentine history. The point to be noted, however, is that they were totally consistent with the policy goals that had begun to develop by 1947. Rather than marking the end of the populist period (as the standard interpretation suggests), these measures appear to have been the extensions of previously submerged policy trends that had begun to form almost as soon as Perón was elected in February 1946. The recession of the 1951–1952 period may have served to underline the need for decisive action in stimulating the basic industry and infrastructure. The recession of 1938 had apparently had a similar effect on at least some portions of the military. Nevertheless, it was the increased pool of potential foreign resources that made possible the actual changes in Argentina's foreign and industrialization policies in the post-1950 period.

Despite the standard interpretation that the 1943–1952 period was characterized by economic nationalism and support for Argentina's consumer goods ISI activities, the evidence cited here reveals a more complex picture. By 1947, Argentina's leaders may have been willing to abandon the nationalistic and consumer goods ISI policies that had been instrumental in bringing them to power. Coalitional pressures may have prevented the elites from abruptly reversing previous policies, however. The inefficiency of the public corporations—and later the shortage of available capital—precluded a rapid expansion into basic industrial development and modernization of the infrastructure. The first successful steps toward stimulating those sectors were not taken until after 1950, when the amount of available foreign capital increased. At that point, actual policy outputs did begin to change even though the goals that gave rise to the "new" policies had begun to form by 1947. The new trends became increasingly pronounced toward the latter stages of the 1947–1955 interval, so that industrialization and foreign policies before and after 1952 differed in degree rather than in their basic direction.

The same picture is characteristic of the policies enacted before and after Perón's downfall in September 1955. The coup brought no changes in the basic directions of Argentina's foreign and industrialization policies. Once again, the differences were in degree rather than in kind. The reliance on foreign capital increased in around 1950. A second jump appears to have occurred in 1954. A third major upward shift is apparent in 1955–1956 after Perón's departure from office. Efforts to promote the nation's basic industries and modernize its infrastructure generally paralleled these shifts. I shall trace the patterns in detail.

Basic Industrial Development After 1954

The overthrow of Perón on September 25, 1955 and his replacement by General Lonardi initiated a series of events which caused Argentina to become increasingly receptive to foreign capital. On October 27, Raul Prebisch, president of the International Monetary Fund, delivered the first of his analyses of Argentina's economic situation. On April 19, 1956 the Aramburu government began proceedings to ratify the 1944 Bretton Woods agreement, which would eventually win Argentina membership in the International Monetary Fund (IMF) and the International Bank for Reconstruction and Development (IBRD, or World Bank). Argentina signed the Act of Paris and thereby consolidated its foreign debts on May 30, 1956. The IMF extended a seventy-five-million-U.S.-dollar credit to Argentina on April 17, 1957 for the purpose of helping the nation pay off its foreign obligations.

In February 1958, Frondizi was installed as Argentina's new president. He acted almost immediately to reduce the budget deficits of Argentina's state-owned corporations, increase Argentina's domestic oil production, and attract foreign capital. In June 1958, for example, Frondizi announced that the government would return to the private sector the German industries that had been confiscated at the end of World War II and since 1947 had been organized in the DINIE. On July 24, Frondizi moved to reduce Argentina's dependency on foreign oil. Just as Perón had done in 1953, Frondizi bypassed the state-owned oil corporation (YPF). In the future, private foreign capital would be utilized to increase domestic oil production. Thus, on August 9, 1958, the first of a series of new oil exploration and production contracts was signed with the Pan-American International Oil Company, an affiliate of Standard Oil of Indiana. Railroad modernization was initiated with a 70-million-U.S.-dollar loan which was obtained from a consortium of Dutch banks. A 140-million-U.S.-dollar credit from a group of British corporations was announced. The funds were to be used for the purchase of oil and industrial machinery and power plant equipment.

On December 30, 1958 Frondizi's Plan for Development and Stability was announced. The plan called for the introduction of a free exchange system, the elimination of price controls and subsidies, increases in the fares and rates charged for public services, new limits on wage increases, a more receptive attitude toward foreign capital, and the restriction of the money supply (Villanueva 1966, 17–19). Specific elements of the plan were enacted even before the plan itself was announced. On December 29, the government revealed that stabilization credits totaling 328.5 million U.S. dollars had been obtained from the IMF and private U.S. banks. That same month, the government moved to enact Laws 14.780 and 14.781. The first granted foreign capital the same constitutional guarantees and legal rights as domestic capital, offered favorable tax advantages to potential foreign investors, and guaranteed the free repatriation of capital. Law 14.781 was designed to stimulate industrial development (Zuvekas 1968, 51).

Retreat from intense promotion of Argentina's consumer goods industries continued to follow its incremental pace. On January 1, 1959 the Argentine peso was returned to the free market exchange rate for the first time in nearly twenty years. By the end of 1959, most import restrictions had been eliminated. The era of intense promotion of the domestic industries that had been initiated by the conservatives in 1933 and intensified by the populists in 1944 was finally at an end.

These government policies were resisted, and public employees were frequently among those leading the fight.[7] At times, the policies appeared to be leading the state toward both increasing and decreasing roles in managing and guiding the national economy. Nevertheless, foreign private direct investments in Argentina increased sharply after 1955.[8] Despite Perón's efforts, foreigners had apparently been unwilling to invest in Argentina through the early 1950s. An average of only 3.16 million U.S. dollars was invested in each year between 1951 and 1955. Because the repatriation of profits was limited during most of that period, it appears likely that most of the increases were simple reinvestments of previous earnings (FIAT 1966, 304).

That situation had begun to change by 1956, however. New private U.S. investments began to arrive in greatly increased amounts in all of Latin America. During the 1951–1955 period, private interests in the United States had invested a total of 1,750 million U.S. dollars in Latin America; between 1956 and 1960, new private direct investments from the United States totalled 3,332 million dollars with 2,200 million dollars of that amount arriving in the 1956–1957 interval (UN Economic Commission on Latin America 1965, 214).[9] Partially as a result of this increased flow of capital from the United States, new investments in Argentina by all private foreign sources rose to an annual average of 165.76 million U.S. dollars between 1956 and 1960.

The majority of the direct private investment in Argentina after 1955 was concentrated in petroleum and consumer-durable, chemical, petrochemical, and pharmaceutical industries whose production was designed primarily for domestic markets (UN Economic Commission on Latin America 1965,

145, 215). Those trends had been set by Perón, but Aramburu and Frondizi carried them to a new extreme. This distribution differed sharply from the pre-1950 pattern, when most of the U.S. and foreign capital was concentrated in the transportation and public utility sectors of the economy.

This post-1955 shift of direct private investments to the petroleum and manufacturing industries does not imply, however, that Argentina's basic industrial and infrastructure sectors were entirely neglected. In fact, new investments in what Ferrer (1967, 191) calls the "social overhead" sectors actually increased sharply after 1955. New loan and credit commitments to Argentina from foreign public sources began to increase dramatically just prior to Perón's downfall in 1955. Under Aramburu the utilization of these sources was sporadic but it was clearly not insignificant. Frondizi drew in large amounts, with greater consistency, and from a larger number of sources than either Perón or Aramburu.[10] Borrowing from foreign public sources continued under Guido, despite the political problems that erupted continuously during his administration. Illia reversed the trend toward increasing utilization of foreign public capital. Both foreign private and foreign public capital flows to Argentina almost ceased during the first years of his administration.[11] Borrowing patterns returned to an upward trend, however, with the arrival of Ongania in June 1966. The shift to Levingston in 1970 coincided with another decrease in the investment commitments which obtained from foreign public sources, but by 1971 the upward trend was reestablished.[12]

These loans and credits from foreign public sources such as the EIB, IBRD, Inter-American Development Bank (IADB), and the Agency for International Development (AID) are generally ignored by researchers because they are relatively small compared to investments from private foreign sources; but they are clearly important. In Argentina, foreign private and foreign public investments have been channeled into very different sectors of the economy. Private capital has gravitated to the areas in which the short-term return on investments was potentially the greatest. There was probably very little that any of the Argentine governments could have done to redirect that flow. They could have forbidden investments in some areas and utilized a variety of profit, tax, and repatriation incentives to encourage them in others. At best, however, government control over foreign private capital could only have been indirect. Critical decisions about whether or not to invest and in what areas and to what degree to expand, would still have been made by the executives of foreign corporations and their local subsidiaries and branches. None of the Argentine governments could have forced foreign private investors to move into areas that did not seem profitable.

With foreign public capital, Argentina's elite political personnel had much more direct control. Regardless of how much or how little a given government obtained in the way of loan and credit commitments from foreign public lenders, the elites were free to allocate the support and control of its disbursal in ways that may have suited their own priorities more closely. When private capital (both foreign and domestic) failed to invest in basic industries and the infrastructure because such investments had low profit potentials, Argentina's elite political personnel borrowed from foreign public sources in order to expand the pool of previously unallocated resources at their command rapidly. They then utilized those resources to promote the expansion of the crucial social overhead sectors of the economy.

Aldo Ferrer argues that Argentina's political elites should have begun earlier to utilize foreign public capital for basic industrial development and that they should have used foreign public capital to a greater degree (1967, 191). It is noteworthy, however, that Argentina's political elites did begin to utilize foreign public capital during the last two years of Perón's administration. As a result, foreign private investments in Argentina's industrial and infrastructure sectors were largely replaced by foreign public capital in the post-1954 period.

New commitments from the EIB, IBRD, IADB, and AID for transportation, steel, power, and water systems projects totaled 1,025.673 million U.S. dollars between 1954 and 1970. Of those credits, 44.5 percent were acquired by the bureaucratic-authoritarian governments of Ongania and Levingston during the last three-and-a-half years of the sixteen-year interval. Between the ousting of Illia on June 28, 1966 and December 31, 1970 Ongania and Levingston obtained new commitments for investments in the four areas at an average daily rate of $276,654 (U.S.). Between February 11, 1954 when Perón obtained approval for a transportation loan from the EIB, and June 28, 1966 the average daily rate was only $126,447.84 (U.S.). Quite clearly, the post-1966 governments obtained new commitments for the four areas of basic industrial and infrastructural development at an appreciably higher rate than did the pre-1966 administrations.

A very different picture emerges when one focuses on borrowing patterns. The governments of the pre-1966 period accounted for 71.8 percent of the commitments obtained to modernize Argentina's transportation systems and 72.6 percent of those obtained for the expansion of the nation's steel production capacity. Finally, the governments of the 1954–1966 interval accounted for 80.6 percent of the commitments which were obtained from the EIB, IBRD, IADB, and AID for the development of Argentina's water systems. Only in the area of electric and hydroelectric power does borrowing by the bureaucratic–authoritarian governments of Ongania and Levingston appear to have been inordinately high.

To a certain extent, even this picture is misleading. While the governments of Perón, Lonardi, Aramburu, Frondizi, Guido, and Illia acquired between 71.8 and 80.6 percent of the commitments for transportation, steel, and water system development, they also accounted for 73.2 percent of the

February 11, 1954–December 31, 1970 period. Because those leaders were collectively in office longer than the post-1966 regimes, it might be argued that they should have borrowed more extensively than Ongania and Levingston. Taken collectively, the pre-1966 governments certainly had a longer period of time—thus a greater opportunity—in which to win new loan and credit approvals.

None of this evidence is at all consistent, of course, with the contention that the post-1966 governments of Ongania and Levingston initiated a new phase of industrialization and modernization of the infrastructure. Whatever else the late Perón-to-Illia governments did or tried to do, they obtained massive new investment commitments from foreign public lenders for critical areas of Argentina's basic industrial and infrastructural sectors. Those administrations might have done more.[13] They might have channeled loans and credits into slightly different areas. In the end, however, the pre-1966 governments at least made a beginning. The post-1966 bureaucratic-authoritarian regimes were not the first to promote basic industrial development in Argentina.

To close this section, two more general points are in order. First, the considerations that stimulated elements of the Argentine military to make special drives for basic industrialization and modernization of the infrastructure may have changed during the post-1954 period. Prior to 1954, the military's concern appears to have been aroused when international security crises developed. The 1929 depression, the 1938 recession, the onset of World War II, the U.S. decision to rearm the Brazilian military in the immediate postwar period, and the Korean crisis are examples of such episodes.

Argentina's military appears to have reacted in the post-1954 period when crises developed that threatened (1) the nation's domestic security situation, (2) its international security, or (3) the military's own organizational interests and integrity. Two examples illustrate this point. An attempted military coup against Frondizi occurred in June of 1959. In September of that year, Frondizi was forced to use loyal troops to remove a dissident commander in chief of the army. Those two events were preceded by a chain of occurrences that, when coupled with the increasing wave of strikes and economic problems in 1959, gave Argentina's military ample reasons to feel insecure. Frondizi was allowed to remain in office, but he yielded ground to the military when he approved a plan placing accused terrorists under military control in March of 1960.

Frondizi also attacked the organizational interests of the military. His oil development plan and the creation of Yacimientos Carboniferos Fiscales (YCF) to control coal production served to bypass the military-dominated YPF. The plan to return DINIE to the private sector, which was announced in June 1958, had the same effect. The first iron and steel development credits that Frondizi obtained (March 12, 1959; May 5, 1960; and June 1960) were not directed toward the military-dominated SOMISA corporation. Instead, they were obtained for the privately owned ACINFER and ACINDAR corporations. On November 27, 1960, Frondizi bypassed Economic Minister Alsogaray and signed a contract with the MISIPA corporation. The agreement called for this consortium of local and foreign firms to develop the iron ore deposits at Sierra Grande which were owned by the military's DGFM (Zuvekas 1968, 54).[14] Finally, on January 12, 1961, the Congress approved a Frondizi-backed bill to increase the private stock subscriptions in the SOMISA iron and steel facilities at San Nicolas.

The second general point is that it was Perón, rather than Ongania or Levingston, who actually initiated foreign-financed basic industrial development in Argentina, when he obtained the 60-million-U.S.-dollar iron-and-steel development credit from the EIB on March 10, 1955. Foreign public investments had been utilized before in Argentina. A trend toward increasing receptivity toward foreign capital began to develop by at least 1947. Efforts to develop Argentina's basic industrial and infrastructural sectors can also be noted by that point. The 1955 iron-and-steel credit is important because it marks an intensification of both of those trends.

The March 10, 1955 EIB credit is important for another reason, however. By the time the commitment was obtained, serious difficulties had developed in a number of sectors of the economy. Agricultural production was lagging. The transportation network had seriously deteriorated. The domestic capacity to produce manufactured goods for the export market was low. Despite all of these problems, Argentina's first major development credit from foreign public sources was allocated to iron and steel development, the one area that was of special concern to the Argentine military. That concern was consistent throughout the 1930–1955 period. It is apparent in the establishment of the Superior Technical School in 1930, the creation and expansion of the DGFM in the 1940–1944 interval, and the approval of the Savio Iron and Steel Plan in 1947. The 1947 plan was not immediately implemented, but Perón's 1955 EIB credit was dispersed to Aramburu. Construction of the SOMISA Iron and Steel Complex at San Nicholas was finally begun in 1956. Production began in June of 1960.

Conclusions

This chapter raises doubts about the standard interpretation of Argentine industrialization and foreign policies. Consumer goods import substitution industrialization was promoted by the traditional authoritarian governments during the 1930–1940 or 1943 interval. Such activities received an effective, if unintended, push by the populist governments of the 1943–1952 period.

From that point, however, the periods identified by the standard interpretation have only limited validity.

Efforts by the military to promote Argentina's basic industrial sectors began to be apparent as early as 1930. They were intensified in the events surrounding the creation and expansion of the DGFM during the 1940–1944 period. Evidence suggests that the "ISI legislation" of June 1944 was intended to promote the types of industrial development that would ensure the nation's defense. The Savio Plan, the creation of a series of public corporations, and the attempt to effect a rapprochement with U.S. and foreign capital in 1947 were consistent with that bias. By 1950, foreign capital was being actively pursued. New legislation in 1953 granted new privileges to foreign investors. By 1954, assistance was being obtained from the EIB for the revitalization of Argentina's rail networks. From that point, Argentina's leaders showed a generally increasing tendency to utilize foreign public capital to underwrite the nation's efforts to expand its basic industries and modernize its infrastructure.

The evidence thus tends to support the integrated formulation. Major policy shifts and realignments occurred prior to the late 1940s, when the Argentine state expanded and became highly bureaucratized. From that point, policy changes were more evolutionary than abrupt or dramatic. When important policy shifts did occur in the post-1954 period, they tended to coincide with two different general types of factors. On the one hand, the "willingness" of certain segments of the military to promote basic industrial expansion and the modernization of the infrastructure tended to increase when crises developed that threatened Argentina's international security, the nation's domestic security, or the military's own organizational interests and integrity. The first factor was important even prior to 1954. All three factors appear to have been important during the ensuing period.

If such concerns tended to increase the *willingness* to industrialize, changes in the availability of resources affected the *opportunities* the military possessed to translate policy goals into actual policy outputs. After 1944, the military attempted to promote basic industrial development by relying sequentially on (1) the domestic private sector (1944–1947), (2) the public sector (1947–1950 or 1954), and (3) a combination of both the private and public sectors (1950 or 1954–1970). During the first two periods, primarily domestic capital was utilized. After 1950—especially after 1954—foreign public capital was relied on more and more extensively. Prior to 1950 or 1954, new developmental efforts therefore developed during periods of economic expansion. They ended during recessionary periods. After 1950 or 1954, new efforts in the actual promotion of basic industrial development ceased to move with national expansion/recession cycles. Major shifts in the availability of foreign capital (as in 1950, 1955 or 1956, and 1961) appear to have been more important in facilitating such efforts.

That important policy shifts did occur after the expansion and bureau-cratization of the Argentine state does not undermine the integrated formulation. It will be recalled that the integrated formulation predicts that Argentina's policies should have displayed incremental trends after the late 1940s except when the political elites were able to increase their pool of previously unallocated resources rapidly. To the extent that such new resources were available, they should have been able to maintain supports for consumer goods industries, retain the "failed" state corporations, and channel the new resources into the basic industries and infrastructure by creating new public corporations and/or by providing direct inducements to the private sector.

This pattern of maintaining previous policies and expanding new ones is exactly what developed after 1950 or 1954, when new foreign public capital became available. The retreat from consumer goods ISI was extended to 1959. With the exception of DINIE, the state never divested itself of any major state enterprises.[15] The new resources were frequently channeled so as to bypass the older, less efficient, more politicized state agencies.

One other set of considerations provides additional support for the integrated formulation. Far from being a monolithic representative of the dominant coalition at each stage of the nation's history, the Argentine state showed increasing signs of internal fragmentation after the late 1940s. Public employees repeatedly resisted policies that would have worked to their disadvantage. The same can be said of the various factions of the military. As a result, the elite political personnel were not infrequently in open conflict with other sectors of the state during much of this period. The public bureaucracy, as much as any other force, blocked elite initiatives and imposed an inertial tendency on public policies that could only be overcome when the elites acquired new resources from foreign public sources. From the point of view of the elite political personnel, it was in fact easier to go forward than to retreat.

Notes

1. According to Abelardo Ramos (1973, 68–71), the Pinedo Plan to "national-ize" the British railroads would have required the British to give up some control to native Argentines. In return, they would have retained direct majority control over the network and a guarantee that the Argentine government would not take 50 percent possession until after thirty years (in 1970) or 100 percent until after sixty years (in the year 2000).

2. The Plan de Pinedo was debated in the Senate on December 17–18, 1940. It passed that body by a vote of seventeen to three but was subsequently rejected by the House of Representatives.

3. According to Whitaker, "This 131–page booklet was the work of the Assistant Secretary of State Braden and his staff. It gave what it called 'incontrovertible evi-

dence' (much of it drawn from recently captured German documents) that 'the present Argentine Government and many of its high officials were so seriously compromised with the . . . enemy that trust and confidence could not be reposed in that government.' Perón himself was prominent among the Argentines against whom such evidence was presented" (1954, 148).

4. Whitaker suggests in two places that the abandonment of the populist nationalist policies may have been even more general. First, he points out that Argentina purchased, rather than expropriated, the foreign-owned rail networks. The distinction is interesting: "The object was to promote Argentina's economic independence without alienating the country's trading partners" (1964a, 123). Nationalism clearly could not be allowed to become too extreme. In another place, Whitaker observes that it is possible to interpret Perón's 1946 inaugural address as a "bid for accommodation with the United States on a 'forget and forgive basis'" (1954, 218).

It is entirely possible, of course, that Perón's foreign policy behavior during this period was totally calculated. His simultaneous initiation and abandonment of pro- and anti-U.S. policies on the domestic scene would have built both popular and military support for his government. Both groups would have had something to gain from Perón and something to lose if he left office. On the international scene, the simultaneous moves toward Washington and Moscow evoked the predictable U.S. response. Argentina thus received benefits of U.S. military support but at the same time retained considerable latitude in its capacity to operate independently in the international scene.

This interpretation may be consistent with much of the existing evidence. It does nothing to undermine the integrated formulation, but its validity would raise new problems for the authoritarian argument. Perón would emerge less as the leader of a classical "populist," Bonapartist coalition than as a consummate politician who was playing a common manipulative political strategy.

5. The March 1947 measure authorized the president to adjust existing tariff rates by as much as 50 percent and to impose import duties as high as 25 percent on items that had previously been duty-free. The 1949 measure increased import restrictions. Finally, in August 1950 the existing nine exchange rates for the Argentine peso were consolidated into three (two official and one free).

6. Indications of the changing situation after 1950 are apparent in the data on cumulative book value of U.S. private direct investments in Latin America at year end which may be obtained in UN Economic Commission on Latin America 1965, Organization of American States 1971, or the U.S. Department of Commerce *Survey of Current Business*. The last source reports that the cumulative book value of U.S. private direct investments in Latin America at year end rose from 4.445 million in 1950 to 14.760 million in 1970.

7. YPF workers reacted to the July 24, 1958 announcement of a new oil policy and the August 9 contract with the Pan American International Oil Company by initiating a strike in October. The Dutch railroad loan (September 5, 1958) may have contributed to the beginning of a strike by the state-owned railway workers on December 3, 1958. Rumors that the government planned to sell the state-owned meatpacking plant were denied by Frigerio on September 19, 1958; but the Buenos Aires municipal meatpackers went on strike in January 1959. Labor reaction to the December 30, 1958 announcement of the Plan for Development and Stability was intense. On Jan-

uary 18, 1959 a general strike was begun. Strikes by bank and insurance workers erupted repeatedly between April and June. By July, the sugar workers were on strike.

8. *Foreign private direct investment* refers here to new capital inflows and reinvestments in enterprises in which foreign investors or parent companies controlled at least 25 percent of the voting stock in foreign subsidiary companies or unincorporated foreign branches.

9. Unlike the cumulative U.S. investment figures mentioned in n. 7, the data here refer to average annual changes in year end book values.

10. Frondizi may have borrowed from a wide range of sources simply because more agencies came into existence during his tenure in office. The EIB was created by executive order of the president of the United States in 1934. The IBRD formally began operations on December 27, 1945. Both Perón and Aramburu had the opportunity to utilize those lending agencies. The IADB did not formally begin operations until October 1960, however. The AID was not created until March 1961 when President Kennedy announced the Alliance for Progress.

11. These declines appear to be at least partially attributable to Illia's petroleum policies. During the election campaign, he promised to free Argentina from foreign financial and economic control and to annul the contracts which Frondizi had signed with the foreign oil companies. In his October 12, 1963 inaugural address, however, the new president adopted a slightly more conciliatory position toward the United States when he approved the initiation of Alliance for Progress projects in Argentina. The United States appeared anxious to cement this compromise. U.S. Undersecretary of State for Political Affairs, W. Averill Harriman, was dispatched to Argentina to meet with Illia on November 9 and 10. He apparently warned Illia that cancellation of the government's contracts with U.S. petroleum firms would jeopardize future investments in Argentina by the U.S. government and U.S. private investors. The problem of possible cancellation of the contracts came up at President Kennedy's press conference on November 14: his response was to say that the United States would insist on adequate compensation. Illia ignored the warnings. On November 15, 1963 he signed a decree canceling oil contracts with eight U.S., two European, and four Argentine oil firms.

12. Two points should be noted. First, a loan or credit commitment is an indication that both the Argentine government and some lending agency were *willing* to enter into the agreement. The decline in Illia's utilization of foreign public capital may therefore be attributable to his own disinclination to apply for such funds, disinclination on the part of lending agencies to grant them, or a combination of both. Second, one should not expect the pattern of utilization to have been incremental. Loans and credits from the listed agencies were obtained in most cases for specific projects that the Argentine governments wished to undertake. There is no reason to expect that because an initial commitment had been obtained, the governments would require subsequent, increasingly larger loans.

13. According to UN Economic Commission on Latin America 1965, Argentina ranked third among Latin American nations in use of the EIB and second in the use of IADB through December 31, 1963 and fourth in use of the IBRD through June 30, 1964.

14. Chilcote (1963, 34) reports that this agreement was signed in January 1961 and that the DGFM deposits at Zapla were also included.

15. Even in the case of DINIE, it is not clear that the state actually succeeded in divesting itself of any major state enterprises. About twenty establishments were returned to the private sector in 1961, but DINIE continues to function as a public enterprise. Much the same can be said in the case of SOMISA. Despite the 1961 plan to increase privately owned stock in the corporation, SOMISA remains a predominantly public enterprise.

SEVEN

Labor Policies

I shall investigate more systematically whether Argentina's labor policies support the integrated formula or not. Additional data and analytic techniques will be used to determine whether the outcomes of Ongania's and Levingston's bureaucratic–authoritarian administrations were in fact distinct from those of previous administrations or whether Ongania and Levingston, like their predecessors, were caught in a pattern of drift.

The Policy Outcomes

The following four indicators are used to operationalize in somewhat more systematic fashion the outcomes of Argentine labor policies: The real income received by the nation's wage and salary earners, the share of the nation's gross domestic product (GDP) received by wage and salary earners, union strike activity, and the level of government employment. The 1930–1970 trends in these four indicators are shown in Figures 7.1–7.4 at chapter's end.[1]

The first three indicators are commonly utilized in studies of labor policy in Latin America, and the fourth will be discussed shortly. At this point, it need only be mentioned that all four of these indicators are properly regarded as policy outcomes or resultants rather than policy outputs—a basic distinction that is often overlooked. When workers' real income and/or share of the GDP fall, for example, scholars have typically concluded that such changes are the result of conscious antilabor biases of the government. Such an interpretation is quite obviously fallacious. The four indicators utilized in this analysis reflect what actually occurred; they may say nothing about what decisionmakers wished to do or actually did.

Government employment levels are included as indicators for several reasons. As was noted earlier, increases in the level of employment in the Argentine public sector were effected at times during the 1943–1952 populist period in order to offset stagnating employment opportunities in the private sector. A total of 349,900 new employees (an increase of over 144 percent) were added to the public payrolls during the 1943–1952 interval. Under Farrell, the major increases appear to have been attributable to the policy of

111

nationalizing foreign-owned industries. Workers who had once been employed by private concerns were transformed into government employees. By 1948–1949, however, the economy had entered a major recessionary period, and public employment surged to new highs. In 1949 alone, 117,900 new workers were hired by the Argentine state so that the level of total government employment rose by 30.25 percent between 1948 and 1949. By 1952, the number of public employees in Argentina had reached an all-time high of 592,300.

The policy of using the public sector to compensate for stagnating employment opportunities in the private sector began to be reversed in the early 1950s. Three sources of pressure for this policy change have already been noted. The inefficient and heavily overstaffed public and semipublic corporations created massive budget deficits that allegedly contributed to the nation's chronic inflation problems. High levels of government employment raised the fixed costs of simply maintaining the state and reduced the pools of resources that the elite political personnel could allocate at their discretion. As a result, the decisionmaking latitude of Argentina's top-level policymakers may have been constrained. Finally, pressure for a reduction in public employment began to come from the International Monetary Fund (IMF) in the period after 1952. As the Argentine economy passed through a series of expansion/recession cycles, the nation was repeatedly forced to rely on the IMF for monetary support. One of the prices the IMF exacted for its assistance was a reduction in the spending of the Argentine government.

All of these factors combine to make government employment levels a useful indicator of labor policy outcomes. The considerations that led to efforts to ignore, mobilize, and then repress labor should have been general across both the public and private sectors. The hypothesized goals of labor policies in general—traditional neglect and patrimonialism, populist inclusion, and bureaucratic–authoritarian exclusion—should therefore be reflected in policies toward employment in the public sector.

Taken together, these four indicators constitute a useful set of measures of the impact of labor policies. They augment a focus on the disruption of labor union activities, labor legislation, the suppression of strikes, and so on. If the authoritarian proposition relating different types of authoritarian political systems with different orientations toward labor is valid, the transition from one type of authoritarian rule to the next should have produced some impact on the patterns displayed by the four indicators through time. I now turn to a systematic examination of this hypothesis.

The 1952 Transition: From Populist Authoritarian Rule to the Era of the Hegemonic Crisis

The results reported here are based on techniques and procedures that have been employed previously in interrupted time series and impact analyses (e.g., Hoole 1976). The focus is on the detection of rather simple slope and intercept changes that may have resulted from the transition between different types of authoritarian rule. The analyses are conducted separately on each of the four indicators, but I employ throughout the discussion the following two basic equations:

$$Y^{\wedge}_t = a + b_1 X_1 + e_t \tag{7.1}$$

and

$$Y^{\wedge}_t = a + b_1 X_1 + b_2 D_i + b_3 (X_1 D_i) + e_t , \tag{7.2}$$

where $Y^{\wedge}_t$ is the predicted value of a given dependent variable in year t, X_1 is the year, a is the intercept of the regression line, b_1 to b_3 are the regression parameters, e_t is an error term that takes into account factors not otherwise included in the equation, and D_i is a variable that "dummies in" the impact of a given transition.[2] In this section, D_i refers exclusively to the 1952 transition. In this section it is coded zero for the 1943–1952 period and one for the 1953–1965 interval.

These equations are utilized for exploring the following slightly more precise versions of the initial question:

1. *When Equation 7.1 is estimated separately on the pretransition and combined pre- and post-transition periods, are the resulting regression parameters the same in the two periods?* If the transition did in fact have an impact on the trend of a given indicator, the parameters in Equation 7.1 should *not* be similar in the two periods.

2. *If the estimation of Equation 7.1 on the combined pre- and post-transition period produces autocorrelation, does the introduction of dummy variables in Equation 7.2 resolve that problem?* Autocorrelation is a technical problem that frequently develops in time series analyses. When it is present, ordinary least squares estimates of the regression parameters are unbiased, but a number of other difficulties arise. If autocorrelation is detected when Equation 7.1 is estimated, one explanation may be that that model is seriously misspecified insofar as (a) it omits the impact of the transition and (b) the inclusion of a variable that taps the transition is important for understanding the pattern of the predicted variable. If that explanation is valid, autocorrelation problems should be reduced when Equation 7.2 is employed.[3]

3. *Does the introduction of dummy variables, that is, the use of Equation 7.2 instead of 7.1, significantly increase the amount of explained variance in the dependent variable?* If a transition did in fact have an impact on the trend of a given indicator, the inclusion in the analysis of variables that tap that transition should yield an increase in the variance for which one can account.

The first step toward answering these questions is taken by estimating Equation 7.1 on the combined pre- and post-1952 transition period (1943–

1965) and the post-1952 transition interval (1953–1965). The results of these analyses are presented in Table 7.1, part a. The initial focus of interest is on the degree of similarity in the regression parameters (*b*s) when the estimation is based on the two different periods. The appropriate technique for determining whether or not the parameters are significantly different in a statistical sense is Chow's *F*-statistic.[4] The results of those tests are presented in Table 7.1, part b. The null hypothesis that the regression parameters are identical when Equation 7.1 is estimated on the 1943–1965 and 1953–1965 intervals is rejected except in the case of strikes. In other words, the conclusion to be drawn from the Chow's *F*-tests is that the parameters from the equation involving workers' real income, workers' GDP share, and the level of government employment were different in the pre- and post-1952 transition periods. The inference is that these parameter shifts are attributable to the 1952 transition from populist authoritarian rule to the era of the hegemonic crisis. This, then, is the answer to the first question. Except in the case of strikes, the evidence is consistent with the hypothesis that the 1952 transition altered the regression parameters.

Consider now the second question concerning the problem with positive first-order autocorrelation. The Durbin–Watson *d*-statistic[5] and the Geary Runs test[6] are used as complementary techniques for detecting this problem. An examination of the last two columns in Table 7.1, part a reveals that the 1943–1965 estimations of Equation 7.1 resulted in the detection of autocorrelation in all but the case of strikes. The introduction of dummy variables, that is, the use of Equation 7.2, helps to reduce the autocorrelation problems, however. The Geary Runs test detects no autocorrelation problems when Equation 7.2, with the dummy variable treatments of the 1952 transition, is utilized (Table 7.1, see part c). The Durbin–Watson *d*-statistic produces somewhat weaker results, but it can at least be said that the null hypothesis of no positive first-order autocorrelation cannot be safely rejected at the .01 level. When autocorrelation problems develop, they are at least partially resolved when the previously omitted effects of the 1952 transition are inserted into the analysis.

What, then, can be said in regard to the third question? Does the introduction of dummy variables increase the amount of explained variance in the dependent variables? One knows, of course, that Equation 7.2, with three independent variables, will produce a higher R^2 than Equation 7.1, with only one predictor. For that reason, $-R^2$ is utilized to correct for the number of independent variables.[7] The appropriate comparisons then involve the R^2 from Equation 7.1 with the corrected coefficients of determination ($-R^2$) calculated from Equation 7.2. If the dummy variables do provide an increase in the explained variance, the $-R^2$ should be greater than its respective R^2 from Equation 7.1.

An examination of Table 7.1, part d reveals that the $-R^2$ is in fact greater

Table 7.1   Labor Policies: Impact of the 1952 Transition

Part a
Overlapping Regressions (Equation 7.1, k = 1)

Dependent Variable	R^2	b	Durbin-Watson	Runs
1943-1965(n = 23)				
Real income	.44	2.469	.60194[a]	6
GDP share	.00	0.170	.38606[a]	3[b]
B.A. strikes	.18	-2.010	1.70587	9
Gov. employment	.58	12.668	.21762[a]	3[b]
1953-1965(n = 13)				
Real income	.10	0.951	1.51964	4
GDP share	.75	-0.696	2.14943[a]	7
B.A. strikes	.05	-1.110	1.22930	6
Gov. employment	.03	-0.937	.73912[a]	3

[a]H_0 of no positive, first-order autocorrelation rejected at the .01 level using the Durbin-Watson d-statistic.
[b]H_0 of random distribution of the residuals rejected at the .01 level using the Geary Sign test.

Part b
Chow's F-Statistics on the Overlapping Periods
1943-1965 and 1953-1965 (Degrees of Freedom 10, 12)

	F	Significance Level
Real income	5.337	p<.01
GDP share	11.402	p<.01
B.A. strikes	2.838	p>.05
Gov. employment	23.938	p<.01

Part c
Dummy Variable Regressions
on the Period 1943-1965 (Equation 7.2, n = 23, k = 3)

Dependent Variable	R^2	Durbin-Watson	Runs
Real income	.65	1.10776[a]	6
GDP share	.81	1.7719	11
B.A. strikes	.26	1.82140	8
Gov. employment	.96	1.24211[a]	6

[a]H_0 of no positive, first-order autocorrelation is in the indeterminant range using the Durbin-Watson d-statistic.

Part d
$\bar{R}^2$ Tests (n = 23)

Dependent Variable	R^2 Eq. 7.1	R^2 Eq. 7.2	$\bar{R}^2$
Real income	.44	.65	.59
GDP share	.00	.81	.78
B.A. strikes	.18	.26	.14
Gov. employment	.22	.96	.95

than the R^2 from Equation 7.1 in the case of workers' real income, workers' GDP share, and government employment. The introduction of dummy variables that tap the effects of the 1952 transition does significantly increase the amount of explained variance in those three indicators. Only in the case of strikes does a consideration of the 1952 shift fail to improve the explanation of the trend.

Summary and Interpretation of the Results

All three tests produce results consistent with the proposition that the transition from populism to the era of the hegemonic crisis produced an impact on the long-term trends in workers' real income, workers' GDP share, and government employment (see Table 7.2). In contrast, the 1952 transition does not appear to have affected the long-term pattern in union strikes.

Table 7.2   Labor Policies: Summary of the 1952 Transition: From Populist Authoritarian Rule to the Era of the Hegemonic Crisis

Dependent Variable	Parameter Change?	Autocorrelation Resolved?	$\bar{R}^2$ Increase?
Real income	yes	yes	yes
GDP share	yes	yes	yes
B.A. strikes	no	—	no
Gov. employment	yes	yes	yes

As predicted by both the authoritarian and integrated formulations, labor benefits apparently did increase during the populist period between 1943 and 1952 (see Figures 7.1 and 7.2 and the regression parameters in Table 7.1, part a). This pattern toward the increasing "inclusion" of labor then shifted during the ensuing 1953–1965 interval.

However, while workers made significant gains in terms of their real income and government employment during the postpopulist period, there were no immediate or abrupt reversals of those trends in the subsequent interval. A steep positive 1943–1952 trend in real income was succeeded by a gentle but still positive slope in the 1953–1965 period. The 1952 shift had a significant impact on real income not because the previous trend was reversed but because the previous trend leveled out.

Government employment followed a similar pattern (see Figure 7.4 and Table 7.1, part a). Sharp increases in the number of employees in the public sector during the 1943–1952 period were followed by decreases between 1953 and 1965. These decreases were only marginal, however. By 1965, the number of government employees in Argentina was only 7.1 percent lower than the 1952 all-time high of 592,300. Despite the pressures for a reduction in public sector employment, in other words, the number of employees was decreased at an average annual rate of only .5 percent between 1953 and 1965.[8]

These results appear to have one obvious implication. At least in the areas of real income and government employment, workers were "included" more rapidly by the populist governments than they were excluded by the 1953–1965 administrations. As will be seen, these remarks also pertain to the GDP share indicator.

These observations do not directly contradict the authoritarian thesis, which is generally mute on the era of the hegemonic crisis. They do support the integrated formulation, however. As expected, it was apparently difficult for the leaders of the post-1952 governments to stop what had already been started. The administrations of Ramirez, Farrell, and Perón mobilized the popular sectors and brought them into the political life of the nation. The leaders of the post-1952 governments were able to halt or slow the advance of those trends, but at least in the areas of real income and government employment Argentina's political elites did not succeed in executing major reversals during the era of the hegemonic crisis. Workers' real income and the number of government employees had been raised to new levels by the populist governments. Those indicators never again returned to their low, prepopulist levels.

One additional point might be noted. Examination of the plots in Figures 7.1 and 7.2 yields the impression that the trends in real income and GDP share may have changed in 1949 rather than 1952. As mentioned earlier, an important change in Perón's labor policy became apparent almost immediately following his election in 1946. Argentina's foreign and industrialization policies began to be altered in 1947. Argentina had begun to abandon its nationalistic, prolabor, and pro–consumer goods import substitution industrialization policies by the onset of a recession in 1948–1949. A finding here that the trends in workers' real income and GDP share occurred in 1949 rather than 1952 would be consistent with those earlier results and tend to support the integrated formulation. The identification of 1949 shifts would also disrupt the logic of the authoritarian thesis. If the long-term patterns of real income and GDP share were altered in 1949, they may have resulted from the economic crisis of the 1948–1949 interval rather than from the 1952 political shift from populist authoritarian rule. The 1949 possibility is therefore examined in some detail. The results of this reanalysis are shown in Table 7.3.

Several interesting findings emerge from these tests. Autocorrelation problems evident for both real income and GDP share are largely resolved when variables that tap a possible 1949 shift are included in the analysis (see Table 7.3, parts a and c). Similarly, the proportion of explained variance in both of these indicators of labor policy is increased when one moves from Equation 7.1 to 7.2. Neither of these results is surprising. Tests on the 1952 transition indicated that that interruption may have had similar effects on real income and GDP share trends, and of course dummy variables based on 1952 and 1949 transition possibilities are highly correlated at .75.

Table 7.3   Labor Policies: Examination of a Possible 1949 Transition

Part a
Overlapping regressions (Equation 7.1, k = 1)

Dependent Variable	R^2	b	Durbin-Watson	Runs
1943-1965 (n = 23)				
Real income	.44	2.469	.60194[a]	6
GDP share	.00	.170	.38606[a]	3[b]
1950-1965 (n = 16)				
Real income	.10	.804	1.44422	5
GDP share	.79	-.639	2.20308	8

[a]H_0 of no positive, first-order autocorrelation rejected at the .01 level using the Durbin-Watson d-statistic.
[b]H_0 of random distibution of the residuals rejected at the .01 level using the Geary Sign test.

Part b
Chow's F-Statistics
on the Overlapping Periods
1943-1965 and 1950-1965 (Degrees of Freedom 7, 15; $p<.01$)

	F
Real income	6.482
GDP share	15.735

Part c
Dummy Variable Regressions
on the Period 1943-1965 (Equation 7.2, n = 23, k = 3)

Dependent Variable	R^2	Durbin-Watson	Runs
Real income	.79	1.35343[a]	7
GDP share	.81	1.92540	11

Note: D_i in Equation 7.2 is coded here to represent a possible 1949 shift. It is zero for the 1943-1949 period and one for the 1950-1965 interval.

[a]H_0 of no positive, first-order autocorrelation is in the indeterminant range using the Durbin-Watson d-statistic.

Part d
$\bar{R}^2$ Tests (n = 23)

Dependent Variable	R^2 Eq. 7.1	R^2 Eq. 7.2[a]	$\bar{R}^2$
Real income	.44	.79	.76
GDP share	.00	.81	.78

[a]D_i in Equation 7.2 is coded here to represent a possible 1949 shift. It is zero for the 1943-1949 period and one for the 1950-1965 interval.

The surprising finding develops from the Chow's F-tests (see Table 7.3 part b). A possible 1949 shift emerges as an authentic rival to the 1952 transition. The hypotheses that the real income and GDP share regression parameters were identical before and after 1952 were rejected, but rejection is also possible when a potential 1949 shift is considered. The implication of this finding is clear. The trend changes in workers' real income and share of the GDP in 1949 during Perón's first term in office cannot be attributed to the 1952 transition from populist authoritarian rule to the era of the hegemonic crisis.

The 1943 Transition:
From Traditional to Populist Authoritarian Rule

I shall focus on the 1943 shift from traditional to populist authoritarian rule, the first of the three Argentine transitions between different types of political systems. The questions and methodologies employed here are nearly identical to those developed in the previous section. Where differences do develop, they will be noted.

The initial focus in these analyses concerns the question of whether the pre- and post-1943 regression parameters are identical or not. This query is considered in Table 7.4, part a. The reader will note that Equation 7.2 is utilized in these initial tests rather than Equation 7.1, as in the previous section. This procedure is dictated by the combined effects of relatively short pre-1943 series for some of the variables and the rather brief period between the establishment of populist authoritarian rule in 1943 and its erosion in 1952. A small-number-of-cases problem arises if one compares a pre- or post-1943 transition regression with one that includes the 1930–1952 period. A solution to this difficulty is finding an appropriate treatment for the 1952 shift and inserting it in Equation 7.2. In this way the post-1943 and pre- and post-1943 periods can be extended to include the 1943–1965 and 1930–1965 intervals, respectively. When the 1930–1965 period is considered in this manner, D_i in Equation 7.2 represents the effects of the 1952 shift and is coded as zero for the 1930–1952 period and one for the 1953–1965 interval. (Equation 7.1 is utilized here in the case of strikes because the analysis in the previous section indicated that the 1952 transition had no detectable impact on that series. The "appropriate treatment" for the 1952 interruption in the case of strikes is thus to ignore it entirely.)

Chow's F-tests for pre- and post-transition parameter changes are reported in Table 7.4, part b. Rejection of the null hypothesis that the regression parameters are identical in the two periods (1930–1965 and 1943–1965) is possible only in the cases of workers' GDP share and government employment. It is not possible to say on the basis of these tests that the 1943 transi-

Table 7.4   Labor Policies: Impact of the 1943 Transition

Part a
Overlapping Regressions

Dependent Variable	Equation[a]	n	k	R^2	Durbin-Watson	Runs
c. 1930-1965[b]						
Real income	7.2	27	3	.78	.98760[c]	7
GDP share	7.2	31	3	.59	.83721[d]	9
B.A. strikes	7.1	36	1	.25	1.81305	15
Gov. employment	7.2	31	3	.94	.54256[d]	6[e]
c. 1943-1965						
Real income	7.2	23	3	.65	1.10776[c]	6
GDP share	7.2	23	3	.81	1.77199	11
B.A. strikes	7.1	23	1	.18	1.70587	9
Gov. employment	7.2	23	3	.96	1.24211[c]	6

[a]D_i dummy variables in Equation 7.2 in this section are treatments of the 1952 shift. They are coded zero for the c. 1930-1952 period and one for the 1953-1965 interval.

[b]Data is available beginning with 1939 for real income, 1935 for GDP share, 1930 for B.A. strikes, and 1935 for government employment.

[c]H_0 of no positive, first-order autocorrelation is in the indeterminant range using the Durbin-Watson d-statistic.

[d]H_0 of no positive, first-order autocorrelation rejected at the .01 level using the Durbin-Watson d-statistic.

[e]H_0 of random distribution of residuals rejected at the .01 level using the Geary Sign test.

Part b
Chow's F-Statistics
on the Overlapping Periods,
c. 1930-1965 and 1943-1965

	F	Degrees of Freedom	Significance Level
Real income	0.487	4, 20	$p > .05$
GDP share	4.405	8, 20	$p < .05$
B.A. strikes	1.044	13, 22	$p > .05$
Gov. employment	8.965	8, 20	$p < .01$

Part c
Dummy Variable Regressions
on the Period, c. 1930-1952

Dependent Variable	n	R^2	Durbin-Watson	Runs
Equation 7.1 $(k = 1)$				
Real income	14	.71	.67439[a]	4[b]
GDP share	18	.48	.48653[a]	3
B.A. strikes	23	.11	1.88657	10
Gov. employment	18	.87	.36907[a]	3[b]
Equation 7.2 $(k = 3)$[c]				
Real income	14	.75	.73794[d]	6
GDP share	18	.86	1.65393	9

B.A. strikes	23	.17	2.09478	10
Gov. employment	18	.98	1.79439	7

[a]H_0 of no positive, first-order autocorrelation is in the indeterminant range using the Durbin-Watson d-statistic.

[b]H_0 of random distribution of residuals rejected at the .01 level using the Geary Sign test.

[c]D_i dummy variables in Equation 7.2 in this section are treatments of the 1943 shift. They are coded zero for the c. 1930-1942 period and one for the 1943-1952 interval.

[d]H_0 of no positive, first-order autocorrelation is in the indeterminant range using the Durbin-Watson d-statistic.

	Part d $\bar{R}^2$ Tests			
Dependent	R^2			
Variable	Eq. 7.1	Eq. 7.2	$\bar{R}^2$	n
Real income	.71	.75	.67	14
GDP share	.48	.86	.83	18
B. A. strikes	.11	.17	.04	23
Gov. employment	.87	.98	.97	18

tion from traditional to populist authoritarian rule altered the long-term trends in either the real income received by workers or strikes.

Consider now the problem of positive first-order autocorrelation. If one focuses exclusively on the 1930–1952 interval, positive first-order autocorrelation problems develop in connection with real income, GDP share, and government employment (see the first four lines in Table 7.4, part c).[9] If, however, one codes D_i to represent the effects of the 1943 transition—zero for the 1942 period and one for the 1943–1952 interval—in Equation 7.2 and reanalyzes the data, the autocorrelation difficulties can be resolved almost completely. In other words, even though the 1943 transition from traditional to populist authoritarian rule apparently did not alter the regression parameters of any of the series except GDP share and government employment, the insertion of variables that tap the effects of that interruption does help to resolve autocorrelation problems when they develop.

Consider now the third question. Does the introduction of dummy variables increase the amount of explained variance in the dependent variables? $\bar{R}^2$ comparisons of the equations reported in Table 7.4, part c are examined in part d. These tests show that the $\bar{R}^2$ is in fact greater than the R^2 from Equation 7.1 in the case of GDP share and government employment. The introduction of dummy variables that reflect the effects of the 1943 transition does increase the amount of explained variance in those two indicators. In the cases of workers' real income and strikes, a consideration of the 1943 transition fails to improve the explanation of the trend.

Summary and Interpretation of the Results

The 1943 transition had somewhat less of an impact on the four indicators than the 1952 transition (see Table 7.5). The shift from populist authoritarian rule to the era of the hegemonic crisis altered the regression parameters in three of the series (workers' real income, workers' GDP share, and government employment). Analyses in this section reveal that the 1943 transition may have had a similar effect on workers' GDP share and government employment. This does not mean that the 1943 transition from traditional to populist authoritarian rule is unimportant for understanding the trend in workers' real income, however.

Table 7.5   Labor Policies: Summary of the 1943 Transition: From Traditional to Populist Authoritarian Rule

Dependent Variable	Parameter Change?	Autocorrelation Resolved?	$\bar{R}^2$ Increase?
Real income	no	yes	no
GDP share	yes	yes	yes
B.A. strikes	no	—	no
Gov. employment	yes	yes	yes

I have shown that the 1943 coalition change did not alter the regression parameters of the real income series and that a consideration of that transition fails to increase the $\bar{R}^2$. Those results were produced using equations that "dummied in" a possible 1952 trend change in real income. As the analyses in the preceding section demonstrated, however, the real income series underwent a trend shift in 1949 at a point prior to the erosion of the populist coalition. This point is important because reanalyses of the 1943 transition using equations that "dummy in" this 1949 shift in real income succeed in producing a significant Chow's F-statistic. In other words, if it is the case that the trend in workers' real income shifted in 1949 instead of in 1952, it is possible to say that the pre- and post-1943 real income regression parameters are distinct. (The remaining tests for autocorrelation and $\bar{R}^2$ increases produce results that are identical to those summarized in Table 7.5. Parallel tests on GDP share also fail to alter the original findings.)

The 1966 Transition: From the Era of the Hegemonic Crisis to Bureaucratic–Authoritarian Rule

The focus in this section is on the impact of the shift from the era of the hegemonic crisis to the period of bureaucratic–authoritarian rule. The questions and methodologies are identical to those developed in the previous sections. Only two changes need be noted. First, there is, of course, a shift in the time periods employed in these analyses. The pre- and post-transition period in this section included the 1953–1970 interval. The results from regressions on that period are compared with those from the pretransition interval,

1953–1965. The second difference here concerns the dummy variable D_i in Equation 7.2. In this section, D_i is coded zero for the 1953–1965 period and as one for the 1966–1970 interval.

The results of Equation 7.1 estimations on the 1953–1970 and 1953–1965 periods are presented in Table 7.6, part a. If the bureaucratic–authoritarian governments of the post-1966 era did in fact move to exclude labor, positive trends obtained on the 1953–1965 regressions should be reversed at least slightly, and negative 1953–1965 slopes should be accentuated when the full 1953–1970 period is included in the analysis.

An examination of Table 7.6, part a reveals that these expectations are satisfied only in the case of strikes. A positive 1953–1965 trend in real income becomes slightly stronger in the positive direction when the post-1965 years are included in the analysis. Negative 1953–1965 trends in GDP share and government employment become weaker when the estimations are based on the 1953–1970 interval.

Because of these results, the findings from the Chow's F tests for pre- and post-1966 transition parameter changes are not surprising (see Table 7.6, part b). In no case is it possible to reject the null hypothesis that the regression parameters are identical before and after the interruption. In other words, the conclusion from these initial tests of the 1966 shift to bureaucratic–authoritarian rule is that interruption did not alter the previous trends in workers' real income, workers' GDP share, strikes, or government employment.

The 1966 transition did produce at least some effects, however. Positive first-order autocorrelation was detected quite frequently in the sections above when Equation 7.1 was estimated on the combined pre- and post-transition periods. This resulted from the omission of variables that tap the important effects of the 1943 and 1952 shifts in authoritarian rule.

In regard to the 1966 interruption autocorrelation problems here are less severe and less numerous than in the sections above. No autocorrelation is detected when real income and strikes are examined on the 1953–1970 period, so that one may conclude that the 1966 shift was probably not of major importance in deflecting the trends in those indicators. If the 1966 transition had little impact, the omission of variables that tap the effects of that shift should not lead to problems with positive first-order autocorrelation.

Autocorrelation is detected, of course, with GDP share and government employment; and the utilization of Equation 7.2 helps to resolve those difficulties at least partially (Table 7.6, part c). The regression parameters of GDP share and government employment may not have shifted, but the 1966 interruption appears to have had at least some impact on those two indicators of labor policy.

The introduction of variables that tap the effects of the 1966 transition to bureaucratic–authoritarian rule seems also to enhance one's ability to explain

Table 7.6   Labor Policies: Impact of the 1966 Transition

Part a
Overlapping Regressions
(Equation 7.1, k = 1)

Dependent Variable	n	R^2	b	Durbin-Watson	Runs
1953-c. 1970[a]					
Real income	16	.17	.980	1.48042	5
GDP share	18	.41	-.335	.96580[b]	6
B.A. strikes	20	.37	-2.074	1.1884	8
Gov. employment	17	.00	.119	.69980[c]	4
1953-1965					
Real income	13	.10	.951	1.51964	4
GDP share	13	.75	-.695	2.14943	7
B.A. strikes	13	.05	-1.110	1.22930	6
Gov. employment	13	.03	-.937	.73912	3

[a]Data is available through 1968 for real income, through 1970 for GDP share, through 1972 for B.A. strikes, and through 1969 for government employment.

[b]H_0 of no positive, first-order autocorrelation is in the indeterminant range using the Durbin-Watson d-statistic.

[c]H_0 of no positive, first-order autocorrelation rejected at the .01 level using the Durbin-Watson d-statistic.

Part b
Chow's F-Statistics
on the Overlapping Periods
1953-c. 1970 and 1953-1970 (p>.05)

	F	Degrees of Freedom
Real income	.406	3, 12
GDP share	3.070	5, 12
B.A. strikes	.253	7, 12
Gov. employment	.251	4, 12

Part c
Dummy Variable Regressions
on the Period,1952-c. 1970
(Equation 7.2, k = 3)

Dependent Variable	n	R^2	Durbin-Watson	Runs
Real income	16	.25	1.64425	7
GDP share	18	.76	2.53317	10
B.A. strikes	20	.40	1.28581[a]	8
Gov. employment	17	.08	.74368[a]	7

[a]H_0 of no positive, first-order autocorrelation is in the indeterminant range using the Durbin-Watson d-statistic.

		Part d$\bar{R}^2$ *Tests*		
Dependent		R^2		
Variable	Eq. 7.1	Eq. 7.2	$\bar{R}^2$	n
Real income	.17	.25	.07	16
GDP share	.41	.76	.71	18
B. A. strikes	.37	.40	.29	20
Gov. employment	.00	.08	.00	17

the variance in the workers' GDP share (Table 7.6, part d). Here again, however, the impact of the 1966 shift does not seem to have been general across all four of the series. In no other case is an explanation enhanced by a consideration of the transition from the era of the hegemonic crisis to bureaucratic–authoritarian rule.

Summary and Interpretation of the Results

The 1966 transition is seen to have had less of an impact than the 1943 and 1952 shifts, when all four indicators of labor policy are viewed collectively (see Table 7.7). The transition from the era of the hegemonic crisis to bureaucratic–authoritarian rule apparently failed to alter the pre- and postinterruption regression parameters. While the inclusion of variables that tap the effects of the 1966 shift helps to resolve autocorrelation problems that develop in connection with GDP share and government employment, the omission of such considerations does not produce difficulties when real income and strikes are considered. Finally, only in the case of workers' GDP share is an increase in the explained variance produced when Equation 7.2 with 1966 dummy variables is utilized.

Table 7.7 Labor Policies: Summary of the 1966 Transition: From the Era of the Hegemonic Crisis to Bureaucratic-Authoritarian Rule

Dependent Variable	Parameter Change?	Autocorrelation Resolved?	R^2 Increase?
Real income	no	—-	no
GDP share	no	yes	yes
B.A. strikes	no	—	no
Gov. employment	no	yes	no

All of these results tend to support the integrated formulation and raise additional doubts about the validity of the authoritarian thesis. Even stronger supportive evidence for the integrated argument might be noted, however. The estimates of the regression slopes in Table 7.6, part a are not sufficiently different to produce significant Chow's F-statistics. However, with the exception of strikes, the parameters change in the wrong direction as one moves from the pre-1966 regressions to the combined pre- and post-1966 estimations. If the authoritarian thesis is valid, positive pre-1966 slopes should be washed out as labor is excluded in the period after 1966. Similarly, negative pre-1966 slopes should become steeper as the Ongania and Levingston governments move to repress labor even more severely. The curious point, therefore, is that, again with the exception of strikes, the marginal slope changes that do develop are in the wrong direction.

During the 1950–1965 interval, real income received by workers improved only very slowly. This trend toward improvement is not reversed when the analysis is extended to include the post-1966 interruption years. Instead, labor's real income actually appears to have climbed at a slightly more rapid pace during the 1950–1970 interval than during the 1950–1965 period. The number of government employees was slightly reduced between 1952 and 1965. The Ongania and Levingston administrations should have accelerated that trend. Instead, the number of employees increased in 1966 and thereafter, so that a negative 1953–1965 slope actually becomes positive during the 1953–1970 period. Labor clearly lost ground in terms of its share of the GDP between 1950 and 1965. However, the decreases in workers' GDP share are seen as being less rapid when the analysis is extended to include the post-1966 interruption period.

The findings in regard to GDP share appear to be altered significantly when that series is reexamined on the basis of the 1950–1970 and 1950–1965 intervals (see Table 7.8). (The selection of these new periods is dictated, of course, by the fact that both the GDP share and real income series were found to have undergone shifts in 1949.) The new starting point does not alter the findings outlined above in connection with the impact of the 1966 transition on the real income received by workers. Autocorrelation and R^2 tests on GDP share, similarly, remain unchanged. The apparently significant departure here is that if one focuses on the 1950–1970 and 1950–1965 periods instead of the 1953–1965 and 1953–1970 intervals, it is possible to say that the transition to bureaucratic–authoritarian rule in 1966 altered the regression parameters in the GDP share series.

This new result is obviously of some interest, but even here a problem for the authoritarian thesis should be noted. An examination of Figure 7.2 reveals that labor suffered decreases in its GDP share during the 1968–1970 era. This is exactly what should be expected if Ongania and Levingston did move to exclude labor but their efforts to do so were delayed. Unfortunately, the pattern is also consistent with the observations in Chapter 4 that state–labor relations may have been largely conciliatory during the early stages of the bureaucratic–authoritarian era. The important point to be noted, however, is that decreases in labor's GDP share in the 1968–1970 interval were preceded by increases between 1965 and 1967. The downward trend between 1967 and 1970 was the norm for the full 1950–1970 period. The

**Table 7.8   Labor Policies: Examination of the
1966 Transition Using 1950 Starting Points**

Part a
Overlapping Regressions (Equation 7.1, k = 1)

Dependent Variable	n	R^2	b	Durbin-Watson	Runs
1950-c. 1970					
Real income	19	.18	.885	1.41580	6
GDP share	21	.56	-.381	1.08141[a]	7
1950-1965					
Real income	16	.10	.804	1.44422	5
GDP share	16	.79	-.638	2.20308	8

[a]H_0 of no positive, first-order autocorrelation is in the indeterminant range using the Durbin-Watson d-statistic.

Part b
*Chow's F-Statistics
on the Overlapping Periods,
1950-c. 1970 and 1950-1965*

	F	Degrees of Freedom	Significance Level
Real income	0.386	3, 15	$p>.05$
GDP share	4.108	5, 15	$p<.05$

Part c
*Dummy Variable Regressions
on the Period, 1950-c. 1970 (Equation 7.2, k = 3)*

Dependent Variable	n	R^2	Durbin-Watson	Runs
Real income	19	.23	1.54944	8
GDP share	21	.80	2.46527	11

Note: D_i dummy variables in Equation 7.2 are coded 0 for the 1950-1965 period and 1 for the 1966-c. 1970 interval.

Part d
R^2 *Tests*

Dependent Variable	$\bar{R}^2$ Eq. 7.1	Eq. 7.2	$\bar{R}^2$	n
Real income	.18	.23	.08	19
GDP share	.56	.80	.76	21

trend toward increasing shares of the GDP that workers received between 1965 and 1967 was the deviation. With the exception of the Peronist years, the redistribution of wealth in the direction of labor was never so rapid as during the Illia administration. Thus, it appears that the dummy variables in Equation 7.2 are detecting a post-1967 return to the norm—a reinstatement of a long historical trend, rather than a sharp departure from a previous trend, resulting from the 1966 coalition change.[10]

None of this minimizes the fact that a consideration of the 1966 shift from the era of the hegemonic crisis to bureaucratic–authoritarian rule is important for understanding pre- and post-1966 trends in the GDP share that labor received. These observations do, however, alter the substantive interpretation of the 1966 interruption. In terms of the share of the GDP that workers received, labor may indeed have been excluded by the bureaucratic–authoritarian regimes of Ongania and Levingston. However, that redistribution of wealth away from Argentina's wage and salary earners was neither immediate nor unique. Labor's GDP share position did not deteriorate until 1967–1968, at a point when Augusto Vandor's faction of the labor movement was losing control; and when it did come, the reversal marked a return to previous policies whose negative effect can be seen throughout the area of the hegemonic crisis. Thus, the analyses in this section do not support the contention that labor was immediately repressed after the June 28, 1966 coup. They do support the contention that workers were not suddenly excluded for the first time by the bureaucratic–authoritarian governments. The policies of previous, nontechnocratic, nonbureaucratic–authoritarian governments had produced similar effects.

Conclusions

An overall summary of the analyses in this chapter is presented in Table 7.9. One characteristic of that review stands out quite clearly. In comparison with the 1943 and 1952 coalition changes, the establishment of bureaucratic–authoritarian rule in 1966 had only a marginal impact on the four labor policy outcomes I have discussed. Although workers' real income and strikes did decline after 1966 (as the authoritarian thesis predicts), the 1966 transition appears to have had no statistically significant impact on those series when even the weakest of the three tests is utilized. Chow's F-tests indicated that only the trend in GDP share was different in the pre- and post-1966 intervals. Even that result was not obtained until I rejected the proposition that the populist coalition was displaced in 1952 and reanalyzed the GDP series using the 1950–1965 and 1950–1970 comparisons. Somewhat surprisingly, the fact that a 1966 shift in GDP share can thus be detected does not provide support for the authoritarian thesis. The transition to bureaucratic–authoritarian rule appears to be important in explaining the series only because wealth was redistributed toward labor during the tenure of President Illia (1963–1966). This improvement in the position of labor was a deviation from what had been the trend in Argentina since 1949. The redistribution of wealth away from labor that eventually occurred under Ongania and Levingston was simply a return to the established trend.

Somewhat similar findings emerged in connection with the impact of the 1966 transition on government employment. Consideration of that interruption did help to resolve an autocorrelation problem. Nevertheless, the bureaucratic–authoritarian coalition that allegedly came to power with the avowed purpose of increasing government efficiency and decreasing the size of the deficits added more workers to the public payrolls. In other words, even though the variables which tap the effects of the 1966 interruption are of use for understanding the trend in government employment, they appear to work for the wrong reasons. Despite the authoritarian prediction that government employment would be reduced in the bureaucratic–authoritarian period, the number of public employees rose incrementally during the post-1966 era.

These findings concerning the 1966 transition from the era of the hegemonic crisis to bureaucratic–authoritarian rule tend to support the integrated argument and raise doubts about the validity of the authoritarian thesis. Labor was not excluded immediately or in any particularly unique fashion when the bureaucratic–authoritarian coalition came to power in 1966. Instead, the policy trends established in the late 1940s or early 1950s remained largely unbroken throughout the remainder of the period. At best, the 1966 interruption served to end deviations from the long-term historical trends that had developed during the immediate pre-1966 years. All of these findings are consistent with the integrated thesis.

It should be added that an almost identical set of results emerged from the more qualitative analyses in the previous chapters. Whether one focuses on qualitative data—the suppression and control of the labor movement, the freezing of wages, the imposition of constraints on collective bargaining, the exclusion of labor union candidates from the electoral process, and so on— (as was done in earlier chapters) or on real income, GDP share, strikes, and government employment, the outcomes of the pre- and post-1966 labor policies were more similar than distinct. The effects of the 1966–1968 changes in the unity of the military and in state–labor relations noted in the previous discussions are also apparent here. Both the constituency of the coalition and the policy mix its members preferred may have evolved in rather significant ways in the period immediately following the June 28, 1966 coup.

The analyses of the 1952 transition also tend to support the integrated formulation. It is true that the evidence is consistent with the hypothesis that the shift from populist authoritarian rule to the era of the hegemonic crisis deflected the trends in real income, GDP share, and government employment. It is also the case that variables tapping the 1952 shift succeed in resolving autocorrelation problems that develop in connection with those three series and that they produce increases in the proportion of the variance in the indicators that can be explained.

The 1952 transition was clearly of major significance, but not for the reasons suggested by the authoritarian argument. The post-1952 trends were not invariably in the directions predicted by that thesis. While workers made

Table 7.9 Labor Policies: Overall Summary

Part a
By Policy Indicator

	Parameter Change?			Autocorrelation Detected?			Autocorrelation Resolved?			R^2 Increase?		
	1943	1952	1966	1943	1952	1966	1943	1952	1966	1943	1952	1966
Real income	y[a]	y	n	y	y	n	y	y	—	n	y	n
GDP share	y	y	y[b]	y	y	y	y	y	y	y	y	y
B.A. strikes	n	n	n	n	n	n	—	—	—	n	n	n
Gov. employment	y	y	n	y	y	y	y	y	y	y	y	n

Part b
By Transition

	Parameter Changes	Autocorrelation Detected	Autocorrelation Resolved	$\bar{R}^2$ Increases
1943 transition	3	3	3	2
1952 transition	3	3	3	3
1966 transition	1	2	2	1

important gains in terms of their real income, GDP share, and government employment during the post-1943 populist period, there were no immediate or abrupt reversals of those trends. A steep positive 1943–1952 trend in real income was succeeded by a gentle but still positive slope in the 1953–1965 period. The 1952 shift had a significant impact on real income not because the previous trend was reversed but because the previous trend leveled out. A sharp positive 1943–1965 trend in government employment was succeeded by a negative but nevertheless shallow slope during the 1953–1965 era. Finally, once the proper break point in the GDP share series has been located in 1949, it becomes clear that the rapid 1943–1949 improvements in labor's position were only slowly reversed in the immediate postinterruption era. Thus, in these areas at least, it is clear that the workers were included by the populist governments more rapidly than they were excluded by the post-transition administrations: it was harder to go back than to go forward.

The analyses also isolated a 1949 break point in workers' real income and GDP share. Certain key economic advisors were replaced in 1949, as the economy deteriorated. It was at that point that Perón began to assemble a massive propaganda apparatus in the office of the president and switch from providing labor with material benefits to providing symbolic benefits. Nevertheless, if the dates associated with the erosion of the populist coalition are correct, the 1949 shift in the real income and GDP share series could not have resulted from the transition from populist authoritarian rule.

This brings one to a consideration of the 1943 transition from traditional to populist authoritarian rule. Both the authoritarian and integrated formulations predict that this shift should have been significant. The analyses provide support for this hypothesis. The impact of the 1943 coalition change is considerably more clear-cut than the 1966 shift and only slightly weaker than that of the 1952 (1949) interruption.

In summary, it appears that the integrated argument performs quite well when tested in the context of real income, GDP share, strikes, and government employment. In the pre-1950 era it predicts, along with the authoritarian thesis, that changing coalitions will produce changes in policy outcomes. That expectation is generally satisfied despite the fact that 1949 shifts can be detected in the real income and GDP share series. In the post-1950 period, the integrated formulation predicts that changes between coalitions will cease to result in alterations in the outcomes of labor policy outcomes. In this period the integrated thesis proves to be more useful than the authoritarian formulation. From approximately 1950 on, three of the indicators ceased to be influenced by changes between different types of authoritarian rule. Only the workers' share of the GDP continued to respond to coalition changes. Even in this area, however, the post-1966 trend was more the reinstitution of an established pattern than a new departure toward authoritarian rule.

Figure 7.1 Real Income

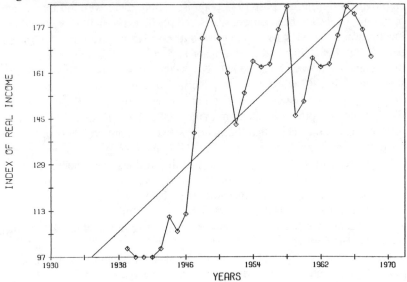

Figure 7.2 Gross Domestic Product Share

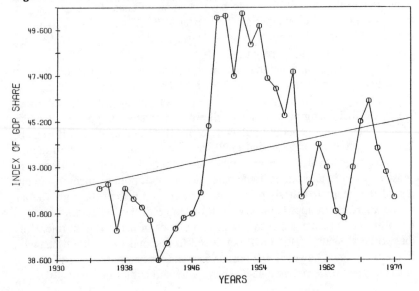

Figure 7.3 Labor Strikes

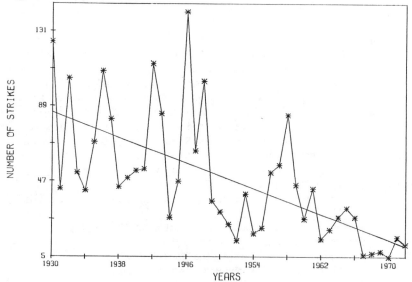

Figure 7.4 Government Employment Levels

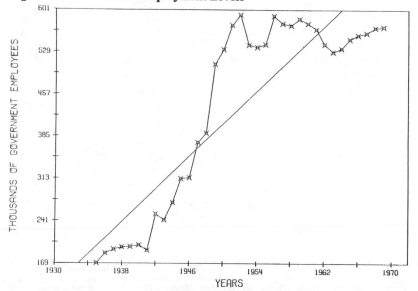

Notes

1. Reports are available for the following periods: real income, 1939–1968; GDP share, 1935–1970; strikes, 1930–1972; and, government employment, 1935–1969. The real income data is a linked series from Diaz Alejandro 1970, 538 and Republica de Argentina, Consejo Nacional de Desarrollo 1970, 154. The GDP share data are a linked series from the Ministry of Economic Affairs 1955, UN Economic Commission on Latin America 1969, 170, Republica de Argentina, Consejo Nacional de Desarrollo 1970, 154, and Siguat 1972, 57, 66. The strike data pertain to the Greater Buenos Aires province only and are drawn from International Labor Organization Yearbooks, Carri 1967, 47, and S. Baily 1967, 180. Information on the number of government employees is from Treber 1971, 521–522.

2. For readings on the use of dummy variables in regression analyses, see Gujarti 1970a and 1970b, and Johnston 1972.

3. For a discussion of the effects of autocorrelation, see Johnston 1972, 246–249.

4. See Chow 1960; Davis, Dempster, and Wildavsky 1966a, 1966b.

5. See Durbin and Watson 1950, 1951.

6. See Geary 1970, and Habibagahi and Pratschki 1972.

7. See Goldberger 1964, 217 and Bohrnstedt and Carter 1971, 129.

8. The low point in the number of government employees during the 1953–1965 period was reached in 1963 when 528,500 workers were on the public payrolls. That level represented a 10.77 percent reduction from the 1952 level of 592,300, or an average annual decrease of .98 percent between 1952 and 1963.

9. Equation 7.1 can be employed at this stage of the analysis because the small-number-of-cases problems noted above can now be avoided.

10. This conclusion is reinforced by the fact that forward stepwise regressions of Equation 7.2 on the 1950–1970 and 1953–1970 periods result in the loading of D_i and the exclusion of the interaction term $(X_i D_i)$. This indicates that the significant Chow's F-results in a post-1966 change in the intercept rather than from a change from the slope of the regression line. If that is the case, the intercept shift seems attributable to the 1965–1967 increases in the GDP share received by labor.

EIGHT

Expenditure and Revenue Policies

An important series of propositions of the authoritarian thesis links transitions between the three different types of authoritarian political systems with changes in governments' overall spending and revenue collection policies, with shifts in the levels of military spending, and with changes in governments' effectiveness in controlling inflation. I shall probe whether or not the shift from one type of political system to the next did in fact alter the policy trends in these four areas.

The changes in the four policy areas that should be observable if the authoritarian thesis is valid can be readily summarized. The transition from traditional to populist authoritarian rule in 1943 should have produced sharp increases in overall expenditures as the governments of Ramirez, Farrell, and Perón created and expanded a variety of expensive social welfare and public works programs as a means for attracting and subsequently maintaining popular support. Revenues should not have kept pace with the increases in spending, so that the 1943–1952 era of populist rule should have been characterized by an ever-widening gap between government resources and expenditures. Partially because the military was included in the populist coalition and partly because the populist governments were extremely nationalistic and hostile to the United States, defense spending should have climbed dramatically as a result of the shift to populist authoritarian rule. Finally, rising government deficits and the slowed expansion of the nation's consumer goods industries should have served to make inflation an increasingly serious problem during the latter stages of the populist period.[1]

Yielding to pressures from the International Monetary Fund for sound fiscal policies,[2] the technocrats of the post-1966 bureaucratic–authoritarian administrations of Ongania and Levingston should have attempted to improve the operating efficiency of the state and balance the budget by decreasing overall spending and increasing government revenues. Those measures, coupled with the initiation of wage controls, should have served to reduce the rate of inflation. Since the military was included in the bureaucratic–authoritarian coalition and a capable military would have been important for effecting the important bureaucratic–authoritarian goal of excluding the popular sectors from the political life of the nation, the authoritarian thesis seems to imply that military spending should have climbed once again after 1966.[3]

The integrated formulation departs from the authoritarian thesis in predicting that sharp policy changes should have been infrequent after the expansion and extensive unionization of the Argentine public sector. The capacities of the newly arriving elites to alter dramatically the trends in Argentina's public policies should have been reduced so that the shift from populist authoritarian rule to the era of the hegemonic crisis in 1952 and the 1966 transition to the domination of the bureaucratic–authoritarian coalition should not have produced major reversals in the policy areas I shall consider. In other words, if the integrated formulation is valid, shifts between coalitions of political elites should have ceased to produce major policy changes in the period after the growth and unionization of the Argentine public bureaucracy. The middle- and low-level bureaucrats should have taken control of the policy-making arena, reducing the political elites who had set "basic" policies in the traditional and populist authoritarian periods to effecting only marginal changes in policies from 1950 on.

The Policies

The following eight policy indicators are used to operationalize the four broad policy areas examined in this chapter:

1. Total government spending
   - Total expenditures of the Argentine national government in 1960 pesos
   - Total expenditures of the Argentine national government in current pesos
2. Total government revenues
   - Total government revenues from all sources in 1960 pesos
3. Defense spending
   - Defense expenditures in 1960 pesos
   - Defense expenditures in current pesos
   - Defense expenditures as a proportion of total expenditures
4. Inflation
   - Cost-of-living index for Buenos Aires
   - Rate of change in the Buenos Aires cost-of-living index.[4]

The indicators in the first two areas seem adequate for tapping the proposition that certain of the Argentine governments sharply increased overall spending while others moved to balance their budgets by reducing expenditures and increasing revenues. (An additional series—the size of the annual operating deficit—is computed on the basis of these indicators.) The hypotheses relating the Argentine military with changing public policy outputs are examined by utilizing the three series listed in the third area.[5] Finally, the arguments linking shifting dominant coalitions with different degrees of success in controlling inflation are examined by employing the indicators in the fourth area. The 1938–1970 trends in the eight policy indicators are shown in Figures 8.1–8.8.[6]

A Methodological Aside: The Policy–Motivation Link

Note that both current (undeflated) and real (deflated) currencies are used to operationalize total expenditures and defense expenditures. Both current and real operationalizations are utilized as a result of the difficulty in interpreting the meaning of year-to-year changes in spending. One focuses on expenditures in the first place because they reflect something about the decisionmakers' motivations and their allocation of values. Unfortunately, there is a potential for a high degree of "slippage" between what decisionmakers "really" want to spend and the amounts that are actually expended in either real or current terms. It is my contention that as long as this potential slippage exists, neither real nor current expenditures allow one to draw inferences about the real goals and policy preferences of the decisionmakers.

The nature of the problem here can be readily explained. In the absence of better information, it seems intuitively plausible that in situations characterized by sporadic bursts of double-digit inflation (such as the Argentine case), the expenditure decisions can be decomposed into at least two parts: (1) the amount that decisionmakers "really" want to spend, which may be expressed in either deflated or undeflated terms; and (2) the increment (or decrement) that must be added to (or subtracted from) the total in part 1 in order to offset the anticipated effects of inflation. If this assumption is valid, it follows that an increase between time t and time $t + 1$ in the undeflated expenditures that decisionmakers allocate to a given area may only partially reflect the way in which they wish to allocate their resources. For example, a 10-percent increase between time t and time $t + 1$ in the undeflated expenditures devoted to defense may not indicate a desire by the decisionmakers to enhance the position of the military if they expected a 10-percent rate of inflation and "padded" their expenditure requests accordingly. Indeed, a 10-percent increase in undeflated military expenditures may actually reflect a "real" desire of the decisionmakers to deemphasize the military if they predicted a 15 percent rate of inflation.

The problem of interpreting through time changes in spending remains because decisionmakers may not always predict the effects of inflation accurately. The question here does not seem to reduce to either of two assertions: that one should use current (undeflated) currencies because decisionmakers "really think" in those terms or that real (deflated) monies should be employed in order to improve the through-time comparability of the data. As was said above, one focuses on expenditures in the first place because they reflect—at least in theory—something about decisionmakers' motivations and their allocations of values. Unfortunately, neither real nor current expenditure figures allow one to draw inferences about the real goals and policy preferences of the decisionmakers unless one is willing to assume that decisionmakers accurately predicted the effects of inflation and "padded" their spending requests accordingly. In situations such as the Argentine case, where inflation is generally high but also extremely sporadic (see Figure 8.8), that assumption may be unrealistic, so that there is room for considerable slippage between decisionmakers' goals and the amounts that they spend in either real or current terms.

This difficulty in interpreting expenditures is of course only an example of the more general problem mentioned earlier. Policy outputs are a thin reed on which to hang our interpretations of why something is done. The possibility that miscalculation, inadvertence, and simple policy failure may have intervened between decisionmakers' goals and actual policy outputs cannot be ignored if one wishes to understand what policymakers attempted to do and why.

The only immediate escape from this problem seems to be to supplement a focus on policy outputs (what is actually done) with a consideration of what the decisionmakers attempted to do. This was done extensively in Chapter 6, where Argentina's actual and intended industrialization policies were reviewed. It is done again in this chapter by employing both undeflated and deflated operationalizations of total and defense expenditures. As the discussion below reveals, this somewhat cumbersome strategy is rewarded by the fact that the results from the real and current spending analyses vary strikingly.

The 1952 Transition: From Populist Authoritarian Rule to the Era of the Hegemonic Crisis

The general question posed in this and the two succeeding sections has already been stated: Did the transition from one type of authoritarian political system to another (that is, from the era of domination by one coalition to that of another) produce an impact on the patterns that public policies display through time? The results reported here are developed by using the techniques and procedures outlined in Chapter 5. The focus is on the detection of rather simple slope and intercept changes that may have resulted from the transition between different types of authoritarian rule. The general question is explored by considering the following three slightly more precise versions of that query:[7]

1. Are the regression parameters (the slope and the intercept) the same in the pre- and post-transition periods?
2. When an equation that ignores the possible effects of a transition is estimated on a combined pre- and post-transition period, does auto-correlation develop and does the introduction of dummy variables that tap the impact of the transition resolve that difficulty?
3. Does the introduction of dummy variables that tap the effects of a transition increase the amount of explained variance in a dependent policy variable?

The focus in this section, of course, is on the policy impacts of the end of populist authoritarian rule in 1952. Specifically, is the evidence consistent with the hypothesis that the erosion of the populist coalition—domestic industrialists, the military, urban workers, and producers of nonexportable agricultural goods—and the onset of an ongoing crisis of authority altered the trends in the policies under consideration? The first step toward answering this question is taken by estimating Equation 7.1, which ignores the possible impact of the 1952 shift on a combined pre- and post-1952 transition period (1948–1965), and the post-transition interval (1953–1965). The results of these analyses are presented in Table 8.1, part a.

The initial focus of interest is on the degree of similarity in the regression parameters when the estimation is based on the two different periods. The appropriate technique for determining whether or not the parameters are significantly different is Chow's F-statistic. The results of those tests are presented in Table 8.1, part b. The null hypothesis that the regression parameters are identical in the two overlapping periods is rejected except in the cases of total expenditures in 1960 pesos (total exp.), total revenues in 1960 pesos (total revs.) and percent change in the cost-of-living index (change CLI). In other words, the conclusion to be drawn from Chow's F-tests is that the parameters in the equations involving total expenditures in current pesos (current exp.), defense expenditures in 1960 pesos (defense exp.), defense expenditures in current pesos (cur. def. exp.), defense expenditures as a percent of total expenditures (def. exp. ratio), and the cost-of-living index (CLI) were different in the pre- and post-1952 transition periods. The evidence is thus consistent with the hypothesis that the 1952 transition from the era of populist authoritarian rule to the era of the hegemonic crisis altered the regression parameters.

Consider now the problem of positive first-order autocorrelation. Chow's F-tests indicated that the trends in total expenditures in 1960 pesos,

Table 8.1   Budget Policies: Impact of the 1952 Transition

Part a
Overlapping regressions (Equation 7.1, k = 1)

Dependent Variable	n	R^2	b	Durbin-Watson	Runs
1948-1965					
Total exp.[a]	18	.24	2439.2632	1.70686	10
Current exp.	18	.78	19,708.2840	.28818[b]	3[c]
Total revs.	18	.45	2,387.8271	1.90094	11
Defense exp.[a]	18	.21	-414.7745	.83547[b]	7
Cur. def. exp.	18	.78	3,087.3369	.30785[b]	3[c]
Def./exp. ratio	20[d]	.76	-.8565	1.02763[a]	7
CLI	18	.78	13.9056	.22047[b]	3[c]
Change CLI	18	.02	.5756	1.75416	5
1953-1965					
Total exp.[a]	13	.22	3,404.9879	1.90162	7
Current exp.	13	.89	30,265.2820	.61423	3
Total revs.	13	.49	3,717.1665	2.29159	6
Defense exp.[a]	13	.02	-63.6659	1.89094	8
Cur. def. exp.	13	.89	4,697.2901	.63579	3
Def./exp. ratio	13	.55	-.5916	2.04921	9
CLI	13	.88	21.2341	.41227	3
Change CLI	13	.05	1.6636	1.71309	3

[a] in millions of 1960 pesos.

[b]H_0 of no positive, first-order autocorrelation rejected at the .01 level using the Durbin-Watson d-statistic.

[c]H_0 of random distribution of the residuals rejected at the point .01 level using the Geary sign test.

[d] in the case of the Def./exp. ratio, the 1946-1965 period was utilized.

[e]H_0 of no positive, first-order autocorrelation is in the indeterminant range using the Durbin-Watson d-statistic.

Part b
Chow's F-Statistics
on the Overlapping Periods
1948-1965 and 1953-1965

	F	Degrees of Freedom	Significance Level
Total exp.	.544	5,12	$p>.05$
Current exp.	4.084	5,12	$p<.05$
Total revs.	.681	5,12	$p>.05$
Defense exp.	14.111	5,12	$p<.01$
Cur. def. exp.	3.918	5,12	$p<.05$
Def./exp. ratio	3.526	7,12	$p<.05$
CLI	3.603	5,12	$p<.05$
Change CLI	.220	5,12	$p>.05$

Part c
Dummy Variable Regressions
on the Period 1948-1965 (Equation 7.2, k = 3)

Dependent Variable	n	R^2	Durbin-Watson	Runs
Total exp.	18	.37	1.94614	10
Current exp.	18	.92	.81734[a]	5
Total revs.	18	.56	2.30453	10
Defense exp.	18	.76	1.86231	11
Cur. def. exp.	18	.92	.82770[a]	5
Def./exp. ratio	20[b]	.89	2.06981	13
CLI	18	.91	.60915[c]	5
Change CLI	18	.08	1.74727	7

[a]H_0 of no positive, first-order autocorrelation is in the indeterminant range using the Durbin-Watson d-statistic.

[b] in the case of Def./exp. ratio, the 1946-1965 period was utilized.

[c]H_0 of no positive, first-order autocorrelation rejected at the .01 level using the Durbin-Watson d-statistic.

Part d
R^2 *Tests*

Dependent Variable	R^2		$\bar{R}^2$	n
	Eq. 7.1	Eq. 7.2		
Total exp.	.24	.37	.24	18
Current exp.	.78	.92	.90	18
Total revs.	.45	.56	.47	18
Defense exp.	.21	.76	.71	18
Cur. def. exp.	.78	.92	.90	18
Def./exp. ratio	.76	.89	.87	20
CLI	.78	.91	.89	18
Change CLI	.02	.08	.00	18

total revenues, and change in the CLI were not significantly different in the 1948–1965 and 1953–1965 intervals. Examination of the last two columns of Table 8.1, part a reveals that the Durbin–Watson d-statistic and the Geary Signs test detect no indications of autocorrelation when Equation 7.1 is used to estimate those three policies on the combined pre- and post-1952 (1948–1965) interval. The results from Chow's F- and autocorrelation tests on these three policies are perfectly consistent. If the 1952 shift from populist authoritarian rule to the era of the hegemonic crisis did not alter the trends in total expenditures in 1960 pesos, total revenues and Change in the CLI, autocorrelation problems should *not* develop when Equation 7.1, which omits the effects of the 1952 transition, is estimated on the 1948–1965 period.

Chow's F-tests revealed that a shift occurred in the pre- and post-1952 patterns of the remaining five policies. If that is the case, autocorrelation problems should develop when Equation 7.1 is used to estimate those policies on the 1948–1965 interval. Here again, Chow's F- and autocorrelation tests produce consistent results. Autocorrelation is detected in connection with total expenditures in current pesos, defense expenditures in 1960 pesos, defense expenditures in current pesos, defense expenditures as a percent of total expenditures, and the CLI. The conclusion that these difficulties may have resulted from the omission of variables which tap the effects of the 1952 transition is reinforced by the findings in Table 8.1, part c. Except in the case of the CLI, the introduction of dummy variables that reflect the 1952 shift (that is, the use of Equation 7.2) at least partially helps to resolve the autocorrelation problems. In other words, with the exception of the CLI, autocorrelation problems that develop are either reduced or eliminated when the previously omitted effects of the 1952 transition are inserted in the analysis. The shift from populist authoritarian rule to the era of the hegemonic crisis does in fact appear to have marked a major turning point in the trends of total expenditures in current pesos, defense expenditures in 1960 pesos, defense expenditures in current pesos, and defense expenditures as a percent of total expenditures.

What, then, can be said in regard to the question whether the introduction of dummy variables increases the amount of explained variance in the dependent variables or not? It will be recalled that if the dummy variables that tap the effects of the 1952 transition provide an increase in the explained variance, the R^2 (which corrects for the number of predictor variables) should be greater than the R^2 from Equation 7.1. An examination of these comparisons in part d of Table 8.1 reveals that the R^2 is in fact greater than the R^2 from Equation 7.1 in the cases of total expenditures in current pesos, total revenues in 1960 pesos, defense expenditures in 1960 pesos, defense expenditures in current pesos, defense expenditures as a percent of total expenditures, and the CLI. The introduction of dummy variables that reflect the 1952 shift does increase the amount of explained variance in these six policy indicators. Only in the case of total expenditures in 1960 pesos and change in the CLI does a consideration of the 1952 transition fail to improve the explanation of the trend.

Summary and Interpretation of the Results

All three tests produce results consistent with the hypothesis that the transition from populism to the era of the hegemonic crisis produced an impact on the long-term trends in total expenditures in current pesos, defense expenditures in 1960 pesos, defense expenditures in current pesos, defense expenditures as a percent of total expenditures, and the cost-of-living index (see Table 8.2). In contrast, the findings indicate that the 1952 shift had only a very marginal effect on total revenues in 1960 pesos and almost no impact at all on total expenditures in 1960 pesos or the rate of change in the CLI.

Table 8.2   Budget Policies: Summary of the 1952 Transition: From Populist Authoritarian Rule to the Era of the Hegemonic Crisis

Dependent Variable	Parameter Change?	Autocorrelation Resolved?	$\bar{R}^2$ Increase?
Total exp.	no	—	no
Current exp.	yes	yes	yes
Total revs.	no	—	yes
Defense exp.	yes	yes	yes
Cur. def. exp.	yes	yes	yes
Def./exp. ratio	yes	yes	yes
CLI	yes	no	yes
Change CLI	no	—	no

The fact that major shifts can be detected in five out of the eight policies appears to provide general support for the authoritarian thesis, which predicts that major policy realignments should have resulted from the 1952 transition from populist authoritarian rule to the era of the hegemonic crisis. Conversely, the findings in this section appear to undermine the integrated formulation, which hypothesizes only minor policy changes as a result of the 1952 transition. However, two additional considerations appear to shift the evidence in favor of the integrated argument.

First, when policy shifts coincided with the erosion of populist authoritarian rule in 1952, the new policy trends did not invariably move in the *directions* predicted by the authoritarian thesis. The integrated formulation predicts only that pre-1952 trends should not have been sharply reversed in the 1953–1965 period. The authoritarian argument implies a number of such directional changes. For example, spending on the military should have increased during the 1943–1952 interval both as a means for safeguarding the security of the nationalistic regimes of Ramirez, Farrell, and Perón and as a means for cementing military support for the populist coalition. According to the authoritarian thesis, the dissolution of the populist coalition in 1952 should have reversed that trend. Defense expenditures should have declined after 1952, as Perón moved away from his nationalistic policies and attempted to reduce his reliance on the military. A focus on defense expenditures in current pesos reveals, however, that military spending actually increased sharply, rather than decreased, after the shift from populist authoritarian rule (see Figure 8.5). Expenditures on defense climbed at an average rate of nearly 3.1 billion pesos during the 1948–1965 period; defense expenditures rose at an average annual rate of 4.7 billion current pesos during the post-transition (1953–1965) interval. Thus, as the integrated formulation predicts, the pre-1952 trend was continued through the 1953–1965 period.

Consideration of the trends in defense expenditures in 1960 pesos and in the proportion of total expenditures devoted to defense reveals similar problems for the authoritarian formulation. Both of these series show downward tendencies in the period after 1952 (see Figures 8.4 and 8.6), but the slopes in Table 8.1, part a indicate that reductions in both policies occurred at a faster rate during the combined pre- and post-1952 transition period than during the 1953–1965 interval. Rather than initiating or even accelerating a shift away from the military, as the authoritarian argument predicts, the 1952 transition simply slowed or dampened the pretransition trends.

The pre- and post-1952 trends in total expenditure also fail to satisfy the expectations of the authoritarian thesis. According to that argument, the populist governments of the 1943–1952 period mobilized and later retained popular support by initiating or expanding a variety of expensive social welfare and public works programs. These massive government outlays and the resultant growth in the government's operating deficit were, in theory at least, partially responsible for the eventual erosion of the populist authoritarian coalition in 1952. Overall expenditures should therefore have declined after the end of populist rule as the new political elites moved to exclude the popular sectors, abandon expensive populist policies, and reduce the government's operating deficit.

The analysis in this section reveals quite a different pattern, more consistent with the integrated formulation. The expensive populist policies were apparently not simply abandoned. Overall spending was not quickly reduced and new revenues were not immediately raised so that the budget could be brought into balance. Instead, expenditures appear to have climbed during the post-1952 interval. During the 1948–1965 period, for example, total expenditures in current pesos climbed at an average annual rate of nearly 20 billion pesos; during the 1953–1965 interval, total expenditures in current pesos rose at an average annual rate of slightly more than 30 billion pesos. Even though the 1952 transition produced no major impact on the trend in total expenditures in 1960 pesos, the same pattern emerges when that indicator is considered. Slight reductions were made through 1955 in total expenditures in 1960 pesos (Figure 8.1), but total expenditures rose at a faster rate during the 1963–1965 period (3.4 billion 1960 pesos per year) than during the 1948–1965 interval (2.4 billion 1960 pesos per year).

The estimates of the average annual increases in total expenditures in 1960 pesos are of course affected by the major increase that occurred in 1958; but the annual operating deficit (total revenues – total annual expenditures) also increased in the period immediately after 1952 (see Figure 8.9). While Perón bankrupted the nation with his expensive social welfare and public works programs, it appears that he actually succeeded in reducing the annual operating deficit during the 1948–1952 interval. After the end of populist authoritarian rule in 1952, total revenues rose on average 312.2-million-1960-pesos faster than total expenditures. The gap between government income and outgo should therefore have continued to narrow as the postpopulist governments raised new revenues faster than they increased spending. The paradox is that the government's annual operating deficit increased, rather than decreased, between 1953 and 1958. The administrations that supposedly came to power with views toward reducing the high, populist period expenditures and balancing the budget actually widened the gap between government resources and expenditures in the period immediately after the end of populist authoritarian rule.

If the integrated formulation is thus more often supported than the authoritarian argument by a consideration of the directions in which policies shifted after 1952, a second major problem with the latter thesis should be noted. Pre- and post-1952 shifts were detected in five of the eight policies. However, the shifts in three of those five policies (total expenditures in current pesos, defense expenditures in current pesos, and the CLI) may be attributable to the fact that those policies are linked with changes in the Argentine CLI. It seems reasonable to assume that total budgeted expenditures, for example, are a function of what the political elites want to spend plus some increment (or decrement) based on their projection of the change in the CLI. If that is the case, it follows that high rates of increase in the CLI may be paralleled by similarly high rates of increase in expenditures. This is precisely what occurred in Argentina. The CLI rose sharply during the 1953–1965 interval, and Equation 7.1 estimations on the 1953–1965 period yield standardized regression coefficients (betas) that are remarkably similar: CLI, .940; total expenditures in current pesos, .945; defense expenditures in current pesos, .945. Given this similarity, it seems plausible that the 1952 shifts in total expenditures in current pesos and defense expenditures in current pesos may have resulted from the post-1952 increases in the CLI rather than from the transition between different dominant ruling coalitions.

This conclusion is reinforced by the analyses of defense expenditures in 1960 pesos, total expenditures in 1960 pesos, total revenues in 1960 pesos, and the rate of change in the cost-of-living index. Although these four policies are outcomes rather than outputs because they compensate for the (possibly unintended) effects of inflation, it is significant that the last three behaved in the manner predicted by the integrated formulation and were only marginally affected by the 1952 transition. In other words, of the five policies that shifted after 1952, only the changes in defense expenditures in 1960 pesos and defense expenditures as a percent of total expenditures may actually be attributable to the erosion of populist authoritarian rule.

A third major problem for the authoritarian thesis appears to arise because a number of the policies displayed in Figures 8.1–8.8 seem to have undergone shifts during, rather than at the end of, the populist period. A 1945 shift from a steeply rising, to a steeply falling, trend is observable, for example, in the proportion of the total expenditures devoted to defense. Shifts from a rising to a falling trend can be noted in 1948 in the series of total expenditures in 1960 pesos, total revenues in 1960 pesos, and defense expenditures in 1960 pesos. A reverse 1948 shift can be noted in the size of the government's operating deficit (Figure 8.9).

The shift in the share of total expenditures devoted to defense would appear to be attributable to the end of World War II and need not create a problem for the authoritarian thesis. It is of interest to note, however, that the 1945 shift coincides almost perfectly with Perón's efforts to effect a secret rapprochement with the United States so that the Argentine military could benefit from President Truman's postwar military assistance programs. The end of the war would have naturally allowed Argentina to shift away from emphasizing military spending. A pragmatic abandonment of the Peron nationalistic, anti-U.S. position and a secret rapprochement with the United States in return for military aid would have facilitated that shift.[8]

If the pre-1952 shifts in the military-related policies do not, therefore, create a problem for the authoritarian thesis, the same thing cannot be said about the apparent 1948 shifts in total expenditures in 1960 pesos and total revenues in 1960 pesos. It will be recalled from Chapter 4 that Argentina passed through a major recessionary period between 1948 and 1949. The discussion in Chapters 5 and 6 showed that it was at that point that Perón substituted material benefits to the popular sector with symbolic benefits and began to build a massive propaganda apparatus in the office of the president. Analyses in the previous chapter showed that the trend in the share of the GDP received by labor and workers' real income shifted in 1949. All of this suggests the possibility that if shifts actually occurred in 1948, they may have resulted from the 1948–1949 recession and its political aftereffects rather than from the 1952 transition from populist authoritarian rule.

In light of this possibility, all eight of the policies were reexamined with a view toward detecting shifts in 1945 and 1948. This work required only a modest extension of the procedures employed above. The examination of possible shifts in 1945 and 1948 now occasionally requires the use of the following equation:

$$Y^\wedge_t = a + b_1X_1 + b_2D_i + b_3(X_1D_i) + b_4D + b_5(X_1D_j) + e_t \qquad (8.1)$$

where all terms are as defined for equation 7.2 and D_i and D_j represent dummy variable codings for the 1952 and 1948 (or 1945) shifts, respectively. (Equation 8.1 is used only in instances in which major policy shifts were detected in 1952. In all other cases, Equations 7.1 and 7.2 are utilized, and D_i is coded to represent the possible 1945 or 1948 shift.)

The important results of the 1945/1948 reanalyses are shown in Table 8.3 and are summarized in Table 8.4. A shift was detected in 1945 only in the case of the proportion of the total expenditures devoted to defense. The only major shift detected in 1948 was in defense expenditures in 1960 pesos. Despite the impression that might be gained from an examination of Figures 8.1 and 8.3, 1948 did not mark a statistically significant turning point in the

Table 8.3   Budget Policies: Examination of Possible Shifts in 1945 and 1948

Part a
Overlapping Regressions

Dependent Variable	Eq.	n	k	R^2	Durbin-Watson	Runs
1943-1965						
Total exp.[a]	7.1	23	1	.52	1.79702	13
Current exp.	7.2[b]	23	3	.93	.80738[c]	5[d]
Total revs.	7.1	23	1	.67	1.80107	12
Defense exp.[a]	7.2[b]	23	3	.17	1.41410	10
Cur. def. exp.	7.2[b]	23	3	.93	.82550[c]	7
Def./exp. ratio	7.2[b]	23	3	.81	1.26924[e]	12
CLI	7.2[b]	23	3	.92	.58745[c]	5[d]
Change CLI	7.1	23	1	.11	1.70885	7
1949-1965[f]						
Total exp.	7.1	17	1	.34	1.88866	10
Current exp.	7.2[b]	17	3	.91	.82068	7
Total revs.	7.1	17	1	.51	2.07946	9
Defense exp.	7.2[b]	17	3	.43	2.13313	11
Cur. def. exp.	7.2[b]	17	3	.91	.83372	5
Def./exp. ratio	7.2[b]	20	3	.89	2.06981	13
CLI	7.2[b]	17	3	.91	.61280	5
Change CLI	7.1	17	3	.01	1.73603	6

[a] in millions of 1960 pesos.

[b] D_i codings in Equation 7.2 are treatments of the 1952 shift.

[c] H_0 of no positive, first-order autocorrelation rejected at the .01 level using the Durbin-Watson d-statistic.

[d] H_0 of random distribution of the residuals rejected at the point .01 level using the Geary sign test.

[e] H_0 of no positive, first-order autocorrelation is in the indeterminant range using the Durbin-Watson d-statistic.

[f] the 1946-1965 interval is used in the case of the Def./exp. ratio.

Part b
Chow's F-Statistics
on the Overlapping Periods
1943-1965 and 1949-1965

Dependant Variable	F	Degrees of Freedom	Significance Level
Total exp.	.706	6,16	$p>.05$
Current exp.	.002	6,14	$p>.05$
Total revs.	.922	6,16	$p>.05$
Defense exp.	16.510	6,14	$p<.01$
Cur. def. exp.	.002	6,14	$p>.05$
Def./exp. ratio	163.281	3,17	$p<.01$
CLI	.006	6,14	$p>.05$
Change CLI	.176	6,16	$p>.05$

Note: In the case of Def./exp. ratio, the overlapping periods are 1943-1965 and 1946-1965.

Part c
Dummy Variable Regressions
on the Period 1943-1965 (n = 23)

Dependent Variable	Eq.	k	R^2	Durbin-Watson	Runs
1943-1965					
Total exp.	7.2	3	.58	1.87975	12
Current exp.	8.1	5	.93	.82079[a]	9
Total revs.	7.2	3	.72	2.07135	11
Defense exp.	8.1	5	.68	2.15802	14
Cur. def. exp.	8.1	5	.93	.83427[a]	8
Def./exp. ratio	8.1	5	.94	2.17055	16
CLI	8.1	5	.92	.61286[b]	7
Change CLI	7.2	3	.14	1.75219	9

[a]H_0 of no positive, first-order autocorrelation is in the indeterminant range using the Durbin-Watson d-statistic.

[b]H_0 of no positive, first-order autocorrelation rejected at the .01 level using the Durbin-Watson d-statistic.

Part d
$\bar{R}^2$ *Tests (n = 23)*

Dependent Variable	R^2		$\bar{R}^2$
	Eq. 7.1/7.2	Eq. 7.2/8.1	
Total exp.	.52	.58	.51
Current exp.	.93	.93	.91
Total revs.	.67	.72	.68
Defense exp.	.17	.68	.59
Cur. def. exp.	.93	.93	.91
Def./exp. ratio	.81	.94	.92
CLI	.92	.92	.90
Change CLI	.11	.14	.00

Table 8.4   Summary of the Possible Shifts in 1945 and 1948

Dependent Variable	Parameter Change?	Autocorrelation Resolved?	$\bar{R}^2$ Increase?
Total exp.	no	—	no
Current exp.	no	yes	no
Total revs.	no	—	yes
Defense exp.	yes	—	yes
Cur. def. exp.	no	yes	no
Def./exp. ratio	yes	yes	yes
CLI	no	no	no
Change CLI	no	—	no

Note: With the exception of the Def./exp. ratio, all results pertain to a possible shift in 1948. The results for Def./exp. ratio pertain to a possible shift in 1945.

series of total expenditure in 1960 pesos and total revenues in 1960 pesos.[9] It is true that deflated expenditures and revenues declined during the 1948–1955 interval, but those reductions were very marginal and are barely detected by the least rigorous of the three tests. It is tempting to attribute the expenditure reductions to Perón's initial efforts in the late 1940s to exclude the popular sectors; but it seems likely that the military bore the burden of the decreasing expenditures between 1948 and 1955, inasmuch as defense expenditures in 1960 pesos dropped by 53.2 percent and total expenditures in 1960 pesos fell by only 26.2 percent over that period. In addition, it seems likely that the declining expenditures may have been partially unintended. The rate of inflation increased between 1948 and 1952, and Argentina's political elites may have been unable to predict those rises accurately. The elites may therefore have actually attempted to increase or at least maintain the level of expenditures during the 1948–1955 interval but have failed to do so in terms of 1960 pesos because they did not compensate adequately for the impact of inflation. In any event, the declining 1948–1955 pattern in total expenditures and total revenues in 1960 pesos did not mark a statistically significant deviation from the 1948–1965 trends. The reductions may have had important political implications, but the predictions of the authoritarian thesis are technically valid. The apparent 1948 shifts in total expenditures in 1960 pesos and total revenues in 1960 pesos were not large enough and did not last long enough to emerge significantly in a statistical sense.

In summary, the analyses of the 1952 transition from populist authoritarian rule to the era of the hegemonic crisis generally seem to support the integrated formulation. The trends of five of the eight policies were apparently affected by the erosion of the populist coalition, as the authoritarian thesis predicts they should have been; but the post-1952 trends were more often in the directions predicted by the integrated argument. Moreover, at least three of the five 1952 policy shifts may have occurred as a result of post-1952 increases in the cost-of-living index rather than the transition from populist rule. A third problem with the authoritarian thesis was found to be more apparent than real. Except in the cases of the proportion of total expenditures devoted to defense and defense expenditures in 1960 pesos, which shifted in 1945 and 1948, respectively, the statistically significant policy realignments during the 1943–1965 period occurred in 1952. Even in the two areas where shifts did occur in 1945 and 1948, however, the key prediction of the integrated formulation is still supported. Basic policy trends established prior to the transition from populist authoritarian rule were maintained and were only dampened by the transition to the era of the hegemonic crisis.

The 1943 Transition:
From Traditional to Populist Authoritarian Rule

I shall focus on the 1943 transition from traditional to populist authoritarian rule. The questions and methodologies employed here are nearly identical to those utilized in the previous section. Slight differences will be noted as the discussion proceeds.

It will be recalled from the previous section that the initial focus in these analyses concerns the question of whether the replacement of the traditional authoritarian coalition (the foreign export sector and export-related industrialists) by the populist alliance (domestic industrialists, the military, urban workers, and producers of nonexportable agricultural goods) altered the trends in the eight policy indicators or not. This query is considered in Table 8.5, part a, where the trends in the overlapping periods 1938–1965 and 1943–1965 are examined. (Note that: Equation 7.1 is utilized in the cases where trend shifts were not detected in 1945, 1948, or 1952; Equation 7.2 where a 1952 shift was previously detected; and Equation 8.1 in the cases of defense expenditures in 1960 pesos and the proportion of total expenditures devoted to defense, which were shown to have undergone shifts in 1948/1952 and 1945/1952, respectively. These procedures are dictated by the necessity of extending the post-1943 transition era to include the 1943–1965 period and the resultant need to "dummy in" treatments of major shifts that occurred during that interval.)[10]

Chow's F-tests for pre- and post-1943 transition parameter changes are presented in Table 8.5, part b. It is possible to reject the null hypothesis that the regression parameters are identical in the two periods (1938–1965 and 1943–1965) only in the case of the proportion of total expenditures devoted to defense. It is not possible to say that the 1943 transition to populist authoritarian rule altered the long-term trends in the remaining seven policy indicators.

This does not mean that the end of traditional authoritarian rule was not important, however. If one estimates equations that ignore the impact of the 1943 transition on the 1938–1952 interval, autocorrelation is detected in the case of total expenditures in current pesos, defense expenditures in current pesos, the proportion of total expenditures devoted to defense, and the CLI (see the first eight lines in Table 7.5, part c).[11] These problems are reduced, however, when equations that tap the effects of the 1943 transition are estimated on the 1938–1952 interval (see the last eight lines in Table 8.5, part c). Thus, even though the 1943 shift from traditional to populist authoritarian rule apparently did not alter the regression parameters of any of the series except the proportion of total expenditures devoted to defense, the insertion of variables that tap the effects of that interruption does help to resolve autocorrelation difficulties when they develop.

The R^2 comparisons of the equations in Table 8.5, part c reflect an even more general impact of the 1943 shift to populist authoritarian rule (see Table 8.5, part d). If a consideration of the 1943 transition improves the explanation of a given series, the R^2 from an equation with variables that tap the 1943 shift should be greater than the R^2 from an equation that ignores the interruption. The results here show that the R^2's are greater than the respec-

Table 8.5   Budget Policies: Impact of the 1943 Transition

<table>
<tr><td colspan="7" align="center">*Part a*
Overlapping Regressions</td></tr>
<tr><td>Dependent
Variable</td><td>Eq.</td><td>k</td><td>R^2</td><td>b</td><td>Durbin-
Watson</td><td>Runs</td></tr>
<tr><td colspan="7">1938-1965 (n = 28)</td></tr>
<tr><td>Total exp.[a]</td><td>7.1</td><td>1</td><td>.71</td><td>3,849.6678</td><td>1.64505</td><td>11</td></tr>
<tr><td>Current exp.</td><td>7.2[b]</td><td>3</td><td>.93</td><td>—</td><td>.79358[c]</td><td>5[d]</td></tr>
<tr><td>Total revs.</td><td>7.1</td><td>1</td><td>.78</td><td>2,891.3923</td><td>1.73615</td><td>13</td></tr>
<tr><td>Defense exp.[a]</td><td>8.1[b]</td><td>5</td><td>.82</td><td>—</td><td>1.58527[e]</td><td>15</td></tr>
<tr><td>Cur. def. exp.</td><td>7.2[b]</td><td>3</td><td>.94</td><td>—</td><td>.81442[c]</td><td>7</td></tr>
<tr><td>Def./exp. ratio</td><td>8.1[b]</td><td>5</td><td>.85</td><td>—</td><td>1.25461[e]</td><td>15</td></tr>
<tr><td>CLI</td><td>7.2[b]</td><td>3</td><td>.93</td><td>—</td><td>.57014[c]</td><td>5[d]</td></tr>
<tr><td>Change CLI</td><td>7.1</td><td>1</td><td>.22</td><td>1.2590</td><td>1.70692</td><td>7[d]</td></tr>
<tr><td colspan="7">1943-1965 (n = 23)</td></tr>
<tr><td>Total exp.</td><td>7.1</td><td>1</td><td>.52</td><td>3,261.2780</td><td>1.79702</td><td>13</td></tr>
<tr><td>Current exp.</td><td>7.2</td><td>3</td><td>.93</td><td>—</td><td>.80738[c]</td><td>5[d]</td></tr>
<tr><td>Total revs.</td><td>7.1</td><td>1</td><td>.67</td><td>2,817.0396</td><td>1.80107</td><td>12</td></tr>
<tr><td>Defense exp.</td><td>8.1</td><td>5</td><td>.68</td><td>—</td><td>2.15802</td><td>14</td></tr>
<tr><td>Cur. def. exp.</td><td>7.2</td><td>3</td><td>.93</td><td>—</td><td>.82550[c]</td><td>7</td></tr>
<tr><td>Def./exp. ratio</td><td>8.1</td><td>5</td><td>.94</td><td>—</td><td>2.17055</td><td>16</td></tr>
<tr><td>CLI</td><td>7.2</td><td>3</td><td>.92</td><td>—</td><td>.58745[c]</td><td>5[d]</td></tr>
<tr><td>Change CLI</td><td>7.1</td><td>1</td><td>.11</td><td>1.0899</td><td>1.70885</td><td>7</td></tr>
</table>

[a] in millions of 1960 pesos.

[b] D_i codings in Equations 7.2 and 8.1 are treatments of the 1952 shift. In the case of Def./exp., D_j in Equation 8.1 is a treatment of the 1948 shift. In the case of Def./exp. ratio, D_j in Equation 8.1 is a treatment of the 1945 shift.

[c] H_0 of no positive, first-order autocorrelation rejected at the .01 level using the Durbin-Watson d-statistic.

[d] H_0 of random distribution of the residuals rejected at the point .01 level using the Geary Sign test.

[e] H_0 of no positive, first-order autocorrelation is in the indeterminant range using the Durbin-Watson d-statistic.

Part b
Chow's F-Statistics
on the Overlapping Periods
1938-1965 and 1943-1965

Dependent Variable	F	Degrees of Freedom	Significance Level
Total exp.	.425	5,22	$p > .05$
Current exp.	.008	5,20	$p > .05$
Total revs.	.214	5,22	$p > .05$
Defense exp.	1.906	5,18	$p > .05$
Cur. def. exp.	.007	5,20	$p > .05$
Def./exp. ratio	5.132	5,18	$p < .01$
CLI	.041	5,20	$p > .05$
Change CLI	.361	5,22	$p > .05$

Part c
Dummy Variable Regressions
on the Period 1938-1952 (n = 15)

Dependent Variable	Eq.a	k	R^2	Durbin-Watson	Runs
Total exp.	7.1	1	.74	1.41248	8
Current exp.	7.1	1	.80	.37611[b]	3
Total revs.	7.1	1	.75	1.11234	8
Defense exp.	7.2	3	.84	1.50666	7
Cur. def. exp.	7.1	1	.90	.93194[c]	5
Def./exp. ratio	7.2	3	.82	.90553[c]	7
CLI	7.1	1	.69	.35141[b]	3
Change CLI	7.1	1	.78	1.83260	9
Total exp.	7.2	3	.78	1.68191	10
Current exp.	7.2	3	.94	1.00942[c]	5
Total revs.	7.2	3	.81	1.43099[c]	12
Defense exp.	8.1	5	.90	2.44874	9
Cur. def. exp.	7.2	3	.96	1.93922	7
Def./exp. ratio	8.1	5	.95	2.24916	11
CLI	7.2	3	.86	.71590[c]	5
Change CLI	7.2	3	.86	2.56508	10

[a]All equations in rows 1 through 8 omit treatments of the 1943 transition period. In the case of Def. exp., D_i in Equation 7.2 is a treatment of the 1948 shift. In the case of Def./exp. ratio, D_i in Equation 7.2 is a treatment of the 1945 shift. All equations in the second section, rows 9 to 16, include treatments of the 1943 transition. The second section equation for Def. exp. therefore includes treatments of the 1943 and 1948 shifts. The second section equation for Def./exp. ratio included treatments of the 1943 and 1945 period.

[b]H_0 of no positive, first-order autocorrelation rejected at the .01 level using the Durbin-Watson d-statistic.

[c]H_0 of no positive, first-order autocorrelation is in the indeterminant range using the Durbin-Watson d-statistic.

Part d
$\bar{R}^2$ *Tests (n = 15)*

Dependent Variable	R^2		$\bar{R}^2$
	Eq. 7.1/7.2	Eq. 7.2/8.1	
Total exp.	.74	.78	.72
Current exp.	.80	.94	.92
Total revs.	.75	.81	.76
Defense exp.	.84[a]	.90[b]	.84[c]
Cur. def. exp.	.90	.96	.95
Def./exp. ratio	.82[a]	.95[b]	.92[c]
CLI	.69	.86	.82
Change CLI	.78	.86	.82

Note: These tests pertain to the equations presented in part c.

[a] Three predictors.

[b] Five predictors.

[c] Corrections on Equation 8.1. R^2 corrections on Equation 7.2 with 3 predictors are Def. exp. (.80) and Def./exp. ratio (.77).

tive R²'s in all but the case of total expenditures in 1960 pesos. Although the improvement is only very slight in the case of total revenues in 1960 pesos, the introduction of dummy variables that detect the 1943 transition effects does increase the amount of explained variance in the remaining series.

Summary and Interpretation of the Results

The impact of the 1943 transition from traditional to populist authoritarian rule was less dramatic than the 1952 shift from populist rule to the era of the hegemonic crisis (see Table 8.6). While the 1952 transition altered the trends in five of the policy indicators (total expenditures in current pesos, defense expenditures in 1960 pesos, defense expenditures in current pesos, the proportion of total expenditures devoted to defense, and the CLI), Chow's F-tests show that the 1943 shift had a similar impact on only the proportion of total expenditures devoted to defense.

A more generalized impact of the 1943 shift is found, however, when

Table 8.6   **Budget Policies: Summary of the 1943 Transition:**
From Traditional to Populist Authoritarian Rule

Dependent Variable	Parameter Change?	Autocorrelation Resolved?	$\bar{R}^2$ Increase?
Total exp.	no	—	no
Current exp.	no	yes	yes
Total revs.	no	—	yes
Defense exp.	no	—	yes
Cur. def. exp.	no	yes	yes
Def./exp. ratio	yes	yes	yes
CLI	no	yes	yes
Change CLI	no	—	yes

one examines the summary results from the tests for autocorrelation and increases in the explained variance. Autocorrelation is detected by the Durbin–Watson d-statistic in four of the series when equations which ignore the 1943 interruption are estimated on the combined pre- and post-transition period. Subsequent inclusion of dummy variables tapping that shift reduces autocorrelation problems in all four instances. Finally, a consideration of the 1943 transition from traditional to populist rule helps to increase the proportion of explained variance in seven of the eight policy indicators.

The first conclusion to be drawn from this section, therefore, is that the erosion of the populist coalition in 1952 had a more dramatic impact on the eight policy indicators than the 1943 transition from traditional to populist authoritarian rule. Nevertheless, the 1943 coalition change is important for understanding the trends in all of the series except total expenditures in 1960 pesos. (Total revenues might also be excluded from the series that were influenced by the 1943 transition.)

This said, note that the post-1943 trends in all eight of the series are in the direction predicted by the authoritarian thesis. Total expenditures and defense expenditures (in both current and real pesos) and the proportion of total expenditures devoted to defense all increased after the populist coalition came to power in 1943. Revenues did not rise sharply until 1947 when the government began to receive income from the recently nationalized corporations in the transportation and communication sectors. Despite a sharp increase at the end of World War II, the cost-of-living index did not begin to rise steadily until the late 1940s, when the economy began to show the effects of the completion of consumer goods import substitution industrialization. Finally, the size of the government's annual operating deficit showed a generally increasing trend through 1948 when the gap between expenditures and revenues began to be closed.

This congruence between the directions of the actual post-1943 trends and the predictions of the authoritarian thesis is of interest because no similar consistency was noted in the preceding section, where the pre- and post-1952 trends were examined. While the 1952 coalition change thus had a more dramatic effect than the 1943 shift from traditional to populist authoritarian rule, the post-1943 trends were more frequently in the directions predicted by the authoritarian formulation.

This finding that the 1943 trend shifts were gradual but in the directions predicted by the authoritarian thesis suggests that the standard interpretation of the populist coalition may be misleading. It should be clear by now that observed policy changes do not permit the researcher to draw inferences about changes in the identities and motivations of the policymakers. Nevertheless, when the evidence from the previous chapters is combined with the results produced in this section, the overwhelming impression is that the populist coalition—domestic industrialists, the military, urban workers, and producers of nonexportable agricultural goods—may not have actually come to power on June 4, 1943 when the military moved to overthrow President Castillo. While certain elements of the populist alliance certainly did take control at that point, it would seem more accurate to argue that the populist coalition was an extremely fragile grouping that evolved only very slowly between 1943 and 1945/1946, existed as an integrated alliance of forces only during the 1946/1947 period, and then began to disintegrate slowly until its apparently abrupt dissolution in 1952. Insofar as one is willing to assume that there was a direct connection between what policymakers wanted to do and what was actually done during this period, such an interpretation of the populist coalition would help to clarify (1) the changes in Argentina's industrialization and foreign policies that began to become apparent in 1947, (2) the shifts in Perón's relations with labor after his election in 1946, and (3) why the post-1943 trend changes in the eight policy indicators examined here were more gradual than abrupt. The 1943 coup may not have marked an immediate shift from the era of domination of one coalition to that of another. While the traditional authoritarian alliance may have been abruptly displaced at that point, there may have been a delay before a new dominant coalition took control. It was during that period of delay that policies—possibly even including the military's interest in promoting basic industries—began to drift in the populist direction.

The exception to this rule of immediate post-1943 drift is in the area of defense spending. Chow's F-tests indicated that the proportion of total expenditures devoted to defense did follow a different trend in the pre- and post-1943 eras. Inspection of Table 8.4 appears to indicate that the trend in defense expenditures in 1960 pesos was also altered in 1943. The abrupt 1943 shifts in these two series are of some significance, of course, because the military was the one element of the populist coalition that actually did come to power in 1943.

It is possible that neither of these shifts was the result of the transition to populist authoritarian rule. The upward trends in both indicators began in 1941, prior to the 1943 coup. Subsequent increases through 1945 may have been more the direct result of World War II than of the change in Argentina's dominant coalitions.

It is quite likely, however, that the 1941–1945 increases in these two indicators might not have been so large had the military not taken power in 1943. The Castillo government (1942–1943) had resisted U.S. pressures to abandon its neutral position and declare war on the Axis nations; but at least some of the military officers of the Castillo administration favored a compromise with the United States that would make Argentina eligible for U.S. Lend Lease aid.[12] A number of these pro-U.S. officers apparently participated in the 1943 coup that ousted Castillo. Had those elements been able to dominate the immediate post-1943 government, it seems likely that U.S. assistance might have been obtained and that there would therefore have been less need for sharp domestic increases in defense spending between 1941 and 1945.

The point here, of course, is that the pro-U.S. faction of the military was quickly subordinated by pro-Axis officers; and the Argentine government consequently took on nationalistic and anti-American characteristics. This shift quite obviously eliminated the option of acquiring U.S. military aid, but Argentina's adoption of an anti-U.S., pro-Axis foreign policy also had the more important effect of increasing the perceived U.S. and Brazilian threats to the nation's security. Had the efforts to obtain Axis military aid been successful, major increases in Argentina's own military spending might still have been avoided. Efforts to obtain German aid were launched but were apparently not successful. Argentina was therefore forced to ensure its national security by increasing its own military spending.

The point is that Argentina's shifting position on the role of the United States in World War II, not the war itself, may account for the sharp

1941–1945 increases in defense spending. If Argentina had become pro-U.S. or even had remained completely neutral, there might have been less impetus to increase military expenditures dramatically. The 1943 coup and the rapid emergence of the pro-Axis officers made the sharp increases necessary.

The 1966 Transition: From the Era of the Hegemonic Crisis to Bureaucratic–Authoritarian Rule

I shall focus on the impact of the 1966 shift from the era of the hegemonic crisis to the period of bureaucratic–authoritarian rule. The questions and methodologies are identical to those developed in the previous sections. Only two changes need be noted. First, there is, of course, a shift in the time periods employed in the analyses in this section. The pre- and post-transition period now includes the 1953–1970 interval. The results from regressions on that period are compared with those from the pretransition period, 1953–1965. The second difference concerns the dummy variable D_i in Equation 7.2. In this section, D_i is coded zero for the 1953–1965 period and one for the 1966–1970 interval.

It will be recalled that the authoritarian thesis maintains that the bureaucratic–authoritarian coalition (large and efficient industrialists, foreign capitalists, a segment of the military, and technocrats) came to power in 1966 with views toward controlling inflation, improving the operating efficiency of the state, and balancing the budget. Inflation should therefore have been slowed in the post-1966 period if the authoritarian thesis is valid. Overall spending should have been decreased. New revenues should have been raised. Since the military was included in the coalition and the Ongania and Levingston administrations were allegedly seeking to exclude the popular sectors from the political life of the nation, the authoritarian thesis also seems to imply that military spending should have increased after 1966.

The post-1966 bureaucratic–authoritarian governments did in fact make progress in a number of these areas. Examination of the slopes from the overlapping regressions in Table 8.7, part a and Figures 8.3, 8.5, 8.8, and 8.9 reveals that total revenues in 1960 pesos and defense expenditures in current pesos increased, while the rate of change in the cost-of-living index and the size of the government's operating deficit declined after 1966. The downward trend in the proportion of total expenditures devoted to defense continued in the post-transition period, but the rate of decrease was at least slowed after 1966 (Figure 8.6). Finally, the gentle downward trend in defense expenditures in 1960 pesos in the 1953–1965 period was actually reversed and became slightly positive when the 1953–1970 interval was examined (Figure 8.4). Only if one focuses on total expenditures in either 1960 or current pesos does a pattern inconsistent with the authoritarian thesis emerge. While total expenditures should have fallen after 1966, they actually rose at an annual average rate nearly 527 million 1960 pesos higher during the 1953–1970 period than during the 1953–1965 interval. Total expenditures in current pesos increased at a rate almost 123.8 percent faster during the 1953–1970 period than during the 1953–1965 interval.

Unfortunately for the authoritarian thesis, only one of the post-1966 trend changes supporting that argument is statistically significant. As the results in Table 8.7, part b show, the null hypothesis of identical pre- and post-1966 regression parameters can be rejected only in three instances (total expenditures in current pesos, defense expenditures in current pesos, and the CLI) when Chow's F-test is applied. In other words, Chow's F-tests permit one to conclude that the regression parameters for these three policies were different in the two overlapping periods, and only one of those significant shifts (the post-1966 increase in defense expenditures in current pesos) was in the direction predicted by the authoritarian thesis. As the alternative integrated formulation hypothesized, none of the 1953–1965 trends in the remaining five series were apparently altered significantly as a result of the 1966 shift to bureaucratic–authoritarian rule.

The lack of impact of the 1966 transition is indicated in another way. When Equation 7.1—which omits variables that tap the effects of the 1966 coalition change—is estimated on the 1953–1970 period, the Durbin–Watson d-statistic and the Geary Sign test detect positive first-order autocorrelation problems only in the cases of total expenditures in current pesos, defense expenditures in current pesos, and the CLI. Although the use of Equation 7.2 helps to resolve these autocorrelation difficulties when they develop (see Table 8.7, part d), the important finding here is that the transition to bureaucratic–authoritarian rule apparently is not an important consideration for understanding the 1953–1970 trends in total expenditures in 1960 pesos, total revenues in 1960 pesos, defense expenditures in 1960 pesos, the proportion of total expenditures devoted to defense, or the rate of change in the cost-of-living index.

This conclusion is modified only very slightly when the R^2's from Equation 7.2 are compared with the R^2's from Equation 7.1 in Table 8.7, part d. The insertion of dummy variables that tap the effects of the 1966 transition to bureaucratic–authoritarian rule increases the proportion of explained variance only in total expenditures in current pesos, defense expenditures in current pesos, CLI, and total revenues in 1960 pesos. Chow's F- and autocorrelation tests had already indicated the impact of the establishment of bureaucratic–authoritarian rule on the first three of these series. Total revenues is an interesting addition; but in no other case is an explanation enhanced by a consideration of the transition from the era of the hegemonic crisis to bureaucratic–authoritarian rule.

Table 8.7   Budget Policies: Impact of the 1966 Transition

Part a
Overlapping regressions
(Equation 7.1, k = 1)

Dependent Variable	n	R^2	b	Durbin-Watson	Runs
1953-1970					
Total exp.[a]	18	.50	3,931.6349	1.91965	8
Current exp.	18	.82	67,726.6550	.19132[b]	3[c]
Total revs.	18	.77	5,531.6123	1.54071	7
Defense exp.[a]	18	.01	28.3978	1.82700	10
Cur. def. exp.	18	.84	9,429.1946	.24628[b]	5
Def./exp. ratio	18	.65	-.4999	1.89278	11
CLI	18	.87	39.4226	.16522[b]	3[c]
Change CLI	13	.00	.3488	1.55144	7
1953-1965					
Total exp.	13	.22	3,404.9879	1.90162	7
Current exp.	13	.89	30,265.2820	.61433	3
Total revs.	13	.49	3,717.1665	2.29159	6
Defense exp.	13	.02	-63.6659	1.89094	8
Cur. def. exp.	13	.89	4,697.2901	.63597	3
Def./exp. ratio	13	.55	-.5916	2.04921	9
CLI	13	.88	21.2341	.41227	3
Change CLI	13	.05	1.6636	1.71039	3

[a] in millions of 1960 pesos.

[b] H_0 of no positive, first-order autocorrelation rejected at the .01 level using the Durbin-Watson d-statistic.

[c] H_0 of random distribution of the residuals rejected at the point .01 level using the Geary sign test.

Part b
Chow's F-Statistics
on the Overlapping Periods
1953-1970 and 1953-1965 (degrees of freedom 5,12)

	F	Significance Level
Total exp.	.020	$p>.05$
Current exp.	54.851	$p<.01$
Total revs.	1.758	$p>.05$
Defense exp.	1.565	$p>.05$
Cur. def. exp.	38.848	$p<.01$
Def./exp. ratio	.629	$p>.05$
CLI	23.160	$p<.01$
Change CLI	.307	$p>.05$

Part c
Dummy Variable Regressions
on the Period 1953-1970 (Equation 7.2, n = 18, k = 3)

Dependent Variable	R^2	Durbin-Watson	Runs
Total exp.	.51	1.92606	10
Current exp.	.99	1.39004[a]	7
Total revs.	.85	2.23255	8
Defense exp.	.07	1.98276	10
Cur. def. exp.	.98	1.03159[a]	5
Def./exp. ratio	.67	2.01197	11
CLI	.99	1.07416[a]	6
Change CLI	.10	1.72390	6

[a]H_0 of no positive, first-order autocorrelation is in the indeterminant range using the Durbin-Watson d-statistic.

Part d
$\bar{R}^2$ *Tests (n = 18)*

Dependent Variable	R^2 Eq. 7.1	R^2 Eq. 7.2	$\bar{R}^2$
Total exp.	.50	.51	.50
Current exp.	.82	.99	.99
Total revs.	.77	.85	.82
Defense exp.	.01	.07	.00
Cur. def. exp.	.84	.98	.98
Def./exp. ratio	.65	.67	.60
CLI	.87	.99	.99
Change CLI	.00	.10	.00

Table 8.8   Budget Policies: Summary of the 1966 Transition: From the Era of the Hegemonic Crisis to Bureaucratic-Authoritarian Rule

Dependent Variable	Parameter Change?	Autocorrelation Resolved?	$\bar{R}^2$ Increase?
Total exp.	no	—	no
Current exp.	yes	yes	yes
Total revs.	no	—	yes
Defense exp.	no	—	no
Cur. def. exp.	yes	yes	yes
Def./exp. ratio	no	—	no
CLI	yes	yes	yes
Change CLI	no	—	no

Summary and Interpretation of the Results

While at least one of the three tests showed that the 1943 and 1952 transitions affected seven and six of the policies, respectively, the 1966 transition to bureaucratic–authoritarian rule had an impact on only four of the series considered in this chapter (see Table 7.8). In terms of the scope of its impact on these policies, the 1966 shift emerges as having been the least significant of the three coalition changes.

It is possible to go a step further. Although the tests in this section revealed that the establishment of bureaucratic–authoritarian rule had at least some impact on the trends in total expenditures in current pesos, defense expenditures in current pesos, the CLI, and total revenues in 1960 pesos, the shifts in the first three of those policies may be attributable to the fact that they are linked with changes in the Argentine cost-of-living index. The CLI did rise sharply over the 1953–1970 period and, once again, the Equation 7.1 estimations on that interval yield standardized regression coefficients that are remarkably similar: CLI, .932; total expenditures in current pesos, .908; defense expenditures in current pesos, .916. This similarity suggests that the post-1966 shifts in the trends may have had more to do with increases in the CLI than with the 1966 transition to bureaucratic–authoritarian rule. This conclusion is supported by the fact that no parameter changes or autocorrelation problems are detected in connection with any of the deflated series. The point here, therefore, is that if one discounts the results from the analyses on total expenditures in current pesos, defense expenditures in current pesos, and the CLI as being falsely attributable to the 1966 transition, the establishment of bureaucratic–authoritarian rule had an impact on only one of the remaining five policies. Consideration of the 1966 transition increases one's ability to explain the variance in total revenues in 1960 pesos. In comparison, the 1943 transition produced one parameter shift, resolved one example of autocorrelation, and provided four increases in the R^2 in the remaining five policies. The 1952 transition resulted in a parameter shift in two of the remaining five series, resolved autocorrelation in two instances, and produced an R^2 increase in three cases.

One additional series of points might be noted. In the discussion above, it was observed that the figures and the parameters in Table 8.7, part a showed that the post-1966 trends had at least moved in the directions predicted by the authoritarian thesis in six series: defense expenditures in 1960 pesos, defense expenditures in current pesos, the proportion of total expenditures devoted to defense; the rate of change in the CLI, the size of the deficit, and total revenues in 1960 pesos. This point is raised here again because the initial post-1966 changes in the first three of these policies were in directions inconsistent with the authoritarian formulation. Although defense expenditures in 1960 pesos generally rose after 1966, for example, defense spending actually fell between 1966 and 1967, so that by 1970 it was only barely above its 1966 level. Although the rate of decline in the proportion of total expenditures devoted to defense was slower in the 1953–1970 interval than during the 1953–1965 period, the share of overall spending that the military received declined steadily between 1966 and its all-time nadir of only 12.46 percent in 1968. Finally, although defense expenditures in current pesos rose steadily after 1966 (as the authoritarian thesis predicts), the rate of increase between 1966 and 1967 was actually slower than it had been between 1964 and 1966 under the civilian, nontechnocratic, nonbureaucratic–authoritarian administration of President Illia.

These findings in regard to the initial post-1966 changes in defense expenditures in 1960 pesos, defense expenditures in current pesos, and the proportion of total expenditures devoted to defense are consistent with two points raised in Chapter 5. First, the predicted increases in these three series did not begin until after the leaders of the 1966 military junta had been removed from their cabinet-level positions. In other words, it was not until the supposedly unified military of the bureaucratic–authoritarian period had begun to show signs of strain that the policy trends associated with bureaucratic–authoritarian rule began to be evidenced. The second point is perhaps more subtle. Although there was an initial wave of popular protest against the policies of the Ongania administration, it was not until 1968–1969 that sustained opposition to the bureaucratic–authoritarian government began to develop. The declining control that Augusto Vandor had over the Argentine labor movement, the decay in the Pax Obrera and the sharp increases in worker opposition to the government coincided closely with the 1968–1969 increases in the three military-related policy indicators. A somewhat analogous post-1966 shift was detected in Chapter 7, where the indicators of Argentine labor policy were reviewed. The share of the nation's GDP received by workers declined during the era of bureaucratic–authoritarian rule, as the authoritarian thesis predicted; but that decline did not begin until 1968.

The point to be noted, therefore, is that while total expenditures in either 1960 or current pesos never moved in the direction predicted by the authoritarian thesis in the post-1966 period, the trends in defense expenditures in 1960 pesos, defense expenditures in current pesos, the proportion of total expenditures devoted to defense, and the share of the GDP received by workers all started out in the wrong direction. In terms of all six of these series, in other words, the bureaucratic–authoritarian administration of General Ongania began by implementing "nonbureaucratic–authoritarian" policies. The post-1966 trends in the last four of these series did eventually shift, of course, in the directions predicted by the authoritarian formulation; but those shifts did not occur until after the original leaders of the 1966 military junta had been replaced and labor opposition had begun to pose a serious threat to the government.

Delays in implementing preferred policies and simple inadvertence may account for these lags between the 1966 coalition change and the trend shifts around 1968. The integrated formulation, of course, predicts that such delays should develop when the public bureaucracies are large and extensively unionized, elites are unable to press their demands and lack pools of previously unallocated resources, and a balance of forces exists in the policy-making arena. It is also possible, however, that changes within the bureaucratic–authoritarian coalition and alterations in the resistance that Ongania faced may account for the trend shifts around 1968. This possibility would suggest that the bureaucratic–authoritarian coalition evolved incrementally toward a bureaucratic–authoritarian policy alignment during the 1966–1968 period. The leaders of the 1966 coup that toppled Illia may not have come to power with precise policy prescriptions in mind.[13] The policies that were eventually adopted may not have been inspired by the initial goals of the leaders of the 1966 coup, as the authoritarian thesis suggests they were. The evidence here is only indirect and extremely tentative, but it is at least consistent with the hypothesis that the standard interpretation of the post-1966 coalition may be misleading. Considerations cited above suggest that the populist coalition may have evolved in significant ways in the period between 1943 and 1952; the evidence outlined here suggests that a similar pattern of evolution and change may have characterized the post-1966 period. The bureaucratic–authoritarian coalition may have been dynamic in even its earliest stages. Its decisionmakers may have been highly pragmatic. The bureaucratic–authoritarian policies that were eventually adopted may have been developed as new elements entered and exited the post-1966 policymaking arena and as the decisionmakers adapted to the real problems they discovered after coming to power. In any event, the bureaucratic–authoritarian government that came to power in 1966 was not bureaucratic–authoritarian in terms of the initial post-1966 changes in total expenditures in 1960 pesos, total expenditures in current pesos, defense expenditures in 1960 pesos, defense expenditures in current pesos, the proportion of total expenditures devoted to defense, or the share of the GDP received by workers.

The three remaining series (the rate of change in the CLI, the size of the deficit, and total revenues in 1960 pesos) did have initial and general post-1966 trends in the directions predicted by the authoritarian thesis. Even in these areas, however, an examination of Figures 8.3, 8.8, and 8.9 shows that the trends under the nonbureaucratic–authoritarian governments of the pre-1966 period were frequently in the same direction as during the administrations of Ongania and Levingston. If in some areas the bureaucratic–authoritarian governments never succeeded in adopting bureaucratic–authoritarian policies and were delayed in adopting such policies in other areas, Ongania and Levingston never succeeded in being more than marginally more bureaucratic–authoritarian than the nontechnocratic, nonbureaucratic–authoritarian governments of the pre-1966 period.

Conclusions

An overall summary of the analyses in this chapter is presented in Table 8.9. In part a, the impact of the three transitions on each of the policy indicators is reviewed (Y = *yes*, N = *no*). Part b summarizes the scope of the impact on the eight series.

The 1966 transition to bureaucratic–authoritarian rule holds few surprises for the integrated formulation. As that thesis predicts, the 1966 shift had only a marginal impact in comparison with the 1943 and 1952 coalition changes that took place prior to, or roughly in conjunction with, (1) the expansion and unionization of the Argentine public sector, (2) the establishment of a tendency toward chronic instability in Argentina's cabinet-level leaders, (3) the exhaustion of the pool of previously unallocated resources that elites had at their disposal, and (4) the initiation of a stalemate in the policymaking arena. True, distinct pre- and post-1966 regression parameters describe the trends in total expenditures in current pesos, defense expenditures in current pesos, and the CLI. However, it is impossible to say whether those parameter shifts resulted from the shift to bureaucratic–authoritarian rule or simply reflect the fact that the Argentine policymakers were including CLI increases in their budget decisions. If the analyses of these three series are therefore discounted, consideration of the 1966 transition serves only to produce a .05 increase in the proportion of the variance explained in total revenues.

Some support for the authoritarian thesis does appear if one considers the direction of the post-1966 trends. Although some of the pre- and post-1966 shifts were only marginal, post-1966 trends in six of the series (defense expenditures in 1960 pesos, defense expenditures in current pesos, the proportion of total expenditures devoted to defense, the rate of change in the CLI, the size of the deficit, and total revenues in 1960 pesos) were at least in the directions predicted by the authoritarian thesis. The initial changes in the first three of these series were in directions inconsistent with that argument, however. The three remaining series had initial and general post-1966 trends in the predicted directions. However, the fact that the trends in those indicators were frequently identical under both bureaucratic–authoritarian and non-bureaucratic–authoritarian administrations raises questions about the uniqueness of the impact of the 1966 transition.

An additional point might be made in connection with the 1966 shift. It is perilous to draw inferences about *why* policies were made on the basis of these policy indicators, and the integrated formulation itself suggests that leaders should meet resistance when they attempt to change policies in bureaucratized contexts. Nevertheless, it should be emphasized that the findings in this chapter are consistent with those obtained in foregoing sections. Specifically, both the qualitative and quantitative evidence suggests that the bureaucratic–authoritarian coalition may have evolved in important ways during the 1966–1968 period. The Ongania administration may not have been bureaucratic–authoritarian in the true sense until the leaders of the original junta had been replaced and increasing labor unrest in 1968 forced the

Table 8.9 Budget Policies: Overall Summary

Part a
By Policy Indicator

	Parameter Change?			Autocorrelation Detected?			Autocorrelation Resolved?			R̄² Increase?		
	1943	1952	1966	1943	1952	1966	1943	1952	1966	1943	1952	1966
Total exp.	n	n	n	n	n	n	—	—	—	n	n	n
Current exp.	n	y	y	y	y	y	y	y	y	y	y	y
Total revs.	n	n	n	n	n	n	—	—	—	y^a	y^b	y^c
Defense exp.	n	y	n	n	y	n	—	y	—	y	y	n
Cur. def. exp.	n	y	y	y	y	y	y	y	y	y	y	y
Def./exp. ratio	y	y	n	y	y	y	y	n	y	y	y	y
CLI	n	y	y	y	y	n	y	y	—	y	y	n
Change CLI	n	n	n	n	n	n	—	—	—	y	n	n

^{a} .01 increase.
^{b} .02 increase.
^{c} .05 increase.

Part b
By Transition

	Parameter Changes	Autocorrelation Detected	Autocorrelation Resolved	R̄² Increases
1943 transition	1(1)^a	4(1)	4(1)	7(4)
1952 transition	5(2)	5(2)	4(2)	6(3)
1966 transition	3(0)	3(0)	3(0)	4(1)

^{a} Bracketed figures are the totals with total expenditures in current pesos, defense expenditures in current pesos, and the CLI excluded.

president to abandon his conciliatory policy toward labor. If so, the period of classical bureaucratic–authoritarian rule in Argentina may have been extremely short. If the bureaucratic–authoritarian policy alignment did not come into existence until sometime in 1968, the bureaucratic–authoritarian coalition was effectively fragmented by the outbreak of major protests in the Cordobazo of 1969.

The statistical findings from the analyses of the 1952 transition from populist authoritarian rule provide support for the authoritarian thesis. That shift was clearly more dramatic than one would expect under the integrated formulation. Nevertheless, the evidence seems to shift in favor of the integrated thesis by reason of the fact that the pre- and post-1952 trend alterations were generally not in the directions predicted by the authoritarian formulation. Only the trend in total revenues in 1960 pesos clearly moved in the direction predicted by the authoritarian argument. In the remaining series, the pre-1952 trends were not reversed. At most, they were only slightly dampened. This evidence is consistent, of course, with the integrated formulation that it is difficult to reverse long-term policy trends.

The authoritarian and integrated formulations provide identical predictions in regard to the impact of the 1943 transition from traditional to populist authoritarian rule. It is in this area that perhaps the most interesting findings emerge. There is overwhelming support for the hypothesis that the populist era is important for understanding the trends in seven of the eight series. However, the fact that only one significant Chow's F was obtained on the 1943 transition suggests that the populist authoritarian coalition may not have come to power as an integrated alliance when the military moved to overthrow President Castillo in 1943. As the more qualitative evidence in Chapters 4–6 suggests, the populist coalition may have evolved only very slowly during the 1943–1945 or 1946 period, existed as an integrated unit only during the 1946/47 interval, and then began to disintegrate slowly until its apparently abrupt dissolution in 1952. It is difficult to work one's way backward along the policy-to-motivation link. Direct evidence is clearly needed to document that interpretation. Nevertheless, such a revised view of the populist period is at least consistent with the evidence reviewed here; the quantitative labor policy indicators discussed in Chapter 5; and the more qualitative discussions of Argentina's labor, foreign, industrialization, and governmental organization policies. As was the case with the bureaucratic–authoritarian period, a dynamic interpretation of the populist period may be more accurate than the existing standard interpretation.

Several additional miscellaneous points might be made. First, the trends in the proportion of total expenditures devoted to defense and defense expenditures in 1960 pesos underwent downward shifts in 1945 and 1948, respectively. The former trend change may have been the result of the end of World War II; but it is of interest to note that it corresponds with an assertion in

Chapter 6 that there was a marked decrease in all but symbolic nationalism shortly after Perón came to power in February 1946. With reduced Argentine–U.S. tensions and the reinsertion of Argentina in President Truman's postwar rearmament programs in June 1947, there may have been less need for Argentina to finance massive military outlays. The 1948 shift in defense expenditures in 1960 pesos corresponds (roughly, of course) with the onset of the 1948–1949 recession and the post-1949 decreases in workers' real income and their share of the GDP, which were noted in Chapter 7. Thus, even though the evidence here is once again not conclusive, it at least suggests that Perón may already have been beginning to dismantle the populist coalition by 1948–1949.

Either of these interpretations of the 1945 and 1948 reductions in the proportion of total expenditures devoted to defense and defense expenditures in 1960 pesos would be reinforced by findings that show similar changes in total expenditures in 1960 pesos and total revenues. Trend alterations in both of these series appear to be evident in Figures 8.1 and 8.3. Those shifts may have had important political implications. Unfortunately, however, even the weakest of the tests fails to detect any statistically significant changes in the pre- and post-1948 trends in these two series.

One final point should be made here. Of all of the policies examined in this and the preceding chapters, the integrated formulation seemed at the outset to have the greatest potential utility for understanding the long-term trends in total expenditures in 1960 pesos, total revenues in 1960 pesos, and government employment. Failure of the integrated formulation in these three areas might have been taken as ample cause for abandoning the argument.

The substantive rationale for focusing on these three series is clear. Since about 1950, high expenditure levels, low revenue totals, resultant government deficits, and high levels of public employment have frequently been seen in Argentina as being among the principal causes of that nation's economic problems. Efforts to reduce overall expenditures, increase revenues, and reduce the number of public employees therefore have frequently held high priority in the policy goals of Argentina's political elites. Unfortunately, these areas are also the ones in which the integrated formulation predicts that successful bureaucratic resistance to elite pressures should be the most likely. The evidence in Tables 7.9 and 8.9 shows overwhelming support for this proposition. With only minor exceptions, changing dominant coalitions had little effect on these three series once (1) the public sector had become large and extensively unionized, (2) the elites lost their ability to press their demands in persistent and unambiguous fashion, (3) the pool of previously unallocated resources that elites had at their command was exhausted, and (4) a balance or stalemate began to exist among the forces in the policymaking arena. In these areas in particular, it really did cease to matter who governed at the top.

Figure 8.1 Total Expenditures in 1960 Pesos

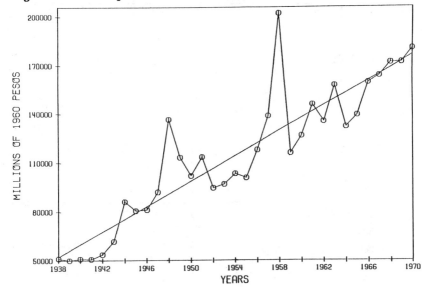

Figure 8.2 Total Expenditures in Current Pesos

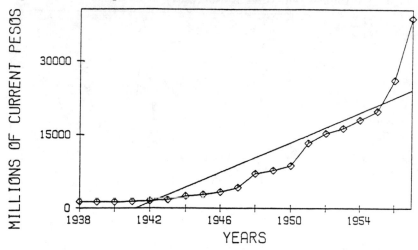

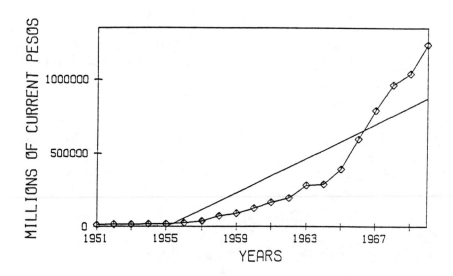

Figure 8.3 Total Revenues in 1960 Pesos

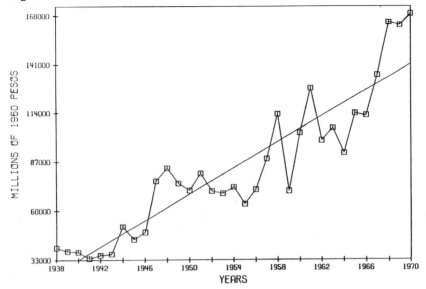

Figure 8.4 Defense Spending in 1960 Pesos

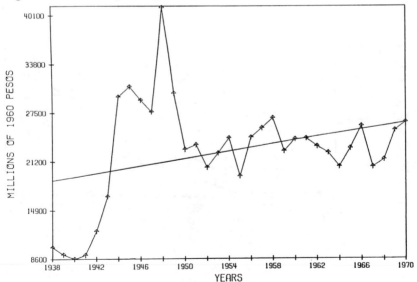

Figure 8.5 Defense Expenditures in Current Pesos

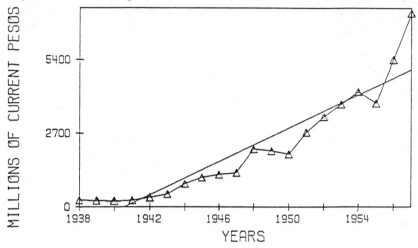

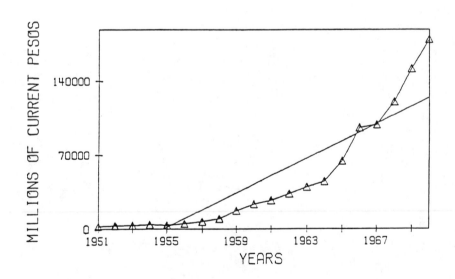

Figure 8.6 Defense Spending-Total Spending Ratio

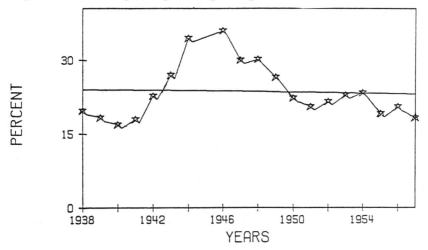

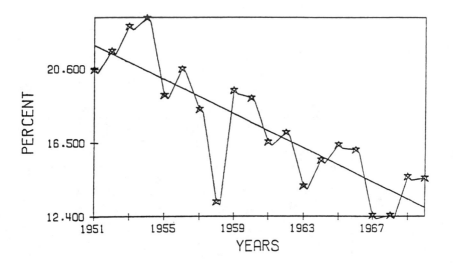

Figure 8.7 Cost-of-Living Index

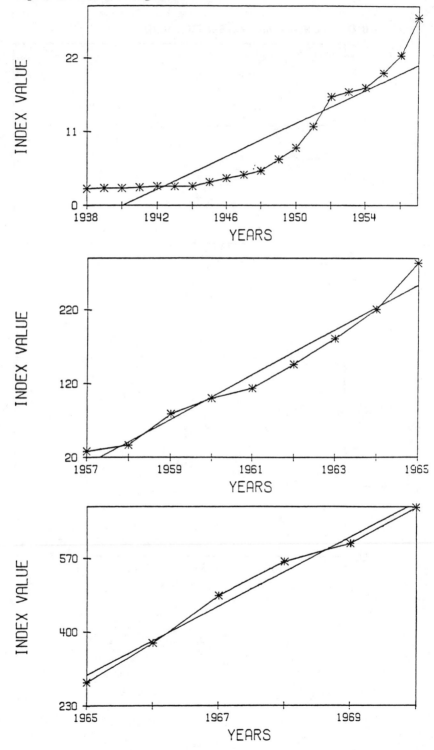

Figure 8.8 Change in the Cost-of-Living Index

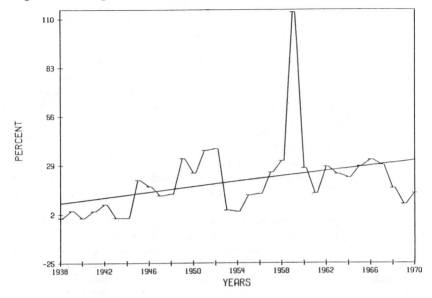

Figure 8.9 Deficit in 1960 Pesos

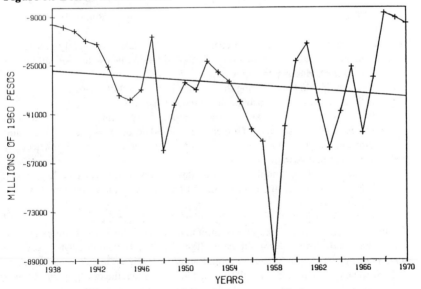

Notes

1. This statement combines the structuralist and monetarist interpretations of the causes of Argentina's inflation problems. It implies a concurrence with Diaz Alejandro (1970), who argues that while Argentina encountered an important economic bottleneck as it neared the completion of its consumer goods stage of import substitution industrialization, the impact of that structural limitation was exacerbated by the government's deficit spending. For a discussion of the economic crisis of the late 1940s, see Chapter 4.

2. For readings on the impact of the IMF, see Braun 1973 and the various selections in Ferrer et al. 1974.

3. The authoritarian thesis is mute, of course, on the effects of the 1952 transition from populist authoritarian rule to the era of the hegemonic crisis. However, mild versions of the 1966 transition effects seem to apply to the immediate post-1952 period.

4. The expenditure and revenue indicators are based on codings from the annual reports of the Argentine Finance and Treasury Ministries. Wherever possible, the original codings were cross-checked with reports in UN, Economic Commission on Latin America, Organization of American States, U.S. Department of State, and Stockholm International Peace Research Institute sources. Corrections were made in all reports to render the figures in calendar, rather than fiscal, years. Data on the Buenos Aires cost-of-living index are from Diaz Alejandro 1970 and various issues of *America en cifras* (published by the Organization of American States). This linked series was used as the deflator in the indicators, which are expressed in 1960 pesos.

5. These indicators supplement the discussion of other military-related factors in Chapters 4 and 5.

6. Even though the CLI and change in the CLI are traditionally considered policy outcomes rather than policy outputs, the discussion below occasionally refers to all eight of the series as public policies.

7. The rationale for exploring these points is presented in Chapter 5.

8. These points are extensively discussed in Chapter 6.

9. Figures 8.1 and 8.3 also appear to indicate a possible 1955 shift in total expenditures in 1960 pesos and total revenues in 1960 pesos. This possible 1955 shift was examined; but once again, even the weakest of the three tests failed to detect any trend changes in that year.

10. The rationale for adopting this procedure is presented in Chapter 7.

11. Note that the results in Table 8.5, part c are based on estimations from the 1938–1952 period.

12. In February 1943 the pro-Ally chief of the Argentine general staff urged President Castillo to arrange an accommodation with the United States so that Argentina could receive U.S. military aid (Potash 1969, 187). Immediately after the 1943 coup, Vice Admiral Segundo Storni, Ramirez's foreign minister, sent a memo to U.S. Secretary of State Cordell Hull in which he argued that the new government was really pro-Ally and requested that the United States begin to supply Argentina with Lend Lease materials. These points are presented with greater supportive detail in Chapter 6.

13. Writing in November 1966, Rowe notes that "At its inception, the movement of June 28, 1966, could be termed a *golpe* with revolutionary pretensions. Ideological vagueness and the lack of an organized cadre of supporters raised some doubt from the beginning as to its ability to evolve into a true revolution. Ideological vagueness plus the heterogeneous participation and support given [to] the movement also made the use of conventional labels . . . dubious at best" (1970, 476).

NINE

Conclusion

In almost all of the policy-related areas examined, the results were consistent with the integrated formulation, which unifies the authoritarian concern for dominant coalitions with the bureaucratic interest in public sector organizations and prior decisions. Argentina's dominant coalitions made a difference in determining what policies were made for whom and at whose expense during the eras of traditional and populist authoritarian rule. Who governed at the top influenced the policies in those years. Except in the areas of industrialization and foreign policies, those two coalitions succeeded in pushing Argentina in directions congruent with the interests of the alliance members.

The political elites failed to execute their desired public policies, however, as soon as (1) employment in the public sector expanded and became extensively unionized, (2) elites in high-level government positions began to show a pattern of chronic instability, (3) a generalized crisis of authority gripped the nation, and (4) government no longer possessed previously unallocated resources. The considerations needed to understand Argentina's public policies underwent a basic change as the new political elites who came to power in the postpopulist era were constrained by these four factors. They found it difficult to effect fundamental policy changes or go forward rapidly in new policy areas. It was almost impossible dramatically to reverse what had already been started.

The integrated formulation performed almost perfectly in areas most closely related to the public sector. Despite repeated efforts to reduce spending, increase revenues, and decrease the level of public employment, it simply ceased to matter very much who governed at the top (and therefore had de facto control). The integrated argument worked less well in other areas. Argentina's leaders from Perón to Levingston, for example, were finally able to begin implementing plans for basic industrial development and modernization of the nation's infrastructure that the military had been promoting since at least 1930. The post-1966 bureaucratic–authoritarian governments were in fact antilabor. These exceptions are important, but they can be explained within the integrated framework. Basic industrial development and modernization of the infrastructure were possible because new resources became available from international lending organizations in the 1950s. Even though the government's domestically available resources were already committed, these newly available funds increased the decisionmaking latitude of Argentina's policymakers. The leaders used the new international capital to expand into basic industrial development. The post-1966 deterioration in the position of labor can be similarly explained. It was a simple return to what had been the norm in Argentina since the late 1940s. While the workers' share of the GDP and real income fell after 1966, similar declines had occurred under nonexclusionary, nonbureaucratic–authoritarian, and even prolabor governments. The methods by which the post-1966 governments sought to exclude labor and depoliticize the system were reprises—intensified versions of repressive policies that had been enacted by previous administrations.

Implications for the Literature on Authoritarian Political Systems in Latin America

The existing literature treats the relationships between changing types of authoritarian rule and shifting public policies in Latin America at abstract theoretical or simple definitional levels. The goals and interests of the dominant coalitions are assumed to be directly and immediately translated into public policy outputs. What is done is done purposefully. "Who governs" determines what policies are made, for whom, and at whose expense.

The results of the present analysis cast doubts on this reasoning. Coalitions and the elites who represent them in the highest levels of government may be *willing* to adopt policies that maximize their gains, but there is no certainty that they will have the *opportunity* to execute the policies they prefer. There is no automatic link between the goals and interests of those who govern at the top and actual policy outputs.

Consequently, the authoritarian/rational argument in general and O'Donnell's (1973) formulation of the bureaucratic–authoritarian thesis in particular are in need of serious reconsideration. Hirschman (1979), Serra (1979), Kaufman (1979), and Collier (1979) suggest that O'Donnell's postulated links between stages of economic development and dominant coalitions—particularly between the perceived need to "deepen" the industrial base (by expanding into consumer-durable and capital goods industries) and the bureaucratic–authoritarian coalition—are questionable. As those analyses create doubts about the economic stage–coalition component of O'Donnell's thesis, my effort raises questions about the coalition-policy linkage. Put most simply, emerging descriptive evidence suggests that neither of the critical linkages in O'Donnell's bureaucratic–authoritarian argument—that between economic changes and coalitions and that between coalitions and policies—seems to hold in O'Donnell's paradigm, or archetypical case.

A major problem is that the focus on dominant coalitions in Argentina has apparently contributed to a general neglect of the important policy changes that occurred during the period in which one or another of the coalitions was dominant. Because "who governs" should be directly related to policies, policy gradations and shifts are almost completely ignored by the proponents of the "who governs" thesis. The policies of the 1943–1952 period, for example, are regarded as having been homogeneously populist because the populist coalition was in power. Only after close examination does one begin to recognize the true heterogeneity of policies during this interval.

A focus on dominant coalitions, therefore, presents a double-edged problem for the policy researcher. On the one hand, concern for dominant coalitions tends to mask the real phenomena we should be seeking to understand. Scholars end up trying to "explain" periods and policy alignments that do not actually exist in the empirical world. Other analysts have to start all over again to discover the authentic policy goals, outputs, and outcomes. On the other hand, a focus on dominant coalitions may be unnecessarily abstract. Those who govern—who have de facto and not merely de jure control of the policymaking arena—could still be important for explaining public policies even if dominant coalitions are not. The emergence of Perón in the post-1943 period, his efforts to consolidate his movement, and the removal of the leaders of the 1966 coup d'état were all important political changes that did result in at least minor policy shifts. Static, monolithic dominant coalitions fail to predict such policy alignments.

The findings here also suggest that reconceptualizations of the state and public policies in Latin America are needed. It is no longer reasonable to regard the state as a unified rational actor that purposefully formulates and executes public policies as a means for co-opting and suppressing supporters and opponents. The integrated formulation predicts the possible internal fragmentation of the state and the resultant breakdown of the unified rational actor/state-centered approach. The integrated thesis is not deterministic. The fragmentation is expected to occur only under certain conditions. If the conditions do develop, however, political elites may be placed in conflict with the low- and middle-level public employees. Public policy outputs may increasingly become the outcomes of intrastate bargaining and conflict. It may no longer be either possible to infer intent on the basis of what is done or reasonable to expect motivations to be translated into policies.

This point can be carried a step further. Scholars typically explain economic and social problems in Latin America on the basis of external determinants such as the difficulties created by delayed dependent development, U.S. imperialism, foreign multinational corporations, and so on. The work here does not minimize the real importance of such factors. It does suggest, however, that simple government mismanagement, poor planning, and faulty and erratic policy implementation may be major contributing factors to the economic and social problems that confront the nations in the region.

A new argument could thus be developed to account for the sequential replacement of one type of authoritarian system by another. Rather than claiming that intermittent social and economic crises associated with intractable problems lead to the continual shifting from one coalition to the next, a new, highly political explanation for the successive assertions of different types of authoritarian rule in Latin America suggests that each new coalition comes to power not because of the social and economic crises per se but because preceding administrations failed to resolve those problems. Authoritarian rule, then, may be a political solution in many ways made necessary by the mismanagement, poor planning, and faulty policy implementation of previous governments.

All of this suggests that it may no longer be fruitful to continue to theorize at the level of the political state in Latin America. It may be necessary, instead, to dissect the state in both theoretical and empirical terms so that its inner workings and final policy products can be examined with greater precision. The four constraints—the size and degree of unionization of the public sector, elite stability, the balance between nonbureaucratic actors, and the availability of uncommitted resources—provide at least an initial agenda for this dissection. Attention should also be paid to the number and efficiency of public and semipublic corporations. Analysts should be sensitive to indications of public employee resistance to elite demands. The means by which elites attempt to ensure bureaucratic obedience and government command-and-control procedures need to be researched with a view toward determining their extensiveness and actual utility. The steps by which the Latin American governments formulate and subsequently attempt to execute public policies should be detailed. Groups within the state that seem most likely to defy elite pressures ought to be identified. Finally, some effort should be made to discover the types of cues that different actors within the state take as guides in their policymaking.

Implications for Research on Public Policies

The analysis here has a number of implications for research on public policies and public policymaking. At one level, this effort to imbed two apparently competing arguments in a common hypotheticodeductive framework has been reasonably successful. The four constraining factors were crude, but they provided some basis for predicting which types of actors—dominant coalitions and political elites or permanent public employees—would dominate the policymaking arena. With those rough predictions, it was then possible to predict with surprising accuracy whether the authoritarian or the bureaucratic model would be useful for understanding public policies. Researchers in other areas may use such an approach to integrate their various economic, political, prior decision, rational actor, bureaucratic politics, and organizational process models.

Work remains to be done, however. The dominant configuration of actors in the policymaking arena—that is, who effectively governs—may play a dual role. On the one hand, it may determine the basic types of policies that are made. On the other hand, it may also serve as a structural condition that in effect selects what variables will be useful for explaining policy variations during the period in which a given configuration of actors is dominant. Because different arenas are dominated by different actors, who respond to different cues in their environment and whose interests and perceptions are affected by different factors, work in this area may further help to clarify why different models work in different policy areas.

On a more basic level, this research serves to sensitize public policy researchers to a number of simple points that appear to have been generally overlooked. For instance, the existing arguments often run into problems for four reasons: (1) they mistakenly equate those who appear to be important with those who actually dominate the arena; (2) they are almost invariably unidimensional in the sense that only one type of actor is assumed to be dominant rather than some possibly complex and shifting combination of elites, bureaucracies, and interest groups;[1] (3) in a related way, they often assume that a particular type of actor is dominant across all issue areas and/or in a given issue area through all time; and (4) many of them overlook the fact that professional middle- and low-level public employees are likely to be the "core" actors in the policymaking arenas of almost any polity. The models tend to ignore the rather obvious points that public employees are often crucial in policy formation and policy execution, that other types of actors must almost invariably struggle with the permanent staffs in order to implement their own policies, and that policy outputs may therefore be the outcomes of intragovernmental bargaining and conflict.

The reasoning here should be carefully understood. If those who effectively control the policymaking arena are critical for explaining public policies but the particular actors that exercise such control also vary across time, space, or different policy issues, none of the existing models presuming the invariant importance of any one or any one combination of actors (rationally acting coalitions or leaders, bureaucratic organizations, elites, interest groups, and so on) will be truly general.

All of these points lend support, of course, to an old conclusion. An improved understanding of public policies is most likely to be achieved by combining a focus on dominant actors in the policymaking arena with a decisionmaking perspective. If one can identify what actors dominate the arena, specify their policy goals and interests, and link those interests with the factors to which the actors are responsive, it may be possible to proceed immediately to develop expectations about what basic policies those actors will pursue and what variables should covary with fluctuations in policy outputs through time.

Policy Implications:
Combating the "Imperial Bureaucracy"

This research provides some insights for political elites who wish to combat the "imperial bureaucracy" (Kristol 1976) and increase their own effectiveness in the policymaking arena. The first point to be noted is that direct assaults on the public employees and their clienteles do not seem to have been particularly successful in Argentina. Repeated efforts to reorganize the structure of the bureaucracy, dismiss employees, abandon or at least curtail established programs, and return publicly owned corporations to the private sector were noticeably ineffective, as the integrated thesis predicted. The Argentine experience may be unique. Elites might be able to move incrementally by restricting their efforts to a succession of narrowly defined portions of the public sector. Nevertheless, it does not appear that direct attacks on the low- and middle-level employees necessarily hold the greatest potential for increasing elite control of the policymaking arena.

Fortunately, at least three alternatives to direct attacks appear to be available. Bureaucratic dominance stems in large part from the fact that public employees are indeed "those that never leave." Given their job security, low- and middle-level public employees may have little reason for being responsive to elite demands. A possible solution to the problem of public employee resistance, therefore, might be to attack the factors that contribute to this security. Placing at least the salary positions of budget proposals on "soft" rather than "hard" money in some sort of sunset bill and a program of cost-effectiveness or zero-based budgeting in which the value of each existing program and agency is periodically reassessed might serve this purpose. In both these ways, the certainty that the employees would never leave might be reduced. Low- and middle-level worker dependency on—hence obedience to—the elites might be increased.

The danger in sunset bills and zero-based budgeting is that like direct assaults on the public sector, such measures might provoke, rather than reduce, resistance. If employee insecurity is made too pervasive, the workers may be afraid to do anything; or they may do little more than engage in incessant attempts to justify their existence. The first result might lead to complete and total inaction. The second could lead to a breakdown of coordination across agencies and to efforts by one agency to swallow up the duties and responsibilities of others. Finally, sunset bill and zero-based budgeting may become routinized. The outcomes of reviews and reassessments may become predictable. The destabilizing and insecurity-inducing effects of these measures might thereby be eroded.

The problem of increasing public employee insecurity might therefore be approached in another way. The merit system of public employment might be abandoned and replaced by at least a threatened return to an extensive form of political patronage. This strategy might be limited to nonmilitary areas. It would not necessarily be limited to nontechnical positions. The main advantage of this approach is that it would enable elites to generate insecurity at a personal level. Whole agencies and programs would not be threatened (as they would be with the sunset and zero-based budgeting measures). Rather, each employee would be individually placed in jeopardy. No worker could shroud himself in the protective cloak of his agency or program. Each would ultimately be dependent on the personal goodwill of the political elites.

An alternative to increasing elite control by increasing public employee insecurity would be to balance the "imperial bureaucracy" with an "imperial presidency." Argentina failed in this area because elite instability became chronic. No stable, powerful alternative existed to counterbalance the public sector or force public employee compliance. An imperial president (and/or a stable, highly ideological mobilizational political party) might be capable of doing these things. The alternative to the "imperial bureaucracy" would have to recognize one critical point, however. In any bureaucratized political system, the enemy may be within the administrative apparatus of the political state itself.

A third and final alternative for increasing elite control would be to circumvent the public sector by avoiding direct conflict with it, moving outside established bureaucratic channels, disrupting those channels, and increasing the pool of previously unallocated resources. Although the importance of these measures was minimized in Chapter 3, they should not be overlooked. They leave the problem of limited elite effectiveness unresolved, but political elites in most polities do have spheres in which they can personally execute policies. They can appeal to the populace and thus attempt to mobilize support for their preferred policies. Elites can and do create informal circles within the government that are personally dependent on them and that are themselves capable of formulating and executing public policies. If new, previously uncommitted resources can be obtained, elites can leave existing agencies and programs untouched and still move ahead to create new programs and agencies which embody their own interests.

All of these steps can be taken. In the end, however, victory over an "imperial bureaucracy" appears unlikely. As was said at the outset, the integrated formulation is a thesis one would prefer to reject.

Note

1. Frankel 1963 and Hoole 1976 are exceptions to this rule.

References

Abelardo Ramos, Jorge. 1973. *Revolucion y Contrarevolucion en la Argentina.* Buenos Aires: Editorial Plus Ultra.

Aizcorbe, Roberto. 1975. *Argentina, the Perónist Myth: An Essay on the Cultural Decay in Argentina After the Second World War.* Hicksville, NY: Exposition Press.

Alexander, Robert J. 1962. *Labor Relations in Argentina, Brazil, and Chile.* New York: McGraw Hill.

———. 1965. *Organized Labor in Latin America.* New York: Free Press.

———. 1968. "Argentine Labor Before Perón and Under Perón. In *Why Perón Came to Power,* ed. Joseph P. Berger. New York: Alfred A. Knopf.

Alker, Hayward, and Cheryl Christensen. 1972. "From Causal Modelling to Artificial Intelligence: The Evolution of a U.N. Peace-making Simulation." In *Experimentation and Simulation in Political Science,* ed. J. A. LaPonce and Paul Smoker. Toronto: University of Toronto Press.

Alker, Hayward, and William J. Greenberg. 1971. "The U.N. Charter: Alternative Pasts and Alternative Futures." In *The United Nations,* ed. Edwin H. Fedder. St. Louis: University of Missouri.

Allison, Graham T. 1971. *Essence of Decisions.* Boston: Little, Brown.

Ames, Barry. 1973. *Rhetoric and Reality in a Militarized Regime: Brazil After 1964.* Professional Paper in Comparative Politics, vol. 4, no. 01-042. Beverly Hills: Sage.

———. 1975. "The Politics of Public Spending in Latin America," Washington University, St. Louis, mimeograph.

———. 1987. *Politicians and Public Policy in Latin America.* Berkeley: University of California Press.

Ames, Barry and Edward Goff. 1975. "Education and Defense Expenditures in Latin America: 1948–68," in C. Liske, W.

Anderson, Charles W. 1965. "'Reformongering' and the Uses of Political Power." *Inter-American Economic Affairs* 19:25–42.

———. 1967. *Politics and Economic Change in Latin America.* New York: Van Nostrand Reinhold.

Anton, Thomas J. 1970. "Roles and Symbols in the Determination of State Expenditures. In *Policy Analysis in Political Science,* ed. Ira Sharkansky. Chicago: Markham.

185

Apter, David A. 1965. *The Politics of Modernization.* Chicago: University of Chicago Press.

———. 1969. *Conceptual Approaches to the Study of Modernization.* Englewood Cliffs: Prentice-Hall.

———. 1971. *Choice and the Politics of Allocation.* New Haven: Yale University Press.

Art, Robert J. 1973. "Bureaucratic Politics and Foreign Policy: A Critique." *Policy Sciences* 4:467–490.

Axelrod, Robert. 1973. Bureaucratic Decision Making in the Military Assistance Program: Some Empirical Findings." In *Readings in American Foreign Policy,* ed. Morton Halperin and Arnold Kanter. Boston: Little, Brown.

Ayres, Robert. 1975. "Political Regimes, Explanatory Variables, and Public Policy in Latin America." *Journal of Developing Areas* 10.

Baer, Werner. 1961–62. "The Economics of Prebisch and ECLA." *Economic Development and Cultural Change* 10:169–182.

Bailey, Thomas A. 1969. *A Diplomatic History of the American People.* 8th ed. New York: Appleton–Century–Crofts.

Baily, Samuel L. 1966. "Argentina: Search for Consensus." *Current History* 51:301–306.

———. 1967. *Labor, Nationalism, and Politics in Argentina.* New Brunswick: Rutgers University Press.

Beechert, Edward D., Jr. 1965. "The Gap Between Planning Goals and Achievements in Latin America." *Inter-American Economic Affairs* 19:59–74.

Bodenheimer, Susanne J. 1971. *The Ideology of Imperialism.* Professional Paper in Comparative Politics, no. 01–015. Beverly Hills: Sage.

Bohrnstedt, George W., and T. Michael Carter. 1971. "Robustness in Regression Analysis." In *Sociological Methodology, 1971,* ed. Herbert L. Costner. San Francisco: Jossey Bass.

Boulding, Kenneth E. 1969. "National Images and International Systems." In *International Politics and Foreign Policy,* ed. James N. Rosenau. New York: Free Press.

Boynton, G. R. 1982. "On Getting from Here to There: Reflections on Two Paragraphs and Other Things." In *Strategies of Political Inquiry,* ed. Elinor Ostrom. Beverly Hills: Sage.

Brady, Linda P. 1974. "Bureaucratic Politics and Situational Constraints in Foreign Policy." Paper presented at the annual meeting of the American Political Science Association, Chicago.

Braun, Oscar. 1973. "Desarrollo del capital monopolista en la Argentina." In *El Capitalismo Argentino en Crisis,* ed. Oscar Braun. Buenos Aires: Siglo Veintiuno.

Braybrooke, David, and Charles E. Lindblom. 1963. *A Strategy of Decision.* New York: Free Press.

Bunge, Alejandro E. 1940. *Una Nueva Argentina.* Buenos Aires: Editorial Guillermo Kraft.

Cafiero, Antonio F. 1961. *Cinco Anos Despues.* Buenos Aires: El Grafico.

Canavese, Alfredo, and Guido Di Tella. 1987. "Inflation, Stabilization, or Hyperinflation Avoidance: The Case of the Austral Plan in Argentina, 1985–87." Mimeo.

Canitrot, Adolfo. 1978. *La vialidad economica de la democracia: Un analisis de la experiencia peronista, 1973–1976.* Buenos Aires: CEDES.

———. 1979. *La disciplina como objetivo de la politica economicia: Un ensayo sobre el programa economico del gobierno argentino desde 1976.* Buenos Aires: CEDES.

———. 1981. "Teoria y practica del liberalismo: Politica antiinflacionaroa y apertura economica en la Argentina, 1976–1981." *Desarrollo economico* 21.

Cardoso, Fernando Henrique. 1973. *Estado y Sociedad en America Latina.* Buenos Aires. Ediciones Nueva Vision.

Cardoso, Fernando Henrique, and Enzo Faletto. 1969. *Dependencia y Desarrollo en America Latina.* Mexico: Siglo Veintiuno Editores.

Cardoso, Fernando Henrique, and Jose Luis Reyna. 1989. "Industrialization, Occupational Structure and Social Stratification in Latin America." In *Constructive Change in Latin America,* ed. Cole Blasier. Pittsburgh: University of Pittsburgh Press.

Carri, Roberto. 1967. *Los Sindicatos Sin Poder.* Buenos Aires: Editorial Sudestada.

Chalmers, Douglas A. 1969. "Developing on the Periphery: External Factors in Latin American Politics." In *Linkage Politics,* ed. James N. Rosenau. New York: Free Press.

Chilcote, Ronald H. 1963. "Integrated Iron and Steel Industry for Argentina?" *Inter-American Economic Affairs* 16:31–46.

Chow, G. C. 1960. "Tests of Equality Between Sets of Coefficients in Two Linear Regressions." *Econometrica* 28:591–605.

Cockcroft, James, André Gunder Frank, and Dale Johnson. 1972. *Dependence and Underdevelopment: Latin America's Political Economy.* New York: Doubleday.

Cohen, Bernard C. 1971. "The influence of Non-Governmental Groups on Foreign Policy Making. In *The Politics of U.S. Foreign Policy Making,* ed. Douglas Fox. Pacific Palisades, CA: Goodyear.

Cohen, Youssef. 1985. "The Impact of Bureaucratic–Authoritarian Rule on Economic Growth," *Comparative Political Studies* 18.

Collier, David. 1975. "Timing of Economic Growth and Regime Characteristics in Latin America." *Comparative Politics* 7:331–359.

———. 1976. *Squatters and Oligarchs: Public Policy and Authoritarian Modernization in Peru.* Baltimore: The Johns Hopkins Press.

———. 1978. "Industrial Modernization and Political Change: A Latin American Perspective." *World Politics* 30:593–614.

———, ed. 1979. *The New Authoritarianism in Latin America.* Princeton: Princeton University Press.

Collier, David, and Richard E. Messick. 1976. "Functional Prerequisites Versus Diffusion: Testing Alternative Explanations of Social Security Adoption." *American Political Science Review* 69:1299–1315.

Collier, David, L. Spencer, and C. Waters. 1975. "Varieties of Latin American 'Corporatism'." Paper presented at the annual meeting of the American Political Science Association, San Francisco.

Collier, Ruth Berins, and David Collier. 1979. "Inducements Versus Constraints: Disaggregating Corporatism." *American Political Science Review* 73:967–986.

Cotler, Julio. 1972. "Bases del corporatismo en el Peru." *Sociedad y Politica* 1:2.

———. 1975. "A New Mode of Political Domination in Peru." In *Continuity and*

Change in Contemporary Peru, ed. Abraham F. Lowenthal. Princeton: Princeton University Press.

Crecine, John P. 1967. "A Computer Simulation of Municipal Budgeting. *Management Science* 13:786–815.

——. 1970. "A Simulation of Municipal Budgeting: The Impact of the Problem Environment." In *Policy Analysis in Political Science,* ed. Ira Sharkansky. Chicago: Markham.

Cyert, R. M., and J. G. March. 1963. *A Behavioral Theory of the Firm.* Englewood Cliffs, NJ: Prentice-Hall.

Dahrendorf, Ralf. 1967. *Society and Democracy in Germany.* Garden City, NY: Doubleday.

Dalto, Juan C. 1967. *Crisis y Auge en la Economica Argentina.* Buenos Aires: Ediciones Macchi.

Davies, John Paton. 1966. *Foreign and Other Affairs.* New York: W. W. Norton.

Davis, Otto A., M. A. H. Dempster, and Aaron Wildavsky. 1966a. "On the Process of Budgeting: An Empirical Study of Congressional Appropriations." In *Papers in Non-Market Decision-making,* ed. Gordon Tullock. Charlottesville: University of Virginia.

——. 1966b. "A Theory of the Budgetary Process." *American Political Science Review* 60:529–547.

Deutsch, Karl W. 1966. *The Nerves of Government.* New York: Free Press.

——. 1970. *Politics and Government: How People Decide Their Fate.* Boston: Houghton Mifflin.

Diaz Alejandro, Carlos F. 1970. *Essays on the Economic History of the Argentine Republic.* New Haven: Yale University Press.

Di Tella, Guido. 1983. *Argentina under Perón, 1973–1976.* London: Macmillan.

Di Tella, Torcuato. 1965. "Populism and reform in Latin America." In *Obstacles to Change in Latin America,* ed. Claudio Veliz. New York: Oxford University Press.

——. 1968a. "Stalemate or Coexistence in Argentina?" In *Latin America: Reform or Revolution?* ed. James Petras and Maurice Zeitlan. Greenwich, CT: Fawcett.

——. 1968b. "The Working Class in Politics." In *Latin America and the Caribbean,* ed. Claudio Veliz. New York: Praeger.

Dos Santos, Teotonio. 1968. "The Changing Structure of Foreign Investment in Latin America." In *Latin America: Reform or Revolution?* ed. James Petras and Maurice Zeitlin. Greenwich, CT: Fawcett.

——. 1970. "The Structure of Dependence." *American Economic Review* 60:2.

Durbin, J., and G. S. Watson. 1950. "Testing for Serial Correlation in Least Squares Regression." Pt. 1 *Biometrika* 37:159–178.

——. 1951. "Testing for Serial Correlation in Least Squares Regression, Pt. 2. *Biometrika* 38:159–178.

Einaudi, Luigi, and Alfred Stepan. 1974. "Changing Military Perspectives in Peru and Brazil." In *Beyond Cuba: Latin America Takes Charge of Its Future,* ed. Luigi Einaudi. New York: Crane, Russak.

Elasser, Edward O. 1955. "Argentine Relations with the Export–Import Bank, 1934–1945." *Inter-American Economic Affairs* 8:87–93.

Engels, Friedrich. 1969. *Germany: Revolution and Counter Revolution*. New York: John Wiley & Sons.

Epstein, Edward. 1987. "Recent Stabilization Programs in Argentina, 1973–86." *World Development* 15.

Erickson, Kenneth Paul. 1972. "Populism and Political Control of the Working Class in Brazil." In *Ideology and Social Change in Latin America*. ed. Juan Corradi and Juno Nash. Millburn, NJ.

Eshag, Eprime, and Rosemary Thorp. 1974. "Las politicas economicas ortodoxas de Perón a Guido (1953–1963)." In *Los Planes de Estabilizacion en la Argentina*, ed. Aldo Ferrer et al. Buenos Aires: Paidos.

Farrell, R. Barry. 1966. "Foreign Policies of Open and Closed Political Societies." In *Approaches to Comparative and International Politics*, ed. R. Barry Farrell. Evanston, IL: Northwestern University Press.

Ferrer, Aldo. 1967. *The Argentine Economy*. Trans. Marjory M. Urguidi. Berkeley: University of California Press.

Ferrer, Aldo, et al. 1974. *Los panes de estabilizacion en la Argentina*. Buenos Aires: Paidos.

FIAT Delegacion para la America Latina. 1966. *Oficina de estudios para la colaboracion economica internacional*. Argentina Economica y Financiera. Buenos Aires.

Forward, Nigel. 1971. *The Field of Nations*. Boston: Little, Brown.

Frank, Andre Gunder. 1966. "The Development of Underdevelopment." *Monthly Review* 17.

———. 1967. *Capitalism and Underdevelopment in Latin America: Historical Studies of Chile and Brazil*. New York: Monthly Review.

Frankel, Joseph. 1963. *The Making of Foreign Policy*. New York: Oxford University Press.

Frenkel, Roberto, and José Maria Fanelli. 1987. "La Argentina y el Fondo en la decada pasada." *El trimestre economico* 56, Mexico City (Enero–Marzo).

Frenkel, Roberto, and Guillermo O'Donnell. 1978. *Los programas de establizacion convenidos con el FMI y sus impactos internos*. Buenos Aires: CEDES.

Furtado, Celso. 1969. "U.S. Hegemony and the Future of Latin America." In *Latin American Radicalism*, ed. Irving Louis Horowitz, Jesus de Castro, and John Gerassi. New York: Vintage.

Garcia-Zamor, Jean Claude. 1968. *Public Administration and Social Changes in Argentina, 1943–1955*. Rio de Janiero: Editora Mory.

Geary, R. C. 1970. "Relative Efficiency of Count of Sign Changes for Assessing Residual Autoregression in Least Squares Regression." *Biometrika* 57.

Gerschenkron, Alexander. 1952. "Economic Backwardness in Historical Perspective. In *The Progress of Underdeveloped Countries*, ed. Bert F. Hoselitz. Chicago: University of Chicago Press.

———. 1966. *Economic Backwardness in Historical Perspective*. Cambridge: Harvard University Press.

Goldberger, A. S. 1964. *Econometric Theory*. New York: Wiley.

Gramsci, Antonio. 1957. *The Modern Prince and Other Writings*. New York: International.

Gujarti, Damodar. 1970a. "Use of Dummy Variables in Testing Equality Between Sets of Coefficients in Two Linear Regressions: A Note. *American Statistician* 24:50–52.

———. 1970b. "Use of Dummy Variables in Testing Equality Between Sets of Coefficients in Two Linear Regressions: A Generalization." *American Statistician* 24:18–22.

Habibagahi, Hamid, and J. L. Pratschki. 1972. "A Comparison of the Power of the Von Neumann Ration, Durbin–Watson and Geary Tests." *Review of Economics and Statistics* 54:179–185.

Haggard, Stephan. 1985. "The Politics of Adjustment: Lessons from the IMF's Extended Fund Facility." *International Organizations* 39.

Halperin, Morton H. 1974. *Bureaucratic Politics and Foreign Policy*. Washington: Brookings Institution.

Halperin, Morton H., and Arnold Kanter. 1973. "The Bureaucratic Perspective: A Preliminary Framework. *Readings in American Foreign Policy,* ed. Morton H. Halperin and Arnold Kanter. Boston: Little, Brown.

Halpern, Manfred. 1962. "Middle Eastern Armies and the New Middle Class." In *The Role of the Military in Underdeveloped Countries,* ed. John Johnson. Princeton: Princeton University Press.

Hanson, Mark. 1974. "Organizational Bureaucracy in Latin America and the Legacy of Spanish Colonialism." *Journal of Inter-American Studies and World Affairs.* 16:199–219.

Hartz, Louis. 1964. *The Founding of New Societies.* New York: Harcourt, Brace, and World.

Hazard, John L. 1951. "Maritime Development in Argentina in the Last Decade." *Inter-American Economic Affairs* 4:48–72.

Henry, Laurin L. 1958. "Public Administration and Civil Service." In *Government and Politics in Latin America,* ed. Harold E. Davis. New York: Ronald.

Hilsman, Roger, 1964. *To Move a Nation: The Politics of Foreign Policy in the Administration of John F. Kennedy.* New York: Dell.

Heymann, Daniel. 1983. "A Study in Economic Instability: The Case of Argentina." Ph.D. diss. University of California, Los Angeles.

Hirschman, Albert O. 1961. "Ideologies of Economic Development in Latin America." In *Latin American Issues,* ed. Albert O. Hirschman. New York: Twentieth Century Fund.

———. 1968a. *Journeys Toward Progress: Studies of Economic Policymaking in Latin America.* New York: Greenwood.

———. 1968b. "The Political Economy of Import-substituting Industrialization in Latin America." *Quarterly Journal of Economics* 82:1–32.

———. 1979. "The Turn to Authoritarianism in Latin America and the Search for Its Economic Determinants." In *The New Authoritarianism in Latin America.* ed. David Collier. Princeton: Princeton University Press.

Hoffman, Stanley. 1968. *Gulliver's Troubles.* New York: Doubleday.

Hoole, Francis W. 1976. "Evaluating the Impact of International Organizations." Indiana University. Mimeograph.

Hopkins, Jack W. 1974. "Contemporary Research on Public Administration and Bureaucracies in Latin America." *Latin American Research Review* 9:109–139.

Hughes, Steven, and Kenneth Mijeski. 1984. *Politics and Public Policy in Latin America.* Boulder: Westview.

Huntington, Samuel. 1971. "The Change to Change: Modernization, Development, and Politics." *Comparative Politics* 3.

Imaz, Jose Luiz de. 1970. *Los Que Mandan.* Albany: State University of New York Press.

Inter-American Development Bank. 1968. *Multinational Investment, Public and Private, in the Economic Development and Integration of Latin America.* Bogota, Colombia: IADB.

———. 1973. *Economic and Social Progress in Latin America, Annual Report.* Washington: IADB.

Iscaro, Rubens. 1973. *Historia del movimiento sindical. Vol. 2, El movimiento sindical argentino.* Buenos Aires: Editorial Fundamentos.

Jaguaribe, Helio, Aldo Ferrer, Miguel Wionczeck, and Theotonio Dos Santos. 1970. *La dependencia politica–economica de America Latina.* Mexico City: Siglo XXI.

Jervis, Robert. 1968. "Hypotheses on Misperception." *World Politics* 20:454–479.

Johnson, John. 1962. *The Role of the Military in Underdeveloped Countries.* Princeton: Princeton University Press.

Johnston, J. 1972. *Econometric Methods.* 2d ed. New York: McGraw–Hill.

Jones, William M. 1964. *On Decision-making in Large Organizations.* Santa Monica: RAND.

Jordan, David C. 1970. "Argentina's New Military Government." *Current History.* 58:85–90, 116–117.

———. 1972. "Argentina's Bureaucratic Oligarchies." *Current History* 62:70–75, 113–114.

Kaufman, Robert R. 1979. "Industrial Change and Authoritarian Rule in Latin America: A Concrete Review of the Bureaucratic–Authoritarian Model. In *The New Authoritarianism in Latin America,* ed. David Collier. Princeton: Princeton University Press.

———. 1985. "Democratic and Authoritarian Responses to the Debt Issue: Argentina, Brazil, and Mexico." *International Organization* 39.

Kaufman, Robert R., et al. 1975. "A Preliminary Test of the Theory of Dependency." *Comparative Politics* 7:303–330.

Kenworthy, Eldon. 1967. "Argentina: The Politics of Late Industrialization." *Foreign Affairs* 45:463–476.

———. 1972. "Did the 'New Industrialists' Play a Significant Role in the Formation of Perón's Coalition, 1943–46? In *New Perspectives on Modern Argentina,* ed. Alberto Ciria et al. Bloomington: Indiana University.

———. 1973. "The Function of the Little-known Case in Theory Formation; or, What Peronism Wasn't" *Comparative Politics* 6:17–45.

———. 1975. "Interpretaciones ortodoxas y revisionistas del apoyo inicial del Peronismo. *Desarrollo economico* 14-749–763.

Kissinger, Henry A. 1969. "Domestic Structure and Foreign Policy." In *International Politics and Foreign Policy,* ed. James N. Rosenau. New York: Free Press.

Kissinger, Henry A., and Bernard Brodie. 1968. *Bureaucracy, Politics, and Strategy.* Security Studies Paper, no. 17. Los Angeles: University of California.

Kling, Merle. 1968. "Toward a Theory of Power and Political Instability in Latin America." In *Latin America: Reform or Revolution?*, ed. James Petras and Maurice Zeitlin. Greenwich, CT: Fawcett.

Kristol, Irving. 1976. "Post-Watergate Mentality, A Dubious Legacy," *New York Times Magazine*, November 14.

Lambert, Jacques. 1971. *Latin America: Social Structures and Political Institutions*. Berkeley: University of California Press.

Lieuwen, Edwin. 1961. *Arms and Politics in Latin America*. Rev. ed. New York: Praeger.

Linz, Juan J. 1964. "An Authoritarian Regime: Spain." In *Cleavages, Ideologies, and Party Systems*, ed. Erik Allardt and Y. Littunen. Helsinki: Academic Bookstore.

———. 1972. "Notes Toward a Typology of Authoritarian Regimes." Paper presented at the annual meeting of the American Political Science Association, Washington.

———. 1975. "Totalitarianism and Authoritarian Regimes." In *Handbook of Political Science*, vol. 3, *Macropolitical Theory*, ed. Fred Greenstein and Nelson Polsby. Reading, MA: Addison–Wesley.

Lipset, Seymour M. 1967. "Values, Education, and Entrepreneurship." In *Elites in Latin America*, ed. Seymour M. Lipset and Aldo Solari. New York: Oxford University Press.

Loehr and J. McCamant, eds. *Comparative Public Policy: Theory, Issues and Method*. Beverly Hills: Sage.

Lissak, Moshe. 1975. "Center and Periphery in Developing Countries and Prototypes of Military Elites." In *Militarism in Developing Countries*, ed. K. Fidel. New Brunswick: Transaction Books.

Lovell, John P. 1970. *Foreign Policy in Perspective*. New York: Holt, Rinehart, & Winston.

McKinlay, R. and S. Cohan. 1975. "A Comparative Analysis of the Political and Economic Performance of Military and Civilian Regimes." *Comparative Politics* 8.

———. 1976. "Performance and Instability in Military and Nonmilitary Regime Systems." *American Political Science Review* 70.

Malloy, James M. 1974. "Authoritarianism, Corporatism, and Mobilization in Peru." *Review of Politics* 36:52–84.

———, ed. 1977. *Authoritarianism and Corporatism in Latin America*. Pittsburgh: University of Pittsburgh Press.

Mamalakis, Markos. 1969. "The Theory of Sectoral Clashes: Commentaries. *Latin American Research Review* 4:9–71.

Manzetti, Luigi. 1988. "The International Monetary Fund and the Argentine Case." Ph.D. diss., University of Iowa.

Manzetti, Luigi, and Marco Dell'Aquila. 1988. "Economic Stabilization in Argentina: The Austral Plan." *Journal of Latin American Studies* 20.

Marx, Karl. 1964. *The Eighteenth Brumaire of Louis Bonaparte*. New York: International.

Merkx, Gilbert W. 1969. "Sectoral Clashes and Political Change: The Argentine Experience." *Latin American Research Review* 4:89–114.

Millington, Thomas A. 1964. "President Arturo Illia and the Argentine Military." *Journal of Inter-American Studies and World Affairs* 6:405–424.

Moore, Barrington, Jr. 1966. *Social Origins of Dictatorship and Democracy.* Boston: Beacon.

Morse, Richard M. 1964. "The Heritage of Latin America." *The Founding of New Societies,* ed. Louis Hartz. New York: Harcourt, Brace, & World.

Most, Benjamin, and Harvey Starr. 1984. "International Relations Theory, Foreign Policy Substitutability, and 'Nice' Laws." *World Politics* 36.

Murmis, Miguel, and Juan Carlos Portantiero. 1971. *Estudios sobre los origenes del Peronismo.* Buenos Aires: Siglo Veintiuno.

Needler, Martin. 1969. "The Latin American Military: Predatory Reactionaries or Modernizing Patriots?" *Journal of Inter-America Studies* 11.

Nelson, Joan M. 1969. "Migrants, Urban Poverty, and Instability in Developing Nations." Cambridge: Harvard University. Occasional Papers in International Affairs, no. 22.

———. 1984. "The Politics of Stabilization." In *Adjustment Crisis in the Third World,* ed. R. Feinberg and V. Kallab. New Brunswick: Transaction Books.

Neustadt, Richard. 1970. *Alliance Politics.* New York: Columbia University Press.

Newton, Ronald C. 1974. "Natural Corporatism and Passing of Populism in Spanish America." *Review of Politics* 36:34–51.

Nordlinger, Eric. 1970. "Soldiers in Mufti: The Impact of Military Rule upon Economic and Social Change in the Non-Western States." *American Political Science Review* 64.

Nun, José. *Latin America: The Hegemonic Crisis and the Military Coup.* Politics of Modernization Series, no. 7. Berkeley: University of California.

O'Donnell, Guillermo. 1973. *Modernization and Bureaucratic–Authoritarianism: Studies of South American Politics.* Politics of Modernization Series, no. 9. Berkeley: University of California.

———. 1974. "A Non-Paper Containing Some Mildly Concerned Reflections on Latin American 'Corporatism.'" Mimeograph, University of California at Berkeley.

———. 1975. "Reflexiones sobre la tendendencias generales de cambio en el estado buricratico–autoritario." Buenos Aires: Centro de Estudios de Estado y Sociedad.

———. 1988. *Bureaucratic–Authoritarianism: Argentina, 1976–1973 in Comparative Perspective.* Berkeley: University of California Press.

Organization of American States (OAS). 1971. *External Financing for Latin American Development.* Baltimore: Johns Hopkins University Press.

Owen, Frank. 1957. *Perón: His Rise and Fall.* London: Cresset.

Pablo, Juan Carlos de 1980. *Economia politica del Peronismo.* Buenos Aires: El Cid.

Paige, Glenn D. 1968. *The Korean Decision.* New York: Free Press.

Peralta Ramos, Monica. 1972. *Etapas de acumulacion y alianzas de clases en la Argentina (1930–1970).* Buenos Aires: Siglo Veintiuno.

Petras, James. 1967. *Politics and Social Forces in Chilean Development.* Berkeley: University of California Press.

Pike, Frederick B. 1974. "Corporatism and Latin American–United States Relations." *Review of Politics* 36:132–170.

Pion-Berlin, David. 1989. *The Ideology of State Terror: Economic Doctrine and Political Repression in Argentina and Peru.* Boulder, CO: Lynne Rienner.

Pion-Berlin, David. 1985. "The Fall of Military Rule in Argentina: 1976–1983." *Journal of Interamerican Studies and World Affairs.*

Portantiero, Juan Carlos. 1971. "Clases dominantes y crisis politica en la Argentina actual." *El capitalismo Argentino en crisis.* Buenos Aires: Siglo Veintiuno.

Potash, Robert A. 1969. *The Army and Politics in Argentina, 1928–1945: Yrigoyen to Perón.* Stanford: Stanford University Press.

———. 1972. "The Military and the Policy Making Process, 1946–1958 (Perón to Aramburu)." *New Perspectives on Modern Argentina,* ed. Alberto Ciria et al. Bloomington: Indiana University.

Poulantzas, Nico. 1973. *Poder politico y clases sociales en el estado capitalista.* Buenos Aires: Siglo Veintiuno.

Purcell, Susan Kaufman. 1973a. "Authoritarianism." *Comparative Politics* 5:301–312.

———. 1973b. "Decision-making in an Authoritarian Regime: Theoretical Implications from a Mexican Case Study." *World Politics* 26:28–54.

Putnam, Robert. 1967. "Toward Explaining Military Intervention in Latin American Politics." *World Politics* 20:83–110.

Pye, Lucian. 1962. "Armies in the Process of Political Modernization." In *The Role of the Military in Underdeveloped Countries,* ed. John Johnson. Princeton: Princeton University Press.

Rakoff, Stuart, and G. F. Schaefer. 1970. "Politics, Policy, and Political Science: Theoretical Alternatives." *Politics and Society* 1:51–77.

Ramos, Joseph. 1986. *Neoconservative Economics in the Southern Cone of Latin America, 1973–83.* Baltimore: Johns Hopkins University Press.

Ray, David. 1973. "The Dependency Model of Latin American Underdevelopment." *Journal of Interamerican Studies and World Affairs* 15:1.

Remmer, Karen. 1986. "The Politics of Economic Stabilization: IMF Stand-by Programs in Latin America, 1954–1984." *Comparative Politics.*

Republica de Argentina. Ministerio de Asuntos Economicos. 1955. *Producto e ingreso de la Republica Argentina.* Buenos Aires.

———. Consejo Nacional de Desarrollo. 1965. *Plan Nacional de Desarrollo 1965–1969.* Vol. 1, *Analisis global.* Buenos Aires.

Republica de Argentina. Consejo Nacional de Desarrollo. 1970. *Plan nacional de desarrollo, 1970–1974.* Vol. 1, *Analisis global.* Buenos Aires.

———. Consejo Nacional de Desarrollo. 1974. *Plan nacional de desarrollo.* Buenos Aires.

Robinson, James A., and Richard C. Snyder. 1966. "Decision-making in International Politics." In *International Behavior,* ed. Herbert C. Kelman. New York: Holt, Rinehart and Winston.

Rockefeller, Nelson. 1969. *The Rockefeller Report on the Americas.* Chicago: Quadrangle Books.

Rodriguez, Carlos Alfredo. 1987. *"Comments on Canavese and Di Tella."* Mimeo.

Rofman, Alejandro, and Luis A. Romero. 1973. *Sistema socioeconomico y estructura en la Argentina.* Buenos Aires: Amorrortu Editores.

Romero, Luis Alberto. 1969. *Los golpes militares, 1812–1955.* Buenos Aires: Coleccion Nuevo Pasado.

Ronfeldt, David. 1974. "Patterns of Civil–Military Rule." In *Beyond Cuba: Latin America Takes Charge of Its Future*, ed. Luigi Einaudi. New York: Crane, Russak.

Rose, Richard. 1973. "Comparing Public Policy: An Overview." *European Journal of Political Research* 1:67–94.

Rottin, Luciano. 1949. *Buenos Aires: Ciudad, patria, mundo*. Buenos Aires.

Rowe, James W. 1970. "Ongania's Argentina." In *Latin American Politics: Studies of the Contemporary Scene*, 2d ed., ed. Robert D. Tomasek. Garden City, NY: Anchor Books.

Salera, Virgil. 1966. "Model-playing with Historical Blinkers: Argentina." *Inter-American Economic Affairs* 20:79–87.

Sarfatti, Magali. 1966. *Spanish Bureaucratic–Patrimonialism in America*. Politics of Modernization Series, no. 1. Berkeley: University of California.

Scenna, Miguel A. 1970. *Como fueron los relaciones Argentino–norteamericanos*. Buenos Aires: Editorial Plus Ultra.

Schilling, Warner E. 1962. "The Politics of National Defense: Fiscal 1950." In *Strategy, Politics, and National Defense Budgets*, ed. Warner Schilling, Paul Y. Hammond, and Glenn Snyder. New York: Columbia University Press.

Schmitter, Philippe C. 1971a. *Interest, Conflict and Political Change in Brazil*. Stanford: Stanford University Press.

———. 1971b. "Military Intervention, Political Competitiveness, and Public Policy in Latin America, 1950–1967." In *On Military Intervention*. edited by Morris Janowitz and Jacques van Doorn. Rotterdam: Rotterdam University Press.

———. 1972a. "Paths to Political Development in Latin America." In *Changing Latin America: New Interpretations of Its Politics and Society*, ed. Douglas A. Chalmers. Proceedings of the American Academy of Political Science 30:4.

———. 1972b. "The Comparative Analysis of Public Policy: Outputs, Outcomes, and Impacts." Paper presented at a meeting of the Social Science Research Council Committee on Comparative Politics, Princeton.

———. 1973. "The 'Portugalization' of Brazil?" In *Authoritarian Brazil*, ed. Alfred A. Stepan. New Haven: Yale University Press.

———. 1974a. "Still the Century of 'Corporatism'?" *Review of Politics* 36:85–131.

———. 1974b. "Notes Toward a Political Economic Conceptualization of Policymaking in Latin America." Paper presented at a meeting of the Social Science Research Council, Buenos Aires.

Schvarzer, Jorge. 1983. *La logica politica de la politica economica*. Buenos Aires: CISEA.

Scott, Robert E. 1974. "Labour Relations in the Public Sector." *International Labour Review* 110:381–404.

———. 1966. "The Government Bureaucrats and Political Change in Latin America." *Journal of International Affairs* 20:289–308.

Serra, José. 1979. "Three Mistaken Theses Regarding the Connection Between Industrialization and Authoritarian Regimes." In *The New Authoritarianism in Latin America*, ed. David Collier. Princeton: Princeton University Press.

Sharkansky, Ira. 1968. *Spending in the American States*. Chicago: Rand McNally.

———. 1970a. "Environment, Policy Output, and Impact: Problems of Theory and

Method in the Analysis of Public Policy." In *Policy Analysis in Political Science,* ed. Ira Sharkansky. Chicago: Markham.

———. 1970b. "Government Expenditures and Public Services in the American States." In *Policy Analysis in Political Science,* ed. Ira Sharkansky. Chicago: Markham.

Sharkansky, Ira, and Richard Hofferbert. 1969. "Dimensions of State Politics, Economics and Public Policy." *American Political Science Review* 63:867–879.

Shils, Edward. 1962. "The Military in Political Development." In *The Role of the Military in Underdeveloped Countries,* ed. John Johnson. Princeton: Princeton University Press.

Siguat, Lorenzo Juan. 1972. *Acerca de la distribucion y niveles de ingreso en la Argentina.* Buenos Aires: Ediciones Macchi.

Silvert, Kalman. 1970. "The Costs of Anti-Nationalism: Argentina." In *Latin American Politics,* ed. Robert D. Tomasek. Garden City, NY: Anchor Books.

Skidmore, Thomas. 1977. "The Politics of Economic Stabilization in Postwar Latin America." In *Authoritarianism and Corporatism in Latin America,* ed. James M. Malloy. Pittsburgh: Pittsburgh University Press.

Smith, Peter H. 1969. "Social Mobilization, Political Participation, and the Rise of Juan D. Perón." *Political Science Quarterly* 84:30–49.

———. 1972. "The Social Base of Perónism." *Hispanic American Historical Review* 52:55–73.

Smith, William C. 1976. "The Armed Forces and the Authoritarian–Bureaucratic State in Argentina." Paper presented at the Inter-University Seminar on Armed Forces and Society, Tempe.

Snow, Peter G. 1969. "The Class Basis of Argentine Political Parties." *American Political Science Review* 63:163–167.

Snyder, Richard C., H. W. Bruck, and Burton Sapin. 1962. *Foreign Policy Decision Making.* New York: Free Press of Glencoe.

Soares, Glaucio Ary Dillon. 1968. "The New Industrialization and the Brazilian Political System," in James Petras and Maurice Zeitlin, eds., *Latin America: Reform or Revolution?* Greenwich: Fawcett.

Sourrouille, Juan. 1983. *Politica economica y procesos de desarrollo: La experiencia Argentina entre 1976 y 1981.* Buenos Aires: CEPAL.

Sprout, Harold, and Margaret Sprout. 1956. *Man–Milieu Relationship Hypotheses in the Context of International Politics.* Princeton: Princeton University.

———. 1957. "Environmental Factors in the Study of International Politics." *Journal of Conflict Resolution* 1:309–328.

———. 1965. *The Ecological Perspective on Human Affairs with Special Reference to International Politics..* Princeton: Princeton University Press.

Starr, Harvey. 1972. "'Organization Process' as an Influence on National Security Policy. *International Relations* (London) 4:176–186.

———. 1978. "'Opportunity' and 'Willingness' as Ordering Concepts in the Study of War." *International Interactions* 4:363–387.

Statistical Abstract of Latin America. Los Angeles: University of California, Los Angeles, Latin American Center.

Stepan, Alfred. 1966. "Political Development Theory: The Latin American Experience." *Journal of International Affairs* 20:223–235.

————. 1973. "The New Professionalism of International Warfare and Military Role Expansion." In *Authoritarian Brazil*, ed. Alfred Stepan. New Haven: Yale University Press.

Stickell, A. Lawrence. 1972. "Perónist Politics in Labor, 1943." In *New Perspectives on Modern Argentina,* ed. Alberto Ciria et al. Bloomington: Indiana University.

Sullivan, G. E. 1972. "Incremental Budget-making in the American States: A Test of the Anton Model." *Journal of Politics* 34:639–647.

Tanter, Raymond, and Richard H. Ullman, eds. 1972. *Theory and Policy in International Relations*. Princeton: Princeton University Press.

Thompson, James D. 1967. *Organizations in Action*. New York: McGraw Hill.

Treber, Salvador. 1969. *La empresa estatal Argentina*. Buenos Aires: Ediciones Macchi.

————. 1971. "El empleo en el sector gubernamental." In *Trabajos presentados en las terceras journadas de finanzas publicas,* ed. Buenos Aires: Ediciones Macchi.

Troncoso, Moises Poblete, and Ben G. Burnett. 1960. *The Rise of the Latin American Labor Movement*. New York: Bookman.

Trotsky, V. 1961. *Por los Estados Unidos Socialistas de Latin America*. Buenos Aires: Ediciones Coyoacan.

Tucker, Harvey J. 1975. "The Budgetary Process in the Commonwealth of Massachusetts, 1950–1973: A Comparison of Three Models." Paper presented at the annual meeting of the Midwest Political Science Association, Chicago.

UN Economic Commission on Latin America. 1954. *A Study of the Iron and Steel Industry in Latin America*. New York: UNECLA.

————. Department of Economic and Social Affairs. 1955. *Foreign Capital in Latin America*. New York: UNECLA.

————. Economic Commission on Latin America. 1965. *External Financing in Latin America*. New York: UNECLA.

————. Economic Commission on Latin America. 1969a. *The Process of Industrialization in Latin America: Statistical Annex*. Santiago de Chile: UNECLA.

————. Economic Commission on Latin America. 1969b. *Economic Development and Income Distribution in Argentina*. New York: UNECLA.

————. Economic Commission on Latin America. 1971. *The External Financing of Latin America*. New York: UNECLA.

U.S. Department of Commerce. 1963. *Statistical Supplement to the Survey of Current Business*. Washington: GPO.

————. 1970. *Statistical Abstract of the United States*. Washington: GPO.

U.S. Department of Labor. Bureau of Labor Statistics. June 1959. *Foreign Labor Information: Labor in Argentina*. Washington: GPO.

————. Bureau of Labor Statistics. 1968. *Labor Law and Practice in Argentina*. BLS Reports, no. 344. Washington: GPO.

Vacs, Aldo. 1986. "Authoritarian Breakdown and Redemocratization in Argentina." In *Authoritarians and Democrats*, ed. James M. Malloy and A. Selgson. Pittsburgh: Pittsburgh University Press.

Valenzuela, Arturo. 1976. "Political Constraints to the Establishment of Socialism in Chile." In *Chile: Politics and Society,* ed. Arturo and J. Samuel Valenzuela. New York: Transition Books.

Veliz, Claudio. 1972. "Centralism and Nationalism in Latin America." In *Contemporary Inter-American Relations,* ed. Englewood Cliffs, NJ: Prentice–Hall.

Villanueva, Javier. 1966. *The Inflationary Process in Argentina, 1943–1960,* 2d ed. Buenos Aires: Instituto Torcuato Di Tella.

Waterston, Albert. 1964. "Administrative Obstacles to Planning." *Economia Lationamericana* 1:308–350.

Weil, Felix J. 1950. "Can Perón Be Bought?" *Inter-American Economic Affairs* 4:27–36.

Whitaker, Arthur P. 1954. *The United States and Argentina.* Cambridge: Harvard University Press.

———. 1964a. *Argentina.* Englewood Cliffs, NJ: Prentice–Hall.

———. 1964b. "Argentina: A Fragmented Society." *Current History* 46:15–18, 51–52.

Wiarda, Howard J. 1973. "Toward a Framework for the Study of Political Change in the Iberic–Latin Tradition: The Corporative Model." *World Politics* 25:206–236.

———. 1974a. "Corporatism and Development in the Iberic–Latin World: Persistent Strains and New Variations." *The Review of Politics* 36:3–33.

———, ed. 1974b. *Politics and Social Change in Latin America: The Distinct Tradition.* Amherst: University of Massachusetts Press.

Wildavsky, Aaron. 1964. *The Politics of the Budgetary Process.* Boston: Little, Brown.

Willner, Ann Ruth. 1970. "Perspectives on Military Elites and Wielders of Power." *Journal of Comparative Administration* 2.

Wogart, Jan. 1983. "Combining Price Stabilization with Trade and Financial Liberalization Policies: The Argentine Experience, 1976–1981." *Journal of Interamerica and World Affairs* 25.

Wynia, Gary. 1978. *Argentina in the Post War Era.* Albuquerque: University of New Mexico Press.

———. 1986. *Argentina: Illusions and Reality.* New York: Holmes & Meier.

Zinnes, Dina A. 1972. "Some Evidence Relevant to the Man-Milieu Hypothesis." In *The Analysis of International Politics,* ed. James N. Rosenau. New York: Free Press.

Zorrilla, Ruben H. 1974. *Estructura y dinamica del sindicalismo Argentino.* Buenos Aires: Editorial la Pleyade.

Zuvekas, Clarence, Jr. 1968. "Argentine Economic Policy, 1958–62: The Frondizi Government's Development Plan." *Inter-American Economic Affairs* 22:45–73.

Index

Abelardo Ramos, Jorge, 64n, 68, 84, 106
Act of Chapultepec, 89, 90
Act of Havana, 86
Act of Paris, 99
Aerolineas Argentinas (ALA), 60, 92
Agency for International Development
    (AID), 101, 102, 108
Aizcorbe, Roberto, 60
"Alberto Hellmuth," 88
Alexander, Robert J., 65n, 66n
Alfonsin, Raul, 13, 14, 16
Alker, Hayward, 42n
Alliance for Progress, 70, 108
Allies (World War II), 87, 95, 175
Allison, Graham T., 27, 42n, 43n
Almos, Amado, 65
Alonso, José (Alonsoistas), 51
Alsogaray, Julio, 52, 53, 71, 104
Alvarez, Brig. Gen. Adolfo Teodoro, 52
Ames, Barry, 7, 24
Anderson, Charles W., 3, 24, 25, 27, 29,
    41n, 42n
Anton, Thomas, 42n
Apter, David A., 3
Aramburu, Pres. Pedro Eugenio, 74, 76,
    101, 104, 108
Aramburu Administration, 53, 59, 66,
    72, 74, 99, 101, 102
Argentine governmental institutions:
    Office of the President, 68, 69, 70, 73,
    76, 79, 131, 146; Courts, 50, 52,
    73–75, 79
Argentine Industrial Credit Bank, 65, 88
Argentine press, 75, 76, 77, 79

Art, Robert J., 42n
Astigueta, Dr. José, 53
authoritarian/bureaucratic thesis, 31, 36,
    45, 54, 55, 56, 63. *See also*
    O'Donnell; bureaucratic-authoritarian
    model
authoritarian/rational thesis, 27, 31, 35,
    36, 45, 47, 51, 63,68, 70, 71, 77, 81,
    111, 112, 116, 117, 125, 126, 128,
    129,131, 135, 136, 143, 144, 145,
    146, 149, 154, 156, 157, 160,161,
    162, 163, 165, 175, 178, 181
authoritarian rule, 20, 23, 24, 26, 27, 41,
    46, 112, 135, 178,180; bureaucratic
    systems, 24, 47, 81; populist systems,
    24,47, 81; traditional systems, 24, 47,
    81, 150
autocorrelation, 113–114, 117, 123, 139,
    141–142, 153
Avalos, Ignacio, 65
Axelrod, Robert, 42n
Axis powers (World War II), 75, 86, 88,
    89, 94, 95, 155, 156
Ayres, Robert, 3

Baer, Werner, 40n
Bailey, Thomas A., 85, 89
Baily, Samuel L., 49, 50, 51, 53, 61, 65n,
    66n, 75, 134n
basic industrial development, 82–85, 88,
    91, 96–99, 177, 178; after 1954, 99,
    102, 103, 105
Beechert, Edward D., 41n
Bignone, Gen. Reynaldo, 13

Bodenheimer, Susanne J., 40n
Bohrnstedt, George W., 134n
Bolivia, 1
Boulding, Kenneth E., 42n
Boynton, G. R., 37
Braden, Sproulle, 90, 106
Brady, Linda P., 42n
Braun, Oscar, 51, 56, 175n
Braybrooke, David, 25, 42n
Brazil, 1, 3, 4, 6, 7, 24, 41, 85–89,
    94–96, 155
Bretton Woods Agreement, 99
Brodie, Bernard, 42n
Bruck, H.W., 42n
Buenos Aires, 74, 79, 85
Bunge, Alejandro E., 58
bureaucratic-authoritarian model, 3–9,
    15, 21, 41, 46, 47, 50,52, 53, 54, 64,
    67–75, 77–82, 88, 102, 103, 122, 123,
    125, 126,128, 129, 136, 156, 159,
    160–165, 177, 178, 181; hypotheses
    of,3–10, 15, 16, 19, 20, 21, 24, 41, 46,
    54, 64, 73, 178, 179. See also O'Don-
    nell; authoritarian/bureaucratic thesis.
bureaucratic/satisficing thesis, 28, 31,
    35–36, 45, 63
Burnett, Ben G., 65n
Busso, Dr. Eduardo, 53
Byrnes, James F., 90

cabinet composition, 54, 56, 67, 68, 69,
    80
cabinet instability, 57–58, 67, 163, 177,
    180
cabinet membership: "in-and-outers,"
    31, 54
cabinet reorganization, 57
Cafiero, Antonio F., 78
California Argentina (Standard Oil),
    97–98
Campora, Pres. Hector, 11, 53
Canavese, Alfredo, 16
Canitrot, Adolfo, 15
Cardoso, Fernando Henrique, 3, 40n,
    41n
Carrera, Gen. Martino Bartolome, 65
Carri, Roberto, 134n
Carter, T. Michael, 134n
Castillo, Pres. Ramon S., 57, 58, 73, 75,
    79, 82, 86, 87, 88, 154, 165, 175
Castillo Administration (1942–1943),
    46, 155

Chalmers, Douglas A., 41n
Checchi, Gen. Julio, 88
China, People's Republic of, 94
Chilcote, Ronald H., 108
Chile, 1, 7, 12
Christensen, Cheryl, 42n
Christian Democratic party, 80
Chow, G.C., 134n
Civil Defense Law, 51, 62
Cockcroft, James, 3
Cohan, S., 2
Cohen, Bernard C., 43n
Cohen, Youssef, 6
Cold War, 90, 94
Collier, David, 2, 4, 5, 9, 19, 40n, 41n,
    178
Collier, Ruth, 41n
Columbia, 6
Communist party, 73, 74, 80
Compulsory Arbitration Act, 77
constitutions: 1898 constitution, 68;
    1949 constitution, 78; Peronist
    Justicialista constitution, 68, 74
Cordoba, 10, 52, 98
corporatist-authoritarian systems
    ("Bonapartist"), 23
Costas, Patron, 73
Cotler, Julio, 41n
coup d'etat: military coup cycle, 7;
    Castillo overthrown (1943),48, 49, 57,
    72, 79, 82, 87, 91, 154, 155, 156, 165;
    Peron overthrown (1955), 76, 98; Illia
    overthrown (1966), 47, 52,53, 59, 62,
    71, 129, 162, 179; Isabella Peron
    overthrown (1976), 11.
Crecine, John P., 42n
cross-national studies, 1, 2, 7, 8
Cuban Revolution, 4
Cyert, R.M., 41n, 42n

Dahrendorf, Ralf, 23
Dalto, Juan C., 83
Davies, John P., 31
Davis, Otto A., 42n, 134n
Dell' Aquila, Marco, 16
Dempster, A.H., 42n, 134n
dependency, 2, 3
Deutsch, Karl W., 42n
Di Tella, Torgnato, 15, 16, 34, 41n, 42n,
    48, 96
Diaz Alejandro, Carlos F., 47, 49, 57, 84,
    88, 134n, 175n

Direccion National de Fabricaciones e
    Investigaciones (DINIE),92, 93, 99,
    103, 106, 109
Directorate of Military Manufacturers
    (DGFM), 64, 86, 88, 91, 92,94, 104,
    105, 108
"dirty war," 13
disjointed incrementalism, 25, 42
Dos Santos, Teotonio, 3, 40n
Durbin, J., 134n

Ecuador, 1
Einaudi, Luigi, 2
Elasser, Edward O., 90
Engels, Friederich, 23
Epstein, Edward, 15
Erickson, Kenneth P., 41n
Eshag, Eprime, 56, 59, 66n
expenditures and revenue policy
    indicators, 136–174
Export-Import Bank (EIB), 80, 90, 93,
    95, 98, 101, 102, 104, 105, 108

Faletto, Enzo, 3, 40n
Falklands/Malvinas war, 13
Fanelli, Jose Maria, 15
Farrell, R. Barry, 42n
Farrell, Pres. Edelmiro J., 49, 53, 66, 75,
    90, 91
Farrell Administration, 67, 87, 88, 89,
    93, 94, 96, 111, 117, 135, 143
feedback, 29
Ferrer, Aldo, 53, 78, 101, 175n
Ferrocariles Argentinas, 92, 97
Forward, Nigel, 37
France, 23, 86
Frank, Andre Gunder, 3
Frankel, Joseph, 43n, 184n
Frenkel, Roberto, 15
Frondizi, Pres. Arturo, 16, 55, 61, 62, 66,
    76, 80, 99, 101, 103, 104, 108
Frondizi Administration, 16, 53, 55, 61,
    62, 66, 68, 70, 101, 102
Furtado, Celso, 40n

Galtieri, Pres. Leopoldo, 12, 13
Garcia-Zamor, Jean Claude, 60
Geary, R.C., 134n
Gelly y Obes, Dr. Carlos, 53
General Confederation of Labor (CGT),
    51, 52, 62, 65, 66, 76, 78
Germany, 23, 41, 72, 86–88, 89, 99

Gerschenkron, Alexander, 3, 23
Goff, Edward, 7
gold reserves, 59, 95
Goldberger, A.S., 134n
government expenditures: measurement
    issues, 136–138
Gramsci, Antonio, 41n, 42n
Great Depression, 3, 48, 49, 82–84, 88,
    89, 103
Greenberg, William J., 42n
Guido, Pres. Jose Maria, 53, 55, 73, 74,
    80
Guido Administration, 55, 59, 73, 101,
    102
Guinazu, Ruiz, 86
Gujarti, Damodar, 134n

Habibagahi, Hamid, 134n
Haggard, Stephan, 6
Halperin, Morton, 31, 42n, 54
Halpern, Manfred, 1
Hanson, Mark, 29
Harriman, W. Averill, 108
Hartz, Louis, 40n
Hayes, M., 7
Hazard, John L., 87
hegemonic crisis, period of (1952–1966),
    46, 47, 59, 63, 64, 114, 116, 117, 119,
    122, 125, 128, 129, 136, 138, 139,
    141, 142, 143, 149, 153, 156, 157,
    159, 175
Henry, Laurin L., 29
Heymann, Daniel, 15, 16
Hilsman, Roger, 43n
Hirschman, Albert O., 3, 4, 24, 26, 40n,
    42n, 178
Hitler, Adolph, 86
Hoffman, Stanley, 31
Hoole, Francis W., 42n, 43n, 113, 184n
Hopkins, Jack W., 43n
Hoz, José Alfredo Martinez de, 11, 12,
    15, 16
Hughes, Steven, 6
Hull, Cordell, 85, 87, 88, 175
Huntington, Samuel, 1, 2

Illia, Pres. Arturo, 10, 47, 52, 61, 62, 17,
    70, 71, 80, 102, 108, 128
Illia Administration, 55, 59, 61, 62, 70,
    71, 73, 77, 101, 102, 103, 127, 161
Imaz, José Luiz de, 55
"imperial bureaucracy," 182–183

import substitution industrialization
    (ISI), 3, 47, 48, 50, 63, 65, 67–68, 80,
    81, 88, 89, 91–98, 104, 105, 106, 117,
    154
incrementalism, 8, 9, 17, 22, 25, 38, 40,
    42, 79
integrated formulation/thesis, 21, 22, 26,
    36–40, 45, 63, 64, 67, 71, 78, 79, 81,
    97, 205, 106, 107, 111, 116, 117, 125,
    131, 136, 143–145, 149, 157, 161,
    163, 165, 166, 177, 179, 183
Inter-American Development Bank
    (IADB), 101, 102, 108
International Bank for Reconstruction
    and Development (IBRD), 99, 101,
    102, 108
International Monetary Fund (IMF), 6,
    12, 14, 53, 99, 100, 112, 135, 175
interrupted time series analysis, 9,
    112–114, 139, 150
Isabelistas, 51
Iscaro, Rubens, 52, 62, 65n, 66n
Italy, 86, 87

Jackman, Robert, 2
Jaguaribe, Helio, 3
Japan, 41, 87
Jervis, Robert, 42n
Johnson, John, 2, 3
Johnston, J., 134n
Jones, William M., 42n
Jordan, David C., 51, 52, 60, 65n
Justo Administration, 75, 83

Kanter, Arnold, 42n
Kaufman, Robert R., 4, 6, 41n, 178
Kennedy, John F., 108
Kenworthy, Eldon, 40n, 47, 48, 49, 64n,
    88, 96
Kissinger, Henry A., 42n
Kling, Merle, 40n
Korean crisis, 103
Krieger Vasena, Adalbert, 17, 51, 52, 53
Kristol, Irving, 182

labor policies: indicators of policy
    outcomes, 114–131
labor unions, 60–62, 66, 67, 78, 84, 106,
    107, 136, 163, 166, 177, 180
Laborista party, 78, 117
Lagomarsino, Rolando, 48, 50
Lamas, Saavedra, 85

Lambert, Jacques, 29, 41n
Lanusse, Pres. Alejandro, 10, 15, 52, 53,
    71
Latin American bureaucracy, 29
Law of Professional Associations, 65,
    66, 77
Lend Lease Act, 86, 87, 94, 155, 156,
    175
Levingston, Pres. Roberto, 10, 15, 50,
    52, 101, 104
Levingston Administration, 52, 53, 54,
    71, 74, 77, 79, 101, 102, 103, 111,
    126, 128, 135, 156, 162, 177
Lieuwen, Edwin, 2
Lindblom, Charles E., 25, 42n
Linz, Juan J., 2, 23, 41n, 42n
Lipset, Seymour Martin, 40n
Lissak, Moshe, 2
Lonardi, Pres. Eduardo, 53, 56, 71, 73,
    74, 75, 76, 98, 99, 102
Lovell, John P., 42n, 43n
Loza, Juan Batista, 65
Luder, Italo, 13

Malloy, James M., 41n
Malvinas (Falkland) islands, 86
Mamalakis, Markos, 41n
Manzetti, Luigi, 15, 16
March, James G., 41n, 42n
Marshall Plan, 91, 95
Martinez, Rodolfo Jr., 80
Marx, Karl, 23
McKinlay, R., 2
Menendez, Benjamin, 66
Merkx, Gilbert W., 5, 9, 41n, 47, 64n, 84
Messick, Richard E., 40n
Mexico, 6
Mijeski, Kenneth, 6
military factions (Colorado and Azul),
    52, 65
military regimes, 1–2
military role in government, 71–73
Miranda, Miguel, 48, 50, 64, 70, 91, 95
modernization theorists, 3, 4
Monroe Doctrine, 89
Morales, Dr. Alfredo Gomez, 70
Moore, Barrington Jr., 23, 41n
Morse, Richard M., 40n
Mosconi, Gen. Enrique, 84
Most, Benjamin A., 8, 9, 15, 17
multinational corporations, 21, 56, 98,
    99, 179

Murmis, Miguel, 56, 83, 84
Mussolini, Benito, 86

National Development Council
  (CONADE), 68, 70, 134
National Security Council (CONASE),
  65, 72, 73, 80
Needler, Martin, 2
Nelson, Joan, 6, 22
neoconservative approach, 12, 15, 16
Neustadt, Richard, 42n
Newton, Ronald C., 41n
non-bureaucratic actors, 32
Nordlinger, Eric, 1, 2
Nun, José, 3, 42n

O'Donnell Guillermo, 19, 34, 40n, 41n,
  59, 64n, 73; bureaucratic-authoritarian
  (b-a) model, 7–10, 15, 21, 24, 46, 50,
  54, 77,178, 179; modernization and
  b-a model, 3–5, 19, 20. See also,
  authoritarian/bureaucratic thesis;
  bureaucratic-authoritarian model;
  "who governs" authoritarian thesis
Ongania, Pres. Juan Carlos, 10, 11, 47,
  50, 53, 56, 62, 65, 71, 77, 80, 101,
  104, 162
Ongania Administration, 15, 16, 51, 52,
  54, 56, 59, 61, 65, 71, 73, 74, 75, 77,
  79, 101, 102, 103, 111, 126, 128, 135,
  156, 161, 162, 163
Ongaro, Raimundo, 52, 65
operationalization, 8, 9
opportunity, 27, 31, 33, 36, 37, 81, 83,
  105, 178
opportunity and willingness framework,
  9, 17
Organization of American States, 107
Ortiz, Pres., 83, 86, 88
Ortiz Administration, 86, 90
Owen, Frank, 60

Pablo, Juan Carlos de, 15
Paige, Glenn D., 42n, 43n
Panama, 7
Pan-American Defense Pact, 89
Pardo, Maria de Pablo, 53
Partido Unico, 78
Pax Obrera, 51, 161
Peralta Ramos, Monica, 65n
Perón, Juan Domingo, 13, 15, 46, 48, 49,
  50, 51, 53, 56, 58, 59, 64, 66, 69, 70,
  72, 73, 74, 75, 76, 77, 78, 79, 82, 89,

90, 91, 92, 93, 94, 97, 98, 99, 100,
  101, 102, 104, 107, 108, 119, 131,
  135, 143, 144, 146, 149, 154, 166,
  177, 179
Peronist Administrations, 15, 58, 59, 61,
  62, 67, 69, 93, 94, 96, 102, 103, 117,
  127, 143
Peronism (Peronist parties), 10, 11, 12,
  13, 15, 49, 51, 52, 53, 73, 74, 75, 76,
  77, 80, 95, 117, 146
Perón, Maria Estela Martinez de, 11, 46,
  66, 75
Peru, 1, 7
Petras, James, 29
Pike, Frederick B., 41n
Pinedo, Federico, 83, 84; Pinedo Plan,
  106
Pion-Berlin, David, 11, 12
Pistorini, Pascual Angel, 52
Plans: Austral Plan, 14, 16;
  Development and Stability (1958
  plan), 107; Four-Year Railroad
  Development Plan, 62; Primavera, 16;
  Pinedo plan, 84; Sanchez Serondo
  plan, 83; Savio Iron and Steel
  development plan, 92, 93, 98, 104,
  105
political elites, background, 55–56
populist authoritarian rule, period of
  (1943–1952), 46, 47, 54, 55, 63, 64,
  67, 68, 81, 89, 91, 98, 104, 107, 112,
  114, 116, 117, 119, 121, 122, 129,
  135, 136, 138, 139, 141–146,
  149,150, 153–155, 165, 175, 177
populist coalition, 3, 4, 139, 150, 154,
  179
populist governments, 33, 34
Portantiero, Juan Carlos, 51, 56, 65n, 83,
  84
postpopulist periods, 34–35
Potash, Robert, 72, 73, 84, 86, 88, 175n
Poulantzas, Nico, 41n, 42n
Pratschki, J.L., 134n
Prebisch, Raul, 98, 99
public (and semi-public) corporations,
  59, 50, 64, 92, 93, 96, 98, 104, 105,
  106, 109, 112
public employees, 58, 111–113, 116,
  117, 166, 177, 180–182
Purcell, Susan K., 24, 25, 41n
Putnam, Robert, 41n
Pye, Lucian, 1

Radical administration, 12–16, 45, 64,
　74, 75, 76
Rakoff, Stuart, 42n
Ramirez, Pres. Pedro Pablo, 46, 65, 75
Ramirez Administration, 61, 67, 87, 88,
　93, 94, 96, 117, 135, 143
Ramos, Joseph, 15, 16
rational actor (unified) approach, 27, 37,
　42, 179
Rattenbach, Gen. Benjamin, 65
Rauch, Gen. Enrique, 65
Rawson, Arturo, 46
Ray, David, 41n
recessions: of 1938, 86, 89, 98, 103; of
　1951–52, 98
regime type and economic stabilization,
　5–7
Remmer, Karen, 5, 6, 9
Repetto, Gen. Hector Alberto, 65
Reyna, Jose Luis, 40n
Revolucion Argentina, 52, -54, 71, 73
"Rights of the Workers," 50, 66, 78
Robinson, James A., 42n
Rodriguez, Carlos Alfredo, 16
Rofman, Alejandro, 84
Romero, Luis Alberto, 72, 84
Ronfeldt, David, 3
Rose, Richard, 42n
Rottin, Luciano, 60
Rowe, James W., 51, 53, 59, 75, 176n

Salera, Virgil, 54
Sapin, Burton, 42n
Saravia, Gen. José Octavio Cornejo, 65
Sarfatti, Magali, 40n
Savio, Gen. Manuel, 84, 86, 88, 92
Scenna, Miguel A., 85, 90
Schaefer, G.F., 42n
Schilling, Warner E., 43n
Schmitter, Philippe C., 3, 22, 23, 24,
　40n, 41n
Schvarzer, Jorge, 15
Scott, Robert E., 29, 60
Senorano, Gen. Eduardo, 65
Serra, José, 4, 178
Sharkansky, Ira, 42n
Shils, Edward, 1
Sigaut, Lorenzo, 12
Silvert, Kalman, 74
Skidmore, Thomas, 6
Smith, Peter H., 49
Smith, William C., 40n, 53, 59, 68, 69,

72, 73, 77
Snow, Peter G., 49
Snyder, Richard C., 42n
Soares, Glaucio Ary Dillion, 40n
Socialist party, 73
Sourrouille, Juan, 15
Soviet Union, 89, 90, 94, 107
Spain, 10, 88
Spencer, L., 41n
Sprout, Harold and Margaret, 42n
Starr, Harvey, 17, 27, 42n
Statute of the Peon, 50
Statute of the Revolution, 52
Stepan, Alfred, 2, 22
Stettinius, Edward R., 89, 90
Stickel, A. Lawrence, 50
Storni, Adm. Segundo, 175
Sullivan, G.E., 42n
synoptic problem solving, 27, 42

Tanter, Raymond, 42n
Thompson, James D., 42n
Thorp, Rosemary, 56, 60, 66n
traditional authoritarian rule, period of
　(1930–1943), 46–48, 54, 55, 58, 63,
　81, 104, 119, 121, 122, 131, 135, 136,
　150, 153–155, 177
Treber, Salvador, 49, 61, 91, 92, 134n
Troncoso, Moises Poblete, 65n
Trotsky, V., 23, 41n, 42n
Truman Doctrine, 94
Truman, Harry S, 80, 91, 146, 166
Tucker, Harvey J., 42n, 43n

Ullman, Richard, 42n
unallocated resources, effects of, 33,
　163, 166, 177, 180, 183
United Kingdom, 86, 87, 94
United Nations, 42, 89, 90; UN
　Economic Commission on Latin
　America (1965), 100, 107, 108, 175;
　UN Economic Commission(1969),
　134
United States, 1, 21, 34, 49, 84–91, 93,
　94, 96, 100, 106, 107, 108, 135, 146,
　155–156, 166, 179
Uruguay, 1, 12
Uriburu, Gen. José E., 45, 46, 71, 74, 75,
　83

Vacs, Aldo, 13
Valenzuela, Arturo, 41n

Vandor, Augusto, 51, 52, 65, 161
Vandoristas, 51, 52, 128
Varela, Adm. Benigno Ignacio, 52
Vedela, Jorge, 11, 15, 16
Veliz, Claudio, 40n
Villanueva, Javier, 100
Viola, Roberto, 12, 16

Waters, C., 41n
Waterston, Albert, 29, 41n
Watson, G.S., 134n
Weil, Felix J., 91
"who governs" authoritarian thesis, 20,
    23–27, 30, 36, 63, 67, 69, 77, 82, 96,
    106, 177–179. *See also* O'Donnell;
    bureaucratic-authoritarian model
Whitaker, Arthur P., 60, 61, 74, 75, 76,
    85, 106, 107

Wiarda, Howard J., 40n
Wildavsky, Aaron, 41n, 42n, 134n
willingness, 27, 28, 36, 37, 40, 81, 82,
    105, 108, 178
Willner, Ann Ruth, 2
Wogart, Jan, 15, 16
World War II, 49, 59, 80, 82, 84–86,
    93–95, 99, 103, 146, 154, 155, 165
Wynia, Gary, 15

Yacimientos Petroliferos Fiscales (YPF),
    52, 60, 84, 91, 94, 97, 99, 103, 107
Yrigoyen, Hipolito, 45, 46, 75, 84

Zinnes, Dina A., 42n
Zone, Luis, 65n
Zorrilla, Ruben H., 65n
Zuvekas, Clarence Jr., 56, 66n 100, 104

About the Book and the Authors

Analysts of authoritarian politics in Latin America have emphasized that particular types of economic and political crises tend to bring to power new dominant coalitions and to produce differing types of authoritarian governments, each pursuing a distinct set of policies in its efforts to solve the problems that it confronts. This image of political change, however, is not entirely consistent with standard descriptions of the policy process in Latin America.

This book explores the links between changing types of authoritarianan rule and shifting public policies in Argentina from 1930 to 1970. Two contrasting arguments—a "who governs" authoritarian and a "who cares who governs" bureaucratic model—are integrated in a formulation that predicts the contexts in which the contrasting theses should be useful for understanding public policies.

Most's study indicates that, although dominant coalitions and political elites were important in determining what policies were made, for whom, and at whose expense, during the early part of the 1930–1970 interval, "who governed" at the top lost much of its significance once the Argentine system became highly bureaucratized, political elites became unstable, resources ceased to be readily available, and a stalemate developed among opposing, nonbureaucratic actors in the policymaking arena. As his integrated thesis predicted, coalitions and leaders came and went, but public policy became increasingly based on what had been before.

In an introductory chapter, Luigi Manzetti situates Most's work within the context of the literature on both authoritarian rule and public policy published during the last half-decade. He also relates it to events in Argentina in the 1970s and 1980s.

Benjamin A. Most was associate professor of political science at the University of Iowa at the time of his death in November 1986. **Luigi Manzetti** is assistant professor of political science at Southern Methodist University.